Streaming *The Sandman*

ALSO OF INTEREST
AND FROM MCFARLAND

Neil Gaiman in the 21st Century: Essays on the Novels, Children's Stories, Online Writings, Comics and Other Works (edited by Tara Prescott, 2015)

Feminism in the Worlds of Neil Gaiman: Essays on the Comics, Poetry and Prose (edited by Tara Prescott and Aaron Drucker, 2012)

Streaming *The Sandman*
Essays on the Netflix Series

Edited by
TARA PRESCOTT-JOHNSON

McFarland & Company, Inc., Publishers
Jefferson, North Carolina

This book has undergone peer review.

LIBRARY OF CONGRESS CATALOGING-IN-PUBLICATION DATA

Names: Prescott-Johnson, Tara 1976– editor
Title: Streaming the Sandman : essays on the Netflix series / edited by Tara Prescott-Johnson.
Description: Jefferson, North Carolina : McFarland & Company, Inc., Publishers, 2025. | Includes bibliographical references and index.
Identifiers: LCCN 2025019722 | ISBN 9781476692807 paperback ∞
ISBN 9781476655222 ebook
Subjects: LCSH: Sandman (Television program : 2022) | BISAC: PERFORMING ARTS / Television / History & Criticism
Classification: LCC PN1995.77.S272595 S77 2025 | DDC 791.43/72—dc23/eng/20250512
LC record available at https://lccn.loc.gov/2025019722

ISBN (print) 978-1-4766-9280-7
ISBN (ebook) 978-1-4766-5522-2

© 2025 Tara Prescott-Johnson. All rights reserved

No part of this book may be reproduced or transmitted in any form or by any means, electronic or mechanical, including photocopying or recording, or by any information storage and retrieval system, without permission in writing from the publisher.

Front cover image: a detail from Rob Cooper's stained-glass creation of "Library of Endless Dreaming" commissioned by Neil Gaiman and currently installed in his home (photograph by Roy Adkins, used with permission).

Printed in the United States of America

McFarland & Company, Inc., Publishers
 Box 611, Jefferson, North Carolina 28640
 www.mcfarlandpub.com

For Molly and Eoin

Table of Contents

Acknowledgments	ix
Introduction: The Allegations Against Neil Gaiman and the Future of Sandman TARA PRESCOTT-JOHNSON	1
Fresh-Faced: The Interpretive Impact of Race, Gender, and Ethnicity in the *Sandman* Series ALEXIS BROOKS DE VITA *and* NOVELLA BROOKS DE VITA	15
The Shadow of Empire: Neil Gaiman's Dialogue with Orientalism AAYUSHI SHAH	33
The Mythopoetic Memorial: Creating and Recreating Myth and Sites of Memory ANGELA CARMELA UY FANTONE	51
"You're as bad … as Desire! Or worse!" Examining the Abject Nature of Death and Desire MELISA MARYANN GOVEAS *and* NAVEEN KELVIN DALMEIDA	67
Superheroes Can Be Children in Footie Pajamas: The Sensible Revisions of Netflix's *Sandman* as Participating Within the Larger Project of DC's Sandmen JOSEPH MICHAEL SOMMERS	78
Turning Toward the Sound of Her Wings: The *Sandman* Series as a Doorway to Grief Literacy DREA LETAMENDI	92

"Calliope": How Off-Screen Sexual Violence Changes
  the Narrative
    PINKY CHUNG-MAN LUI   102

The Therapeutic Value of Hope Shining through the Lens
  of *Sandman*
    SAMARA V. SEROTKIN   122

Cautionary Tails: Animation and the Human/Nonhuman
  Animal in "Dream of a Thousand Cats"
    COLIN WHEELER   137

A Cat of a Thousand Dreams: A Research Assistant's Perspective
    SARA MISATO AOKI   151

A Dreaming of Our Own: How Fandom Adapts Multiple
  Canons to Create a New Fanon
    ADRIENNE E. RAW   163

Sandman *Episode Guide*   183
About the Contributors   191
Index   195

Acknowledgments

Many people poured their time, energy, and love into making this collection happen and I am grateful to all of them, but especially to the individual authors: Alexis Brooks de Vita, Novella Brooks de Vita, Aayushi Shah, Angela Carmela Uy Fantone, Melisa Maryann Goveas, Naveen Kelvin Dalmeida, Joseph Michael Sommers, Drea Letamendi, Pinky Chung-Man Lui, Samara V. Serotkin, Colin Wheeler, Sara Misato Aoki, and Adrienne E. Raw. Thank you for entrusting your work to me.

I'm especially grateful for my editor at McFarland, Layla Milholen. It has been such an honor to work with Layla over three books and many years, and I'm indebted to her support, guidance, and tolerance for missed deadlines.

I'd like to thank Neil Gaiman, of course, for all of the stories he creates, and for granting permission to use the cover image of "Library of Endless Dreaming." Gaiman commissioned this stained-glass window for his home from stained-glass artist Rob Cooper. Thank you, Rob, for sharing this gorgeous work and thank you to Roy Adkins for photographing it for all the world to enjoy.

My eternal thanks goes to Katie Van Heest of Tweed Editing for once again helping me polish the literary silver (and organize the utensil drawers). James Epps, a doctoral student in Information Studies at UCLA, has been instrumental in guiding me through conversations about citation justice. Briita Simms offered valuable feedback on the introduction and Gabriel Gianola provided animation insight and industry expertise relevant for the "Dream of a Thousand Cats" essays. I'm also grateful to the students of Honors 87W: The Worlds of Neil Gaiman at UCLA. Each year, these talented, funny, and insightful undergraduates gather and teach me new ways to see and experience the works of Neil Gaiman. I'd also like to offer my gratitude for institutional support at UCLA: this project was supported by a Unit 18 Faculty Professional Development Award as well as an award from Dean Alexandra Stern's Professional Development Fund.

This project could not have happened without my partner, Bjorn, who supports all of my endeavors and curls up on the couch with me to watch *Sandman* and *Good Omens* once the kids have gone to bed. He recently took care of our two young children for a week so that I could fly to Dublin to see the UK tour premiere of *The Ocean at the End of the Lane* and then again so I could go to St. Louis to see Gaiman accept the Saint Louis University Literary Award. Thank you for everything, Bjorn. I promise to watch the kids any time you want to go to bluegrass camp.

And finally, to the cast, crew, writers, showrunners, and everyone else who contributed to Netflix's *Sandman*. Whether your name appears on the end credits, the IMDB page, or not at all, you helped create something powerful that really matters to a lot of people. If you're ever in Culver City, I will buy you a cup of coffee at the Conservatory. Or if you'd like to wait a hundred years, we can meet at the White Horse Tavern. I'll be at the table in the back.

Introduction

The Allegations Against Neil Gaiman and the Future of Sandman

Tara Prescott-Johnson

It was July 2024 and I was relaxing on an Adirondack chair in upstate New York. I had just submitted the final manuscript for the book you are about to read and was eager to crack open Stephen King's *11/22/63*. The promise of three blissful weeks by the lake stretched out ahead of me: no internet, no social media, no news. Then the texts started.

"Have you heard?"

"Did you see it?"

"Are you okay?"

And that's how I learned about the sexual assault allegations against Neil Gaiman.

It would take a while before I could bring myself to listen to the six episodes of the podcast *Master: The Allegations Against Neil Gaiman*, reported by Rachel Johnson and Paul Caruana Galizia. *Master* came from Tortoise Media, a UK-based source I'd never heard of. Like many scholars and fans, I hardly knew what to think when I first heard the news. I hoped it wasn't true. But regardless of the outcome of the allegations, I could feel it, heavy and deep in my stomach: nothing was going to be the same.

Gaiman denied the sexual assault claims, both through his legal representation and, six months later, on his personal blog ("Breaking the Silence"). He maintained that the sexual relationships he had with the women covered in the podcast were consensual. But then more women came forward and more horrific details emerged. All the relationships had enormous differentials in age, income, authority, and power. Two of the women were his employees. As Vera Wylde put it, "That is an irreconcilable power gap, between an employer and an employee. There is no way to make that work…. There is no way to engage with that ethically." Many fans who grew up with Gaiman's stories, who shared beloved paperbacks like talismans and turned to his works for guidance and comfort, now had to figure out what to do with all this information. *What is your relationship to works whose creators have—allegedly or definitively—done bad things? How do you decide?* It was strange, grieving over the loss of something that most of the world hadn't heard about yet. The story sat for quite some time—a minor *Rolling Stone* article that just repeated what the podcast had revealed, a few small stories that noted pauses on or cancellations of Gaiman-related projects (including *Dead Boy Detectives*, *Good Omens*, *Graveyard Book*, and *Sandman*). Many months passed. With no new information coming from mainstream media, fans filled the vacuum on their own, trying to process the information together on Reddit, in Facebook groups and TikToks, and on their blogs and podcasts, including Vera Wylde's thorough analyses on *Council of Geeks*.

And then, in January 2025, the Gaiman news went supernova. Lila Shapiro's article "There Is No Safe Word" became the cover story for *New York* magazine and its companion website *Vulture*. This time, there was new reporting, revealing the last name of one accuser, and graphic to the point that some readers couldn't finish the piece. A story that had been quietly rocking the science fiction and fantasy fandom for months had finally gone mainstream. And it triggered an avalanche of new articles exhausting every possible angle, from #MeToo to the mundane (e.g., "You Have a Neil Gaiman Tattoo. Now What?"). In February 2025 another bomb dropped: Gaiman's former nanny filed a rape and human trafficking lawsuit against Gaiman and his estranged wife, Amanda Palmer. Power imbalances, large gaps in age and income, a celebrity feminist writer and his fiercely loyal, devoted fans. It was the stuff of fiction—literally. The parallels with the *Sandman* issue "Calliope" were inescapable. In this standalone story, an author celebrated for being a feminist secretly rapes a Greek muse. In 2012, I published a close reading of this issue, include the following line: "At the very least, Gaiman asks readers to more actively question which authors and works they read as 'feminist'—including his own." I had no idea how prescient it would be.

An unexpected silver lining of the media attention on the sexual assault allegations was that it sparked vital conversations. Friends and colleagues contacted me to share their own experiences with what happened when works they loved turned out to have been created by people who had done immoral or reprehensible things. A teenage girl told me about her pilgrimage to Munro's Books (Alice Munro's own shattering story of abuse and neglect broke the same week as the Gaiman news). A grad school friend shared what it was like being a lonely young girl in rural Northern California, clinging to Woody Allen movies as her only connection to a promised world of really smart conversation in New York. My neighbor, a celebrated producer, confessed how much *The Cosby Show*'s portrayal of a successful, loving Black family meant to her when she was growing up. The list of fallen creators seems endless, but strangely, this horrible shared experienced surfaced valuable stories I'd never heard before. I hadn't realized that many of my friends had grappled with this issue long before me. *Why does it keep happening? When will it ever stop?*

My friends also shared their different ways of coping with the news. They agreed that certain films could still be enjoyed (especially if the topic of the film and the nature of the perpetrator's crime didn't overlap), but others were simply impossible to watch. In the same way, some creators were much more obviously taboo—Roman Polanski, Harvey Weinstein— and others remained more ambiguous (J.K. Rowling). One theme that quickly emerged: there's no right way to react when a favorite creator falls from grace. We all respond in our own ways. And our different choices as fans and scholars are valid.

My colleague, Nathan Deuel, wrote about his own ambivalent, vacillating, confused reactions to the breaking news that Cormac McCarthy had had a relationship with a 16-year-old girl when he was 42. In his essay, Deuel struggles to define his reaction to the news, both as a reader and as a male college instructor:

> I'm walking and trying to puzzle out how I feel and why I think I am so mad. What do we search for in stories? It's one thing to teach Bradbury's ideas about state control and personal freedom. It's another thing to walk to class and try to privately mourn ... what? That Cormac was a bad dude? That one of my favorite writers was a monster? Here's the deal: I do not know what to think and I can't say exactly why.

Here, Deuel perfectly captures how "bad news" about beloved writers hits so particularly, and the difficulty in deciding what it means. As Emily Nussbaum puts it, "What should we do with the art of terrible men?" It's not as simple as "separating the art from the artist" or dismissing parasocial relationships. There are many, many fans who grew up alongside Gaiman's comics and novels, who turned to them for solace, who later named their children after his characters. His books are so infused with his voice, so unabashedly his, that even when they aren't semi-autobiographical (like *The Ocean at the End of the Lane*), they still sound like Gaiman reading directly to you.

Gaiman has always invited his readership in: he was the first major writer to interact with fans extensively via Twitter and became famous for never-ending book signings where he wouldn't leave until every fan had a book inscribed, a photo taken, a story shared. There's even a documentary, *Dream Dangerously,* about Gaiman's 2013 signing tour, where his right hand was so damaged from overuse that he had submerge it up to the elbow in ice after every signing. This makes the recent news even harder to bear: one of the women in the *Master* podcast first met Gaiman at a signing, when she was just a teenager, and began a sexual relationship with him shortly thereafter.

In an essay for NPR, frequent Gaiman podcaster and writer Glen Weldon describes his own struggle with the news, and the contradictory feelings. He writes:

> Here's my personal approach, whenever allegations come out about an artist whose work is important to me: I see the moment I learned of them as an inflection point. From that very instant, it's on me.
>
> The knowledge of the allegations will color their past works, when and if I choose to revisit them in the future. It won't change how those works affected me back then, and there's no point in pretending it will. But my newfound understanding of the claims can and will change how those works affect me today, and tomorrow.

Weldon's approach gives grace to fans who long to hold onto the memories of these stories, while acknowledging they may not be able to reread those same stories in the same way again. Many Gaiman fans have experienced a collective loss of innocence.

Understandably, people within Gaiman's inner circle have mostly remained silent during this period. The musician Tori Amos, in an interview for *The Guardian*, was both diplomatic and circumspect, walking a careful line that acknowledged the suffering of the alleged victims without explicitly saying Gaiman was guilty. She said:

> And if the allegations are true, that's not the Neil that I knew, that's not the friend that I knew, nor a friend that I ever want to know. So in some ways it's a heartbreaking grief. I never saw that side of Neil. Neither did my crew. And my crew has seen a lot.

Throughout the interview, Amos uses deliberate, careful phrasing. Which makes it even more shocking towards the end of the interview, when Kira Cochrane asks Amos about battling sexism and ill treatment from men,

> [Amos'] steely side comes out. "I won't tolerate it. I won't tolerate it with the crew…" You won't let it happen around you? "No. No." And people know that? "Oh yeah. Yes. But possibly there are wolves in sheep's clothing." She gives me a meaningful look. "And clearly we talked about that earlier."

This passage concludes the interview, implying that one of the "wolves in sheep's clothing" could possibly be Gaiman.

In a 2003 children's picture book, *The Wolves in the Walls*, Gaiman writes the refrain "When the wolves come out of the walls, it's all over."

One could argue that, over the past year, the wolves have come out. But is it all over? *Even if we can figure out our relationship to the single-authored works, what about the collaborations and adaptations?* For years, I was active in the Joss Whedon academic community, formerly known as the Whedon Studies Association. After the fallout from the misconduct accusations against Whedon, the community renamed itself Buffy+ to focus on the collaborative worlds his works built rather than their shared literary ancestor. I saw the same impulse reflected in the Neil Gaiman Fans Facebook group, which rebranded itself as Fans of the Works of Neil Gaiman. *Buffy the Vampire Slayer*, sans Whedon, is now on the verge of a much-anticipated reboot. Could the same happen for Gaiman's film or television work?

The Netflix series *Sandman* is the result of a collaboration of many writers, artists, actors, and creators, concentric rings of people who were not involved in Neil Gaiman's life but are now part of the expanding aftermath of the allegations. I feel for the *Sandman* actors and writers in particular. They have already weathered the SAG-AFTRA strike, which lasted for an astonishing 146 days. The current state of the industry is bleak: many writers and actors are facing the prospect that their careers are over. And if any were lucky enough to have work connected to Gaiman-related properties, well, those projects are basically dead in the water.

Which brings me to the fate of *Sandman*'s Season 2, which was released in July 2025. After the allegations gained traction, it was conceivable that the first season would also become the last. Certainly, it was the only *Sandman* season to have existed in a world generally unaware of Gaiman's alleged transgressions. The essays in this collection were also written in that world. (Although I made a few minor edits for the authors' sake, this introduction is the only piece written post-allegations.) Because the show is a collaboration, and in honor of everyone who contributed to it, I believe it is still worthy, despite everything, to examine the social, artistic, and literary accomplishments that Netflix's *Sandman* achieved. In some ways, the changes between the original comics and the television series are even more important, particularly the "Calliope" episode, given what has recently surfaced.

Therefore, I present *Streaming* The Sandman: *Essays on the Netflix Series*, where scholars of many kinds celebrate and critique what the showrunners, staff, cast, and crew of *Sandman* achieved in its first season. Their work stands on its own. This whole experience is a difficult but important reminder that these works of art are created by many people, not just a sole creator, and it is important to acknowledge them. So before jumping in to the essays themselves, here is the rationale for how the *Sandman* comics and television episodes will be credited in this collection, to honor and name as many people as possible.

Collaboration and Credit

Netflix's *Sandman*, like the original comics, is a richly collaborative work of art that involves a great number of contributors, many of whom don't get much recognition for their work. The *Sandman* television series is based on the original comics published by DC Comics (and later Vertigo) that ran from January 1989 to March 1996. Over the course of seventy-five issues, the story of *Sandman* was shaped by many people, and their shared vision in turn inspired the look and feel of the Netflix adaptation.

Neil Gaiman was the writer and creator of *Sandman*, but he refashioned characters created by other writers and collaborated with dozens of artists, letterers, inkers, pencillers, and editors. *Sandman*'s large body of artists included Sam Kieth, Mike Dringenberg, Malcolm Jones III, Chris Bachalo, Chris Riddell, Charles Vess, Jill Thompson, Bryan Talbot, Michael Zulli, and Kelley Jones. Its distinctive lettering was done by Todd Klein, and its multimedia covers, in the style of Joseph Cornell's Wunderkammer art, were created by Dave McKean (who later created the end credits in the same style for the *Sandman* television series). The project was relentlessly shepherded by editor Karen Berger, notably at a time when there were few prominent women represented in the major comics publishers.

Writing about artistic collaborations is tricky, and there are challenges specific to writing about comics. Because there are many different editions of the original *Sandman* comics (the original "floppy" issues, reprints, trade paperbacks, and the Deluxe, Omnibus, and Absolute editions), the authors in this collection cite whichever version is their preference. The essays in this collection focus on the first season of Netflix's *Sandman*, which covers narrative arcs from the first three collected trade paperbacks: *Preludes and Nocturnes*, *The Doll's House*, and *Dream Country*. Where possible, page numbers have been included, but not all editions have pagination. The authors will sometimes informally refer to *Sandman* as Gaiman's creation, or list him first on the References along with (w) to indicate that he wrote the story. This is mostly for the ease of readability, as there were dozens of people involved in the creation of the original comic and even more for the show. When an essay in this collection cites specific issues, then the names of the primary collaborators are included in the references, as they were first credited in the individual "floppy" issues [e.g., writer (w), artist (a), colorist (c), penciller (p), and inker (i)] and are listed in numerical order by issue number under Gaiman for easy reference (rather than alphabetical by contributor names). When an essay cites a collected volume (such as the *Sandman* trade paperbacks) that contains many different sets of contributors, the reference simply uses "Gaiman, Neil (w), et al."

To try to capture as many of the contributors to the television series,

I have included the names of the showrunners, writers, story editors, and main performers for each episode in the episode guide at the back of this book. When you are viewing the episodes themselves, I encourage you to click on the button that allows you to view the final end credits instead of jumping to the next episode. Not only will you be treated to Dave McKean's gorgeous kaleidoscopic art, but you'll also have time to reflect on the contributions of all those individuals.

Scholarship about comics and television also has other genre-specific quirks that impact this collection, so I will explain them here. Although the comic, show, and eponymous main character's names are all preceded by "The" (e.g., *The Sandman*), most people drop the article in conversation, which is a convention I follow here. In the same way, I have left off the chapter numbers at the start of episode titles ("Chapter 1: Sleep of the Just") because most people refer to them by the second half of the title, which usually is the same as the corresponding comic issue.

Guiding Principles of This Collection

Streaming The Sandman: *Essays on the Netflix Series* is also a collaboration and, like its subject matter, it is more than the sum of its parts. I have had the honor of captaining the ship, and I would like to share the principles that have guided my process. In this collection, I have not only selected works by established scholars in their respective fields; I have also sought to give space to voices that have been traditionally left out of the conversation. Some of the contributors in this collection come from fields outside of literature or media studies (which tend to dominate the scholarship on comics and television). Some are emerging scholars, just starting out on their professional journeys. Some are non-native speakers of English. Some claim identities or backgrounds or nationalities that are under-represented in American academic publications. All have unique, valuable insights and engaging perspectives to share.

In soliciting essays for this collection, I aimed for a sampling of disciplines, topics, and critical frameworks. I wanted some industry-specific discussion but also analyses of the characters and plots that matter the most to viewers. And, perhaps following the lead of the television series which threw in an oddball surprise at the end, I also included two essays about cats—because they're fun and I guarantee they're unlike anything else you've read about *Sandman*.

To address my own position as editor, I am situated within the U.S. university system, siloed within Writing Programs (composition has traditionally been taught by women and female-identifying contingent instructors who often work for low pay and no benefits and have to juggle classes at different institutions), and therefore I identified strongly with the plight of the striking television writers. My own union, UC-AFT, and the union of the graduate student workers at my institution, UAW 2865, have both gone on strike in the last few years to fight for basic job protections and fair compensation. These issues—the exploitation of academic labor, the exploitation of screenwriters, the lack of representation of people of color and LGBTQ actors and creators in film and TV—are not isolated phenomena.

It is essential that creators of television and film as well as media scholars examine these issues. The Netflix adaptation of *Sandman* took many steps that shouldn't be considered bold—such as casting Black women and non-binary performers in lead roles. Inclusive practices—both behind the scenes and in the production—should be standard. But they're not.

I am proud of the work the contributors to this book have done to provide new perspectives on a serial form of art while it was still in progress. In order to thrive, to continually reflect on popular culture productions and practices, we must hold the producers of content we consume, as well as ourselves, accountable to doing better than our predecessors, and striving for equity and inclusion. I believed this to be true before the Gaiman accusations surfaced, and even more so now.

Overview of the Essays: As it aired, Netflix's *Sandman* quickly gained attention for its diverse and inclusive casting, breakout fan-favorite characters, its updating of a comic from the late '80s and early '90s for a modern audience, and the surprise double episode at the end of the first season. The essays in this collection are roughly arranged to explore each of these areas and more.

Perhaps the aspect of the *Sandman* television series that garnered the most press coverage was the decision to cast non-European actors, particularly those of African descent, in several major roles. In the first chapter of this collection, Alexis Brooks de Vita and Novella Brooks de Vita train their critical gazes on the far-reaching effects of these inclusive casting choices, both on the story and on the viewers. "Fresh-Faced: The Interpretive Impact of Race, Gender, and Ethnicity in the *Sandman* Series" digs much deeper than the "diversity is good" argument, calling our attention to the fact that *Sandman*'s racially diverse performers are "playing the roles they are assigned in the economically colonialist era in which the Netflix series debuted." In doing so, the creators not only correct the one-sided nature of some of the original storytelling (which mainly featured white characters) but also add new layers of complexity. This powerful chapter, which offers an engaging overview of vital scholarship from several writers of African descent, examines the show through a womanist, anti-racist, de-colonialist lens, revealing how "visual racial diversity amplifies and clarifies the socio-historical commentary, educational significance and relevance to current sociopolitical issues of *Sandman*'s sweeping and unrelenting vision."

The Othering of non-white people and the corollary exoticization of their stories is also examined by Aayushi Shah in "The Shadow of Empire: Neil Gaiman's Dialogue with Orientalism." In this essay, Shah applies Edward Said's critical theory to three different works by Gaiman (*Stardust*, *Sandman*, and *The Graveyard Book*), which have all been in the process of adaptation to screen and have grappled with or unintentionally perpetuated damaging Orientalist tropes. The original *Sandman* comics did not tell many stories featuring Black, Indigenous, and People of Color (BIPOC), with a few notable exceptions. Shah focuses on two stories in particular: issue #20, "Façade," and issue #50, "Ramadan," neither of which has yet made it into the Netflix series. In looking at how *Stardust*, *The Graveyard Book*, and *Sandman* have presented "The East" and its peoples and cultures, both in the original context and in their adaptations, this essay offers a call to action for filmmakers and producers as they tackle these types of stories in the future.

Sandman does not just reframe the way people and cultures are viewed. It also repurposes and repackages myths, and that is the focus of Angela Carmela Uy Fantone's essay, "The Mythopoetic Memorial: Creating and Recreating Myth and Sites of Memory." Applying methods from the field of memory studies, Fantone examines the ways that the original *Sandman* functions as a memorial of earlier stories and tales, and then itself becomes memorialized in the television series. Unearthing the relationship between the parent and ancestral texts sheds new light on how the new television series influences the way that audiences remember the source text.

Viewers' memories of the first season of *Sandman* will be heavily influenced by the show's outstanding performers, many of whom come from traditionally underrepresented identities. *Sandman*'s casting is remarkable not only for its inclusion of BIPOC but also for its initial steps into gender-inclusive casting, most notably the addition of nonbinary actor Mason Alexander Park. As Park (2022) notes, *Sandman* is "one of the most unapologetically queer shows on television and was honestly very overlooked by queer press. Probably has more out LGBTQ+ lead characters than any current show in the fantasy genre." Park's delicious portrayal of Desire quickly became a fan favorite and is testament both to the strength of the script and to Park's ability to steal every scene they are in. In "'You're as Bad … as Desire! Or Worse!' Examining the Abject Nature of Death and Desire," Melisa Maryann Goveas and Naveen Kelvin Dalmeida use Julia Kristeva's theory as a critical framework to examine

Death and Desire's often contradictory qualities and the different reactions these characters elicit from audiences.

This move toward gender-inclusive casting is one way to re-envision and update stories, myths, and narrative for new audiences. Grappling with a story's past is an inherent challenge for any adaptation, but it is exponentially so with a work like *Sandman*, which is itself built upon and interconnected with an enormous web of stories and characters borrowed from many sources. Like several of the contributors in this collection, Joseph Michael Sommers recognizes the ways in which the *Sandman* series now has the task of updating and acknowledging traditions in line with modern audiences. Before he was Morpheus (or Dream King, Dream of the Endless, Oneiros, Kai'ckul, etc.), the Sandman was Wesley Dodds, a crimefighter who first appeared in comics in the 1930s. Drawing upon iterations of several Sandmen that predate the Netflix one created by Tom Sturridge, "Superheroes Can Be Children in Footie Pajamas: The Sensible Revisions of Netflix's Sandman as Participating within the Larger Project of DC's Sandmen" looks at the ways that the Netflix version responds to and reinvents this title character and his story. Because of the challenges of continuity, access to expensive and out of print materials, and the overall depth of material needed to understand decades of comics publications, this essay is also particularly useful for a quick overview of the history and lineage of the Sandman as a character.

The next essay in the collection, by Drea Letamendi, takes a turn away from Dream to focus on his elder sister, Death. Letamendi is a psychologist, Comic-Con International and the American Psychological Association speaker, and cohost of the podcast *The Arkham Sessions*, where she offers a psychologist's take on superhero narratives. In "Turning toward the Sound of Her Wings: The *Sandman* Series as a Doorway to Grief Literacy," Letamendi applies this perspective to arguably the most beloved and celebrated *Sandman* story, "The Sound of Her Wings," which features the first appearance of Dream's sister Death. Using this episode as her guide, Letamendi works to build our grief literacy, examining the show's examples of grief phobia, grief companions, death doulas, continuing bonds, post-traumatic growth, dispositional gratitude, and parasocial relationships. Guided by transformative psychology with an emphasis on holistic psychological resilience, this essay provides a very enlightening exploration of a topic that large parts of American culture try to avoid at all costs.

Working towards the end of the first season, the final essays in this collection examine the surprise bonus episode, "Calliope / A Dream of a Thousand Cats." Pinky Chung-Man Lui tackles perhaps the biggest surprise of the season, the representation of Calliope's story. The source material in the comics, as I pointed out in *Neil Gaiman in the 21st Century*, is problematic by modern standards, both in the visual representation of sexual violence and in the narrative's use of it as a plot device. These problems are now exponentially worse in light of the sexual assault allegations. In "'Calliope': How Off-Screen Sexual Violence Changes the Narrative," Lui offers a historical survey of sexual violence representations in film and TV, from the early days of *General Hospital* to *Buffy the Vampire Slayer, Game of Thrones, I May Destroy You,* and *Promising Young Woman,* before positioning Netflix's *Sandman* as "a feminist example that respects the viewers' ability to comprehend a story about rape without showing them the act, and proves that compelling storytelling can be powerful enough on its own merits."

The reverberations of the changes to "Calliope" also inspire the next essay of the collection, "The Therapeutic Value of Hope Shining through the Lens of *Sandman*." Like Letamendi, Samara V. Serotkin is a practicing psychologist with a deep professional and personal investment in the *Sandman* universe. In her practice, she regularly asks new clients about books that have mattered to them, which has led to many conversations about *Sandman*. Her contribution to this collection looks at the healing effect these stories have had on her clients, and the important ways that catharsis, representation, and especially, hope, work within the series and beyond.

Whereas Serotkin pays particular attention to a traumatic story from "Calliope," Colin Wheeler addresses the lighter second half of the episode, "Dream of a Thousand Cats." Tucked into the end of the first season, this short is notable for lots of reasons: its status as the only animated episode, its surprise gift to fans, and the fact that it's the only episode told from a non-human, non-Endless perspective. In "Cautionary Tails: Animation and the Human/Nonhuman Animal in 'Dream of a Thousand Cats,'" animator Wheeler offers a one-of-a-kind analysis of a one-of-a-kind episode that privileges the non-human animal experience.

Like Wheeler, Sara Misato Aoki's professional experiences initially drew her to "Dream of a Thousand Cats," but she takes the episode in a completely different and unexpected direction. In "A Cat of a Thousand Dreams: A Research Assistant's Perspective," she blends personal observation, scientific study, and literary analysis to offer her literally on-the-ground perspective on feral cats, trap-neuter-return policies, and how fictional and nonfictional experiences with cats map onto our understanding of this most beloved yet surprisingly elusive species.

With all episodes of the first season now examined, Adrienne E. Raw closes out the collection by exploring what fans have contributed to the *Sandman* universe since the release of *Sandman*'s first season. Throughout the world, communities of fans have been building *Sandman* fanfiction specific to the show, creating new fan canons, or fanon. "A Dreaming of Our Own: How Fandom Adapts Multiple Canons to Create a New

Fanon" gives readers a peek inside the complex, celebratory, passionate, and enthralling world of the *Sandman* fanon.

Looking Ahead

At this point, it is very difficult to predict what the legacy will be for works written by Neil Gaiman or adapted from them. It is clear that the imperial phase of Gaiman-related properties has ended: it included the shows *American Gods*, *Good Omens*, *Dead Boy Detectives*, and *Sandman*, as well as *Anansi Boys*, *The Graveyard Book*, and other anticipated works that never made it to screen. That was the moment in which the current volume was conceptualized and composed. What started as a collection of essays on one of the newest adaptations of Gaiman's work now feels like a snapshot documenting the end of an era. *Sandman*'s legacy, for better or for worse, is connected to Neil Gaiman's. But one of the goals for this collection is examining how Netflix's *Sandman*, informed by the efforts of movements such as #MeToo and Black Lives Matter, made important contributions to televised art. And it is my hope that, in the recognition of what the show has done well, these contributions will continue to grow and inspire others.

References

Amos, Tori, interview by Kira Cochran. 2024. "Tori Amos on Trauma, Trump and Neil Gaiman: 'It's a Heartbreaking Grief.'" *The Guardian*, December 3.

Carras, Christi, and Stacy Perman. 2024. "We Checked in with Hollywood Writers a Year after the Strike. They're Not OK." *Los Angeles Times*, May 13.

Deuel, Nathan. 2024. "Writers I Have Met; Or, On Learning That Cormac McCarthy Was a Creep." *Lit Hub*, December 11.

Fonseca, Ryan. 2024. "The Hollywood Writers' Strike Ended. Writers' Struggles Have Not." *Los Angeles Times*, May 13.

Gaiman, Neil. 2025. "Breaking the Silence." www.neilgaiman.com. January 14.

Klee, Miles. 2025. "You Have a Neil Gaiman Tattoo. Now What?" *Rolling Stone*. January 16.

Meaney, Patrick, dir. 2016. *Dream Dangerously*. Vimeo. July 2.

Nussbum, Emily. 2019. "Confessions of the Human Shield." *I Like to Watch*. Random House.

Park, Mason Alexander (@MasonAPark). 2022. "The Sandman is one of the most unapologetically queer shows on television and was honestly very overlooked by queer press. Probably has more out LGBTQ+ lead characters than any current show in the fantasy genre. Makes me happy to see this celebrating the queerness of our series." Twitter, November 6. https://twitter.com/MasonAPark/status/1589198334287572992.

Shapiro, Lila. 2025. "There Is No Safe Word: How the Best-Selling Fantasy Author Neil Gaiman Hid the Darkest Parts of Himself." *New York*, January 13. https://www.vulture.com/article/neil-gaiman-allegations-controversy-amanda-palmer-sandman-madoc.html.

Weldon, Glen. 2025. "One Longtime Neil Gaiman Fan on Where We Go from Here." www.KQED.org. January 21.

Wylde, Vera. 2024. "About Those Neil Gaiman Allegations (and the Podcast that Originally Broke the Story)." *Council of Geeks*. YouTube. July 27.

Fresh-Faced

The Interpretive Impact of Race, Gender, and Ethnicity in the Sandman *Series*

Alexis Brooks de Vita *and* Novella Brooks de Vita

Netflix depicts key characters in its *Sandman* series as being of non–European descent delivering several impactful jolts that need analytical detangling to help the series' diverse audience understand potential discomfort as well as the education and catharsis these depictions offer.[1] When asked about his casting preferences for the television series, Neil Gaiman is clear that that when he originally wrote the comic, he peopled it with characters similar to his acquaintances and associates at the time, made up of a variety of races, ethnicities, and gender identities (N. Brooks de Vita 2023). However, when *Sandman* became a televised series after thirty-six years, some fans of the more monoracially illustrated comics reacted with mixed emotions at the sight of characters who were not of purely European descent, questioning the inclusion of races and ethnicities not solely and recognizably European. Gaiman makes it clear in "Building Inclusive Worlds and Global Representations in the Works of Neil Gaiman" (N. Brooks de Vita 2023) that he played an integral part in Netflix's casting choices and supported ethnically and racially diverse casting (128–30), highlighting the visibly Africanist woman representing Death, Kirby Howell-Baptiste, whose performance most personified Death to the show's creators. When Death was first illustrated by Mike Dringenberg in *Sandman* issue #8, the character had pale skin and straight, spiked hair, a primary characterization that has previously remained fairly consistent throughout her representations by various artists throughout the series, until recently. Netflix and Gaiman's decision to cast Howell-Baptiste offered this iteration of Death a new, fresh face, raising some audience questions. However, Death was not the only character vital to the interpretation of *Sandman*'s events that Netflix chose to cast as a non–European person. In an interview with Robert K. Elder, Gaiman explained that the character of Death is intended as "a character who would be everything the Sandman wasn't" (64).

Many loyal fans have embraced Gaiman's support of *Sandman*'s racially diverse casting choices as a celebration of talent best suited to the spirit of each character, tending to cite tolerance, inclusion, and the unreality of a solely European fantastical universe. In "Literature and Public Life," Toni Morrison (2019a) critiques this kind of literary escapism as "participation in a wholly illusory community shaped by fear and unquenchable desire" (99). However, other fans see the inclusion of a significant percentage of non–European performers in casting rather than a token or irrelevant smattering of ethnically diverse characters as a challenge to their interpretation of the series. Gaiman's pursuit of representative diversity in his cast can be understood in contrast to his series character Richard Madoc, the villain in "Calliope" who performatively requests displays of ethnic diversity and gender balance, even while indulging his egoistic misogyny and narcissism in private.

While agreeing with and celebrating Gaiman's inclusive and diversity-rich casting choices, we diverge in this analysis from discussion of multiracial casting as an embrace of diversity that implies that racial integration is a positive that does not need further interpretation, an obvious benefit in a globalized interracial and international society without nuanced analytical meaning. Instead, this analysis seeks to excavate the particular relevance of the *Sandman*'s racially diverse cast playing the roles they are assigned in the economically colonialist era in which the Netflix series debuted. Deliberate consideration of the implications of the non–European races of several major characters in the Netflix series exposes the impactful relevance of the *Sandman*'s multiracial casting in its exposure of socio-historical antiracist messaging potentially inherent in the writing but occluded by the printed illustrations of the original *Sandman* texts. The goal of this excavation and these arguments is to establish the analytical necessity of interpreting these characters' racialized depictions as deliberately specific elements impacting understanding of the events in Netflix's adaptation of *Sandman*.

Gaiman has stated that the illustration of Death in the inaugural comic departs from his initial personification. While Gaiman wrote the text that defined Death's attitude and manner of speech, Mike Dringenberg, the original artist for Death, chose to provide his own visual interpretation of Death modeled on Cinamon Hadley. This deviated from Gaiman's initial prompts to draw a Death inspired by rocker Christa

Päffgen's performance persona Nico, as he explains when interviewed in Hy Bender's *The Sandman Companion* (1999). Death's series of illustrated manifestations clarify that the only consistent identifier for this immortal has been personality. Each *Sandman* artist's interpretation of the Endless supports Gaiman's concept that everyone sees these anthropomorphic characters differently. Each artist offers altered ways to perceive these characters, even as they remain loyal to foundational characteristics.

Gaiman's Death is not and has never been static. Lanette Cadle describes *Sandman*'s Death as "laboring through the centuries, through the initial sadness, the rejection of her role, her reborn acceptance, and through her continuing return to a temporary humanity, she has earned an irrepressible joy" (45). Prone to change, Death is recognizable by how she thinks and acts. Howell-Baptiste's Africanist Death exemplifies comfort, calm, and beauty, forcing the query of ethnic alliances and socialized racial codes, recalling with her ankh and loving approach to each newly dead person the loveliness and allure of pre–Adamic Continental African goddesses of Death such as Isis and her sister and iterations Nephthys, Bast, and Hathor/Sekhmet, as well as West African goddesses including Oya and Mami Wata. In *Myth, Literature, and the African World* (Soyinka 1992), *Moorings and Metaphors: Figures of Culture and Gender in Black Women's Literature* (Holloway 1991), and *Mythatypes: Signatures and Signs of African/Diaspora and Black Goddesses* (A. Brooks de Vita 2000), Wole Soyinka, Karla F.C. Holloway, and Alexis Brooks de Vita, respectively, examine these and more Africanist and Black goddesses of Death as beautiful, seductive, representative and bestowing of fecundity, motherhood, protection, and love, as well as ushering the soul on its journey from the physical to the spiritual worlds. Howell-Baptiste's Death immediately and viscerally evokes this prehistory of African goddesses.

The reinstatement of *Sandman*'s Death as attitudinally and visually precolonialist in her self-confident, identifiable African-ness nudges the viewer to bear in mind that continent's precolonial histories of power in its advanced Egyptian, Carthaginian, Ethiopian, Sudanese, and Malian civilizations, to name a few, that were envied by and influential to Europe's culturally foundational Greeks, Romans, and Crusaders as well as feared and emulated by European fiefdoms conquered, colonized and educated by Medieval Moors of African descent. The choice to cast Howell-Baptiste's Death forces one to face the centuries-long systematic process of misrepresentation, whitewashing, and widespread miseducation necessary to construct European colonialist racialism and its concomitant racism, a suppressed history painstakingly reconstructed in works such as Emmanuel Chukwudi Eze's (1997) anthology *Race and the Enlightenment* and Ned and Constance Sublette's (2015) *The American Slave Coast: A History of the*

Slave-Breeding Industry. The current contrast between unstated assumptions of relative powerlessness and demonstrated power that characterize the appearance and interpretation of Howell-Baptiste as Death, exuding a quiet, ancient power viewed in a late capitalist economically colonized global society, imbue *Sandman*'s resultant storyline with relevance to complex current and historical events, encourage suspicion of politically motivated racist propaganda, and invite personal efforts at psychological and emotional decolonization.

Perhaps the *Sandman* character whose unspoken frustrations and motives are most readily explained by considering its racialized Netflix personification is Desire, portrayed by Mexican American and Indigenous trans actor Mason Alexander Park. Gaiman's directing of Park to casting director Lucinda Syson has resulted in the embodiment of an Endless symbolic of a whitewashed yet pervasive history of inequity and exploitation, someone who straddles polarized realities as described by Gloria Anzaldúa (2007) in *Borderlands*. On Twitter, Park (2023) explained, "It just reminds me that most fans/the media only celebrate white AFAB gender creative people. As a Mexican/indigenous non-binary person who's been a lead in 3 large fantasy/sci-fi shows in the past 2 years, we need to do better." Park's symbiotically embattled interpretation of Desire is at once, therefore, not only the living symbol of hundreds of years of enemy nations having blended inseparably together but also masculine and feminine, the exploiting and the exploited, the one character ethnically ambiguous enough to appear and act as both instigator and recipient of unreasoning and relentless aggression inseparably coupled with the assumption of rejection. Park (2023) queries, "What kind of message are we sending to young queer kids who might be gender creative by continually uplifting a specific idea [of] what non binary people look like, while ignoring artists of color or of size or of different ability who are working just as much or as hard?" Desire's infamous but unexplained resentment of Dream makes intuitive sense given Park's and Tom Sturridge's visible ethnicities, with Anglo Dream's theft or abuse of some secret thing having caused Desire's eons of wanting to avenge that wrong.

This sibling antipathy cannot help but be overshadowed by and evocative of the historical Anglo U.S. takeover of Indigenous and Mexican territories while erasing those descendants' protections in the face of the U.S.'s de facto and de jure persecutions of those populations. Ian Haney Lopez (1998) posits that "the assignment of racial boundaries arises in the form of social practices, and so reveals itself to be a highly contingent, historically specific process" which "resulted in the racialization of Mexican Americans" (184). Exploring and embracing this racialization, Park (2023) comments, "Trans people are allowed to discuss privilege and the systems that might purposefully exclude certain parts of our community, without this being a personal attack on any of the actors." Desire embodied as an irresistible and yet despised Indigenous/Mexican American character exudes powerlessness to the same degree that it seems they should be powerful, suffering in feeling themselves to be resisted, rejected, and reviled by the very sibling who, it seems, once loved, sought out and embraced them, their intimate distancing festering with each act of treachery. Park concludes the long thread by reflecting, "So if for some reason you are misinterpreting or misrepresenting my discomfort with how certain 'palatable' ideas of queerness are rewarded while others are ridiculed or ignored, know that it's a reflection of the world at large."

Racial hierarchizing, imbalanced power dynamics, racially gendered opportunities, imposed professional limitations, and sociopolitical influences on interpersonal relationships become predominantly featured as well as supremely relevant in contemplating Lucienne's loyal wait for Morpheus's return, as interpreted by Vivienne Acheampong. Lucien of the comics was originally drawn as a tall, thin man of European descent with pointed ears and similarly pointed auburn hair, the human form Lucien selected after retiring as Morpheus's first Raven. Via Acheampong, Morpheus's most trusted Raven in the *Sandman* universe, has transformed into a woman of African descent. Acheampong's Lucienne preserves all she can of her immortal employer's home and library that she has catalogued and arguably understands better than he does, exemplifying the inconsistent and unreliable employability of highly educated women of African descent in formerly colonized societies. Patricia Hill Collins (2002) in *Black Feminist Thought* and Paula Giddings (1988) in *When and Where I Enter: The Impact of Black Women on Race and Sex in America* analyze the hierarchizing and extreme skewing of power dynamics in the U.S. as being historically and sociologically established upon the gendered racial disempowerment and devaluation of skills and qualifications of women and girls of African descent. What profession, what social niche, might Africanist Lucienne safely secure for herself, brilliant bibliophile that she is, if she were not able to identify herself as being of such crucial importance to the powerful Morpheus that she has become his placeholder and symbol of his imminent return, his unwaveringly loyal stand-in, in his absence?

Frantz Fanon (1952), in *Peau Noire, Masques Blancs* (*Black Skin, White Masks*), argues that a woman of African descent in a racially hierarchized post-chattel enslavement society worldwide may align herself with a man of European descent, even to her personal detriment and when their societal misalignment causes her increased psycho-emotional suffering, in a sustained effort to secure protection and relative social empowerment by association. Morrison (2019e) confronts and further details women's forced fidelity, employment dependency on men of European descent, and the combined suppressive forces of U.S. racism and sexism in "Women, Race, and Memory." Sociohistorical analysis contextualizes and clarifies why Acheampong's Lucienne might reasonably and obviously prefer to dwell in Morpheus's crumbling mansion, guarding his library as she awaits his return, rather than seek new employment or venture out elsewhere, unmoored, and encounter unknowns. Lucienne's choice to continue her implied affiliation with the dreaded Morpheus, seen by most with whom Lucienne interacts as being a male of European descent, would in this context grant her sufficient status and protection from revenge, humiliation, and degradation that might otherwise have been visited upon her by her employer's enemies, who have already stolen his relics, murdered his newest Raven, and imprisoned his person, were she to abandon that affiliation or wander from the disintegrating remnants of his home. Alone in the world, Lucienne's deliberately separating her identity from that of Morpheus might be analogous to putting herself in a situation similar to that of lynch- and rape-targeted, newly emancipated Reconstruction-era African American women.

However, being targeted by Morpheus's enemies is not the only endangerment a woman of African descent chosen by Morpheus may face if she abandons the association he has offered her. For confirmation of the perils uniquely visited upon a woman of African descent whom Morpheus previously loved, pre–Ethiopian Queen Nada's rejection of Morpheus has resulted in her ten thousand unrelieved years' imprisonment in Hell by her rejected lover's decree. When she pleads for release, Morpheus insists to the grieving Queen Nada that he has "not yet forgiven" her for her rejection of him; this communication between Morpheus and the millennia-condemned woman whose only infraction against him was her decision not to remain his lover are spotlighted by Peter S. Rawlik, Jr., (2007) as "the only person who requests a boon from our hero and is denied" (37). Acheampong's unflaggingly faithful Lucienne allows the audience a moment of renewed reflection and realization of the danger of being a woman of African descent who abandons Morpheus, however reasonable might be the motive for her rejection of the role he has chosen for her.

As Jeanine T. Abraham (2022) points out, racially mixed casting carries an obligation to be aware of the roles played and the messaging inherent in watching people of those races interact in the ways in which they are scripted to interact, particularly when the storyline incorporates sex and power in a racialized society in which dominance and relative powerlessness are often sexually intertwined. Under the pseudonym Linda Brent (1861), Harriet Jacobs, a woman who escaped chattel enslavement to her captor's serial rapist husband, wrote the autobiographical *Incidents in the Life of a Slave Girl*. Jacobs recounts a violent riot during which the poor people of European descent in her community raid, pillage, and destroy the homes of freed African Americans. This is a community resented by poorer European immigrants for its comparative education, skilled labor, and often blood relationship to and ongoing association with the landowning gentry who may have freed them or their ancestors, most probably in consideration of their being blood kin, from chattel slavery. During the riot, Jacobs recalls, one of her grandmother's landowning Anglo-American male relatives goes to stand guard at her grandmother's house, to make sure that the racist rioters pass by her home and do not feel free to loot, burn, or otherwise destroy it or harm her. Similarly, though unseen in the first season, Morpheus once played this protective role in offering Nada escape from the destruction of reality as a consequence of their relationship. Like Linda Brent's wealthy slaveholding relative protecting only her grandmother from the raging mob, Morpheus's rejected offer was extended only to the person he cared about, Queen Nada. Her rejection, in favor of protecting her community, is the cause of his rage and her imprisonment in Hell. This is the moment when Morpheus has gone from protective caretaker to punishing captor of the woman he loves and desires, no more Brent's relative, but her sexually predatory enslave.

Jacobs also details the personal humiliation and anguish of her choice to voluntarily submit herself as an adolescent child to the sexual usage of a Senator more powerful than her owner's husband, a local doctor, as a maneuver to shield herself from rape by her owner's husband and protect her future children from sale by his wife. This pattern of domestic assault and sexual usage followed by the sale of the resulting children is explained and recounted not only by Jacobs, a chattel slavery survivor writing in hiding as Brent, but also by other witnesses, victims and analysts of the U.S.'s chattel enslavement system, including Hannah Crafts (2002) in *The Bondwoman's Narrative*, William Wells Brown (1853) in *Clotel; Or, the President's Daughter*, Solomon Northup (1853) in *Twelve Years a Slave*, and in documents collected and analyzed by Stephanie E. Jones-Rogers (2019) in *They Were Her Property: White Women as Slave Owners in the American South*. The teenage Brent's/Jacobs's calculations of comparative power and her autobiographical defense of her choice to align herself with the more powerful man of European descent, choosing between the two such men who vie for access to her body rather than waiting to have that choice usurped by the one in whose house she is forced to live, makes it possible for Brent/Jacobs to checkmate the serial rapist married to her owner. There is no one in her queendom as powerful as she and no one in existence more powerful than Morpheus to whom Queen Nada can turn to protect herself and her people from the destruction of reality or Morpheus's vengeance.

Brent/Jacobs gives herself to and gives birth to the children of the U.S. Senator by her own underage consent, thus empowering herself to the extent that she can, rather than to the doctor attempting to take her by intimidation who desists only when a more influential Anglo-American man lays claim to her. The entirety of Brent's/Jacobs's young adult life is then spent struggling to secure her own and her children's freedom from bondage after the doctor refuses to sell them to the Senator, who promises to free them, rather than avoiding rape and the sale of her children away from her, which she witnesses happening to other captive women, girls and children born of rape. As with Morpheus's imprisonment of Queen Nada, if Dr. Flint cannot sexually possess Jacobs, he nevertheless insists on his right and power to attempt to find and keep her captive until they are both of such advanced age that he dies.

Race in the televised *Sandman* becomes an even more inescapably relevant and impactful factor in interpreting the false imprisonment of the orphaned boy, Jed, as interpreted by Eddie Karanja. Originally illustrated and colored as a European American child in the comics, the story explores the child's suffering at the hands of supposed family friends, while the Netflix *Sandman* casting allows audiences to consider racialized foster abuse. Jed's extreme brutalization mirrors the emotional, physical, and sexual abuse often visited upon and suffered by institutionalized African American children. This reflects a real-world legacy of further dehumanizing the abandoned and orphaned child of African descent in U.S. households and institutions by the inflicting of unpredictable and often unimaginable acts of cruelty.

This horrific pattern is depicted in Harriet Wilson's (1859) account of her nearly fatal foster care experience of severe physical abuse accompanied by denigration and constant racial denunciations—as witnessed by the name her foster family gives her, which she uses to title her autobiographical novel *Our Nig*. It is again found in the debilitating psychological racism that was inflicted on Malcolm X (1990) as a seven-year-old child in an orphanage, a child who once wanted to grow up to be an attorney, in *The Autobiography of Malcolm X*, as well as by Antwone Quenton Fisher's (2001) childhood subjection to repeated acts of sexual assault and physical torture in foster care recounted in *Finding Fish*. Unfortunately, time has not lessened these tortures, as the horrific real-life torture and exploitation of the Hart foster/adopted children in Oregon and their pleas for intervention until their murder in 2018 illustrates (Smiley 2018). The pervasive fears and almost incomprehensible realities of institutionalized racist abuse targeting orphaned and incarcerated African American children make up the backstory of *The Keeper* by Tananarive Due and Steven Barnes (2022), and the documented historical horrors of *The Reformatory* by Due (2023). These real world and fictionalized accounts of and by African Americans in the United States show how common such heinous foster and adoptive occurrences are, adding grave veracity to Jed's suffering in isolation and indicating how little surveillant protection he has. Jed's casting as an African American child makes this otherwise inexplicable betrayal of his dead parents' trust by a former friend tragically credible.

Tanya Asim Cooper (2013) explains in "Racial Bias in American Foster Care: The National Debate" that African American and Native American children risk greater maltreatment and abuse in foster care and are more likely to suffer secondary harm from the foster system itself, than children of other races. Netflix's *Sandman* accompanies the brutalities potentially to be suffered by an institutionalized child of African descent in the United States by concurrently and accurately depicting the increasingly desperate efforts made by abused or disempowered women attempting such a child's rescue, as in Crafts' *Bondwoman* and Brown's *Clotel*. Crafts' *Bondwoman* particularly hints at and gestures toward more frequently and clearly than most extant texts of the enslavement era the sexual predation to which adults and children in the relatively helpless state of chattel bondage or government control are subjected, a persistent problem of literary silencing addressed not only in-text by both Crafts and Jacobs but also still queried in the twentieth and twenty-first centuries by Morrison (2019b) in such reflections as "The Site of Memory." Therefore, as Crafts' text and the prehistory informing Morrison's (1988) *Beloved* make clear, there may well be traumatized women attempting to rescue African American children from abuse at the hands of owners or, more contemporaneously, court-appointed caretakers, if anyone tries or manages to save them. This racialized historical reality is excruciatingly faithfully depicted by the convergence of forces—some working against each other—necessary to save Jed in Netflix's *Sandman*.

This scenario of the disadvantaged woman or girl trying to save the abused child plays out in the analysis of Karanja's Jed bearing the prehistory of Jed's and Rose's great-grandmother, Unity, as played by Sandra James-Young. In "It's Pretty Graphic," Tara Prescott (2012) points out that Gaiman "draws to the surface issues that are normally erased in order to force us to see them and question them" (77). In this vein, great-grandmother Unity is a survivor of pedophiliac rape, her backstory foreshadowing and establishing the verisimilitude of Jed's experience of abuse decades after her own, while she was institutionalized due to worldwide Sleeping Sickness caused by Morpheus's capture. Unity's succumbing to Sleeping Sickness, though inspired by historical cases of Encephalitis

Lethargica, recalls the tsetse-fly borne, parasitic wasting disease known as African sleeping sickness or African trypanosomiasis, a worldwide epidemic that nods toward the relevance of Unity's Africanist representation in the Netflix series. In "'Calliope': How Off-Screen Sexual Violence Changes the Narrative,'" Pinky Chung-Man Lui examines the kind of off-screen sexual violence that viewers realize must have victimized Unity and that awaits Jed.

Unity's newly found great-granddaughter—the human vortex Rose, played by Vanesu Samunyai—carries on the tradition of autonomous womanism in the face of abandonment or when facing a hopeless case alone that recognizes racial and sexual legacies inherently referenced in casting choices. Rose's use of her otherworldly gifts to find Jed, risking ripping the universe apart, echoes the self-sacrificial determination to destroy everything, if necessary, for the sake of a doom-defying devotion to loved ones and those in peril that is reminiscent of historical African American women human rights activists such as Frances Ellen Watkins Harper, Ida B. Wells-Barnett, Mamie Till-Mobley, and Anne Moody.

Harper (2004) writes about the horrors and racism African American women endured not only during chattel enslavement but into Reconstruction, challenging the U.S.'s self-congratulatory turning of a blind eye to its de facto as well as de jure racial segregation and ongoing racially targeted persecutions meant to drive liberated African Americans to flee the United States following the Emancipation Proclamation. Wells (1892, 1900) risks being lynched herself in her efforts to expose and outlaw the bloody practices of the U.S.'s racially targeted national self-identification with and ongoing practice of violent vigilantism described in detail in such texts as *Southern Horrors* and *Mob Rule in New Orleans*. Similarly, Rose welcomes possible annihilation in pursuit of her brother's liberation.

Half a century later, not much changed. Till-Mobley finds herself catapulted into a media frenzy of hostile publicity that features the slandering and libeling of her murdered adolescent son within weeks of having sent him from Chicago to visit relatives for the summer in Mississippi (Till-Mobley and Barr 2006). Despite what must have been an insurmountable degree of combined shock, grief and horror, Till-Mobley nevertheless dedicates herself for decades to the exposure of machinations that got her son tortured and murdered by an attention-seeking married woman, and then obstructed the mother's effort to recover her son's horrifically mutilated body. Her search exposed lies and coverups that revealed not only her son's savage murder but also those of Civil Rights activists in Mississippi who disappeared while trying to assist African Americans to register to vote nearly one hundred years after Emancipation. In "Superheroes Can Be Children in Footie Pajamas: The Sensible Revisions of Netflix's

Sandman as Participating in the Larger Project of DC's Sandmen," Joseph Michael Sommers rebuilds the pre–Gaiman amalgamated evolution of Gault as the entity who does not want to be a nightmare, but instead a child's dream of rescue. Cast as an African-descent woman, Gault continues Till-Mobley's legacy of search and protection in the guise of Jed's deceased mother. Gault's rescue strategy reflects a specific African American community tradition of women acting as *othermothers* to African American children in need.

As we see Gault risking the rage of Morpheus an eternal incarceration, Moody, like many African American human rights activists, risks repeated incarceration in potentially fatal circumstances as well as the fear of police violence not only to get out the vote in sixties-era Mississippi but also to spend her tiny budget on clothing and school supplies to make sure that impoverished African American children can go to school. Beyond schooling, Moody is working to make sure that children can report incidents of rape while employed as child laborers, just as Gault works to equip Jed to believe he can self-protect.

Thelma Bryant-Davis et al. (2010) construct how transgenerational trauma affects African American women in "Struggling to Survive: Sexual Assault, Poverty, and Mental Health Outcomes of African American Women," analyzing how these legacies of abuse and trauma have historically hurt and continue to affect this particularly targeted group. As with Netflix's depiction of Rose, Gault, and Unity, these women's acts of courage in an effort to save or vindicate their own or others' endangered children often bring about increased persecution before they result in public awareness, concern, legal protection, and, hopefully, empowering alliances that can lend effective support.

Kristine Larsen (2012) explains that, in Gaiman's multiverse, "not only does the cosmos affect our actions, but our very actions have the power to shape, create, and even destroy universes" (262) before going on to describe Jed's intrepid older sister Rose Walker as "a sort of psychic or supernatural black hole who has the power to destroy worlds—a powerful modern cosmological goddess indeed" (271). Rose, acting on a seemingly irrepressible legacy of courage that is apparently her cultural inheritance, initially relies on an attorney friend, Lyta Hall, played by Razane Jammal, whose widowhood has overwhelmed her and causes her to abandon Rose's search for Jed in favor of languid indulgence in dreams of her dead husband. Sommers reconstructs the history of Lyta, her dead husband Hector Hall, and their interrelationship with Morpheus in the inception of their dreamed pregnancy in his essay in this volume. This abandonment by Lyta, upon whom Rose is counting to assist her in finding and rescuing Jed, is made ironic and hypocritical by the fact that the baby Lyta carries is another fatherless African American child, the same as Jed, based on the combination of the visible race of the child's deceased father and the U.S.'s historical one-drop rule of racial identification for African Americans. In short, the literally daydreaming attorney's death or incapacitation could leave her own child institutionalized, entrapped and neglected, or victimized just like the child she is willfully neglecting to help find and rescue: Jed. The racialization of these roles makes vivid the cyclic nature of this racialized history of abuse facilitated by neglect to follow up with investigation and rescue.

Jed is terrified and held captive in a rat-infested basement, threatened when noticed at all by the foster-parent caretakers who were once his father's friends. At one point, he reaches out to plant a plea for help in the purse of the social worker whose responsibility it is to ensure his safety. Jed's captor intercepts his note, instigating still more vicious acts of aggression. Rose's and Jed's efforts to get help from Lyta and the social worker, overwhelmed or self-concerned by their own challenging circumstances, fail. But while Rose and Unity are attempting to figure out whom they can trust and to whom Rose can turn for effective assistance in finding and liberating her brother, Jed is sustained by the self-empowering dreams gifted to him by an Africanist—not only physically of African descent, but also demonstrating the values of traditional African concepts of community, care and obligation to a child—female figure of nightmare, known as Gault, played by Ann Ogbomo. While the death-dealing Corinthian and universe-connecting Rose race to search for Jed, Gault has already found the boy and abandoned her post as butterfly-winged nightmare to educate Jed.

Disguised as his mother, Gault offers Jed dreams of being a superhero that imbue him with self-reliance, resilience, hope, and courage, teaching him levels of self-confidence that bolster him to survive in his waking world. In her self-appointed role as Gault's *othermother*, a term Collins (2002) explains is used to describe women of African descent who become protectors, mentors, and succorers for the vulnerable trapped in toxic conditions, Gault, like Rose, acts out a self-assured defiance of authority and flagrant disregard of punitive consequences that Alice Walker (1984) labeled with the alternative feminist term *womanism*. Womanism, Walker argues, characterizes uniquely African-descent women's resistant approach to the dually applied threats of racism and sexism that confront them and that throw up obstacles to acting autonomously on their own assessments, ethics, consciences, and best interests. Jed is empowered by Gault's *othermother*-facilitated and womanist-inspired dreams to believe that he has the ability to save others and provide rescue, defying and denying the physical reality of his helplessness. Sommers analyzes the prehistory of Jed's superhero costume and its significance to Jed's adopting the self-image of Sandman, thanks to Gault.

Gault teaches Jed to defy victimization by self-definition, just as she herself has chosen to do. For this reason, the terrorized boy feels emboldened enough to trust his own instincts and keep trying to save himself. Even after his failed attempt to get his social worker to rescue him, Jed goes on to resist the appeals of the horrifying Corinthian as chillingly interpreted by Boyd Holbrook. Though the Corinthian kills the boy's tormentors and appears to liberate Jed, thanks to Gault, he is not the first being to rescue the boy from his imprisonment and offer him solace, companionship, and protection. When Jed encounters the Corinthian, he has already been taught in Gault's arenas of power-filled fantasy to believe in himself as a liberator and agent in securing freedom for others. This translates into Jed's realization that he can and now must, when faced with the Corinthian and the Cereal Convention, think for, protect, and free himself.

Not only is the cannibalistic Corinthian's appetite a threat to Jed, but it has been figuratively foreshadowed in Jed's foster father's desire to degrade and destroy the boy in his care. In *The Delectable Negro*, Vincent Woodard (2014) describes a power hunger that has driven the historic torture and brutalization of—specifically—men and boys of African descent in the U.S. This is the situation in which Jed has been trapped by his late father's former friend, Barnaby Farrell, played by Sam Hazeldine. In an act of ritualistic castration and ingestion that hearkens back to historic U.S. lynching and torture rituals, the dangers Jed faces from both men recall eighteenth- and nineteenth-century U.S. cannibalism as an element of domination.

The targeted African-descent boy and the "ritualized punishment" he is forced to succumb to serve to "reify and ennoble" the racist persecutor, his foster father, whom Woodard describes as "parasite and consumer" (60, 61). Jed's "terror" unwittingly and perhaps unwillingly has fed Barnaby's sense of "authority and power" and secured him in his "white male identity," leaving the abusive male with "powerful feelings of satiation, leisurely comfort, and pleasure" (60, 61). In the frontispiece, Justin A. Joyce quotes Woodard's mention of "US frontiersmen and soldiers" eating and "harvesting the flesh" of Native Americans in their expansionist push, in reflections on "the Coda of the book 'Cannibal Nation'":

> I branch out in the conclusion to suggest how the consumption of black persons coincided with the literal and cultural consumption of other groups seen as expendable or marginal to the US nation-making endeavor.

This broader description of U.S. hierarchical dominance established based on who may eat and consume what or whom is also enacted in episode 5 of the first season, "24/7." In one scene, a Filipina businesswoman, Kate Fletcher (Lourdes Faberes), intimidates her African American husband Gary (James Udom) out of ordering the hamburger he clearly desires, instead forcing him to settle for the vegetarian salad she will allow him. Their interaction increasingly reveals his complete and absolute subservience to her in her relative position near the top of the U.S. societal food chain.

Kate, defying stereotypes that deny her agency and credit for her accomplishments, intentionally acts against biases about women of her ethnicity as submissive, if not invisible, sexual companions, fighting for recognition of her successes and choices. She seizes control by mimicking the soul-consuming dominance exercised by those for whom capitalism is structured to serve, acting out in accordance to ruby/reality manipulator John Dee's (David Thewlis) racially privileged perspective. Angelo Ancheta (2008) clarifies in *Race, Rights, and the Asian American Experience* the importance of identifying "subordination" in issues of racial discrimination, as racial subordination is

> an expression of power based on race in which a dominant person, group, or institution acts to place another person, group, or institution in a lesser or subordinate position relative to the dominant entity. Power and inequality are thus at the root of racial subordination [18].

Kate counters what is popularly considered to be the model minority script that undervalues her hard work and sacrifice and the erasure not only of Kate's business leadership but her presence. Tiffany Yip, Charissa Cheah, Lisa Kiang, and Gordon Nagayama Hall (2021) explain in "Rendered Invisible" that "Asian Americans remain marginalized and invisible in scientific endeavors and the public sphere" (576). Kate's efforts to assert herself over Gary, the partner whom others may assume is responsible for her leadership and business acumen but who is, in reality, a man who supports and credits her for her accomplishments, manifest at every opportunity to dominate and belittle, as if bullying her fellow ethnic minority whom she does not want to receive praise for her success will finally grant Kate the right and pseudo–Anglo-male standing to receive credit for it, herself.

These descriptions fit, as well, the cannibalistic, drawling Southern gentleman appearance of the Corinthian, who attempts to win and feed on Jed's affection, gratitude, and trust. Following his dramatic rescue, Jed is thus placed in the immediate and further danger of being "literally ingested" by the same Corinthian who has just delivered him from what Woodard (2014) describes as the "emotional and spiritual consumption" (61) he has been forced to endure from his foster father but now also faces from the various murderers gathered at the Cereal Convention, discussing and whetting their sexual, physical, emotional, and spiritual appetites. In this comparative context, it becomes clear that both males of European descent who have pursued and attempted to entrap Jed—Barnaby and the Corinthian—have done so because they view him, as Woodard explains, as an "expendable, consumable object" (75), specifically due to the child's combined race and sex as an African American boy.

Gault, secure in the confidence of her womanist actions' rightness in teaching Jed self-rescue, if not their legality in Morpheus's realm, is condemned by Morpheus to eternal imprisonment as punishment for abandoning her post to rescue Jed. Morpheus's condemnation to eternal imprisonment of another female figure of African descent who has attempted rescue of the endangered is a judgment that revisits and reasserts his ten millennia-ongoing sentence in Hell of Queen Nada. It now falls to the immoveable, impeccably dedicated Lucienne to counsel Morpheus to accept change. Change is the watchword and religious core of Octavia E. Butler's (1993, 1998) *Parables*, recalling one of the best-known series by an author who, Gaiman discusses in his interview with Novella Brooks de Vita (2023), he met and admired. Like Butler, Gaiman centers change—its inevitability, and the need to adapt to it—as the necessary framework upon which the future may be built and the multiverses may continue to function. Using that word "change" in describing Gaiman's insertion of "unending transformation" (218), Prescott (2015) explains in "Warming Up the Strings" that Gaiman pushes *Sandman*'s multivalent boundaries, forcing readers to adapt to his own breaking of rules:

> Gaiman created *Sandman*, exceeding all of our expectations, but he still reserves the right to change or even uncreate his creation however he sees fit (with or without the permission of the fans) [227].

Lucienne's argument in favor of accepting change persuades Morpheus to reverse his most recent anti-womanist condemnatory judgment and free Gault to once again haunt the realm of the Dreaming. More to the point of this essay is that, in arguing for embrace of change, Gaiman—through Gault's disruption and Lucienne's reasoning—perhaps offers an apt metaphorical philosophical encapsulation of the process of reconsideration potentially undergone by viewers initially resistant to the racial diversification of *Sandman*'s characters in the Netflix series. In "Speaking the Cacophony of Angels," Rachel R. Martin (2012) observes that "Gaiman operates within and utilizes the phallocentric discourse in his creation and depiction of women ... utilizing the dominant discourse to critique and problematize its own assumptive frameworks" (12).

Considered in the context of this argument, it would appear that the multiethnic array of performers interpreting *Sandman*'s characters facilitates Gaiman's transcendence of the discourse limitations of the page by sharing unique world perspectives through the medium of interpretive actors as discursive instruments. Marilyn "Mattie" Brahen (2007) explains that "Neil Gaiman's works abound with dualistic transmutations" such that "everything is real and everything is an illusion, and somehow the world is, if not always better for it, at least more meaningful because of that union" (145). Taking the possibilities of this dualistic transmutation an interpretive step further, Chris Dowd (2007) argues in "An Autopsy of Storytelling" that "for Gaiman, metafiction is a surgical tool" that "shows us something we could never have seen otherwise" (104). Gaiman's own embrace of change may bring the plurality of his series' fans to appreciate the nuance and profundity with which visual racial diversity amplifies and clarifies the socio-historical commentary, educational significance and relevance to current sociopolitical issues of *Sandman*'s sweeping and unrelenting vision.

Note

1. The European Enlightenment's ethnic distinction erasure in its colorization of people and its adopting of the term "White" for Europeans is highly offensive, particularly when consulting dictionary definitions of these words and finding their literal meanings reflected in ongoing social stereotypes and skewed human and civil rights. We try to avoid using colorized terms for people, particularly people of African descent, and I (Alexis Brooks de Vita) have tried since publishing *Mythatypes* to help academia adopt regional and continental rather than misrepresentative colorized terms for ethnic and racial groups.

References

Abraham, Jeanine T. 2022. "Review: *Good Luck to You, Leo Grande*: A Character Study about Sex, Aging, and Objectification." *Black Girl Nerds*. December 31. https://blackgirlnerds.com/review-good-luck-to-you-leo-grande-a-character-study-about-sex-aging-and-objectification/.
Ancheta, Angelo N. 2008. *Race, Rights, and the Asian American Experience*. Rutgers University Press.
Anzaldúa, Gloria. 2007. *Borderlands/La Frontera: The New Mestiza*. 3rd ed. Aunt Lute Books.
Bender, Hy. 1999. *The Sandman Companion*. 1st ed. Vertigo/DC Comics.
Brahen, Marilyn "Mattie." 2007. "The Thin Line Between." In Schweitzer 2007, 140–48.
Brent, Linda [Harriet Jacobs]. 1861. *Incidents in the Life of a Slave Girl*. Project Gutenberg, 2004. https://www.gutenberg.org/files/11030/11030-h/11030-h.htm.
Brooks de Vita, Alexis. 2000. *Mythatypes: Signatures and Signs of African/Diaspora and Black Goddesses*. Greenwood.
Brooks de Vita, Novella. 2023. "Building Inclusive Worlds and Global Representations in the Works of Neil Gaiman." *Journal of the Fantastic in the Arts* 33, no. 3, 103–30.

Brown, William Wells. 1853. *Clotel: Or, The President's Daughter*. Project Gutenberg, January 1, 2000. https://www.gutenberg.org/cache/epub/2046/pg2046.html.epub.
Bryant-Davis, Thelma, Sarah E. Ullman, Yuying Tsong, Shaquita Tillman, and Kimberly Smith. 2010. "Struggling to Survive: Sexual Assault, Poverty, and Mental Health Outcomes of African American Women." *American Journal of Orthopsychiatry* 80, no. 1 (January): 61–70. https://doi.org/10.1111/j.1939-0025.2010.01007.x. PMID: 20397989; PMCID: PMC3870142.
Butler, Octavia E. 1993. *Parable of the Sower*. Four Walls Eight Windows.
———. 1998. *Parable of the Talents*. Seven Stories Press.
Cadle, Lanette. 2012. "The Power of the Perky: The Feminist Rhetoric of Death." In Prescott and Drucker 2015, 32–46.
Collins, Patricia Hill. 2002. *Black Feminist Thought: Knowledge, Consciousness, and the Politics of Empowerment*. Routledge.
Crafts, Hannah. 2002. *The Bondwoman's Narrative*. Warner Books.
Dowd, Chris. 2007. "An Autopsy of Storytelling: Metafiction and Neil Gaiman." In Schweitzer 2007, 103–20.
Due, Tananarive. 2023. *The Reformatory*. Gallery/Saga Press.
Due, Tananarive, and Steven Barnes. 2022. *The Keeper*. Harry N. Abrams.
Elder, Robert K. 2007. "Gods and Other Monsters: A *Sandman* Exit Interview and Philosophical Omnibus." In Schweitzer 2007, 54–78.
Eze, Emmanuel Chukwudi. 1997. *Race and the Enlightenment: A Reader*. Wiley-Blackwell.
Fanon, Frantz. 1952. *Peau noire, masques blancs*. Editions du Seuil. https://archive.org/details/peau-noire-masques-blancs-by-frantz-fanon/mode/1up.
Fisher, Antwone Quenton. 2001. *Finding Fish: A Memoir*. William Morrow.
Gaiman, Neil (w), et al. 2022a. *Sandman Book One: Preludes and Nocturnes*. DC Comics.
———. 2022b. *Sandman Book Two: The Doll's House*. DC Comics.
———. 2022c. *Sandman Book Three: Dream Country*. DC Comics.
———. 2022d. *Sandman Book Four: Season of Mists*. DC Comics.
Gaiman, Neil, David S. Goyer, and Allan Heinberg, creators. 2022. *Sandman*. Season 1. Netflix.
Giddings, Paula. 1988. *When and Where I Enter: The Impact of Black Women on Race and Sex in America*. Bantam.
Harper, Frances Ellen Watkins. 1853. *Iola Leroy; Or, Shadows Uplifted*. Project Gutenberg, 2004. https://www.gutenberg.org/cache/epub/12352/pg12352.html.
Holloway, Karla F. C. 1991. *Moorings and Metaphors: Figures of Culture and Gender in Black Women's Literature*. Rutgers University Press.
Jones-Rogers, Stephanie E. 2019. *They Were Her Property: White Women as Slave Owners in the American South*. Yale University Press.
Larsen, Kristine. 2012. "Doors, Vortices, and the In-Between: Quantum Cosmological Goddesses in the Gaiman Multiverse." In Prescott and Drucker 2015, 261–79.
Lopez, Ian Haney. 1998. "Race and Erasure: The Salience of Race to Latinos/As." In *The Latino/a Condition: A Critical Reader*, edited by Richard Delgado and Jean Stefancic, 180–95. New York University Press.
Martin, Rachel R. 2012. "Speaking the Cacophony of Angels: Gaiman's Women and the Fracturing of Phallocentric Discourse." In Prescott and Drucker 2015, 261–79.
Moody, Anne. 1992. *Coming of Age in Mississippi: The Classic Autobiography of Growing Up Poor and Black in the Rural South*. Dell.
Morrison, Toni. 1988. *Beloved*. Plume.
———. 2019a. "Literature and Public Life." In Morrison 2019c, 96–101.
———. 2019b. "The Site of Memory." In Morrison 2019c, 233–45.
———. 2019c. *The Source of Self-Regard: Selected Speeches, Essays, and Meditations*. Alfred A. Knopf.
———. 2019d. "Unspeakable Things Unspoken: The Afro-American Presence in American Literature." In Morrison 2019c, 161–97.
———. 2019e. "Women, Race, and Memory." In Morrison 2019c, 86–95.
Northup, Solomon. 1853. *Twelve Years a Slave: Narrative of Solomon Northup, a Citizen*

of New-York, Kidnapped in Washington City in 1841, and Rescued in 1853, from a Cotton Plantation near the Red River in Louisiana. Project Gutenberg, 2014. https://www.gutenberg.org/cache/epub/45631/pg45631-images.html.
Park, Mason Alexander (@MasonAPark). 2023. "It just reminds me that most fans/the media only celebrate white AFAB gender creative people. As a Mexican/indigenous non-binary person. . ." Twitter, February 12. https://twitter.com/MasonAPark/status/1624868802537345024.
Prescott, Tara. 2012. "It's Pretty Graphic: Sexual Violence and the Issue of 'Calliope.'" In Prescott and Drucker 2015, 64–80.
_____. 2015. "Warming Up the Strings." In Prescott and Drucker 2015, 216–31.
Prescott, Tara, and Aaron Drucker, eds. 2015. *Feminism in the Worlds of Neil Gaiman: Essays on the Comics, Poetry and Prose.* McFarland.
Rawlik, Peter S., Jr. 2007. "The King Forsakes His Throne: Campbellian Hero Icons in Neil Gaiman's *Sandman.*" In Schweitzer 2007, 30–50.
Schweitzer, Darrell. 2007. *The Neil Gaiman Reader.* Wildside.
Smiley, Lauren. 2018. "Two White Moms. Six Black Kids. One Unthinkable Tragedy. A Look Inside the 'Perfect' Hart Family." *Glamour,* September 6. https://www.glamour.com/story/hart-family-tragedy-jen-and-sarah-hart-case.
Soyinka, Wole. 1992. *Myth, Literature, and the African World.* Cambridge University Press.
Sublette, Ned, and Constance Sublette. 2015. *The American Slave Coast: A History of the Slave-Breeding Industry.* Lawrence Hill Books.
Till-Mobley, Mamie, and David Barr III. 2006. *The Face of Emmett Till.* Dramatic. https://www.dramaticpublishing.com/media/pdf/excerpts/exFaceEmmettTillF93.pdf.
Walker, Alice. 1984. *In Search of Our Mothers' Gardens: Womanist Prose.* Houghton Mifflin.
Wells-Barnett, Ida B. 1892. *Southern Horrors: Lynch Law in All Its Phases.* The New York Age Print. Schomburg Center for Research in Black Culture, Manuscripts, Archives and Rare Books Division, The New York Public Library, Digital Collections. Retrieved April 21, 2023. https://digitalcollections.nypl.org/items/634281e0-4abc-0134-346c-00505686a51c.epub.
_____. 1900. *Mob Rule in New Orleans: Robert Charles and His Fight to Death, the Story of His Life, Burning Human Beings Alive, Other Lynching Statistics.* Project Gutenberg, 2005. https://www.gutenberg.org/files/14976/14976-h/14976-h.htm.
Wilson, Harriet. 1859. *Our Nig: Or, Sketches from the Life of a Free Black, in a Two-story House, North: Showing that Slavery's Shadows Fall Even There.* Project Gutenberg, 1996. https://www.gutenberg.org/cache/epub/584/pg584-images.html.
Woodard, Vincent. 2014. *The Delectable Negro: Human Consumption and Homoeroticism Within US Slave Culture.* New York University Press.
X, Malcolm, and Alex Haley. 1990. *The Autobiography of Malcolm X.* Ballantine.
Yip, Tiffany, Charissa S. L. Cheah, Lisa Kiang, and Gordon C. Nagayama Hall. 2021. "Rendered Invisible: Are Asian Americans a Model or a Marginalized Minority?" *American Psychologist* 76, no. 4: 575–81. https://doi.org/10.1037/amp0000857.

The Shadow of Empire
Neil Gaiman's Dialogue with Orientalism

AAYUSHI SHAH

In the pilot episode of Netflix's *Dead Boy Detectives,* Kirby Howell-Baptiste's Death recites a portion of Kipling's "The Sack of the Gods" to a tortured ghost-soldier who technically died in India 100 years ago. "He never wasted a leaf or a tree. Do you think He would squander souls?" she says comfortingly to the man before she escorts him into the Sunless Lands (Krieger 2024). This small moment in the adaptation, which features characters who originated in the *Sandman* comic and actors from the Netflix *Sandman* cast, touches on persistent themes in works by and adjacent to Neil Gaiman: the complicated legacy of Kipling, the power dynamics of empire and colonialism, and the stubborn persistence of Orientalism. Noah Berlatsky (2011) notes that Gaiman, his *Sandman* collaborator P. Craig Russell, and *Habibi* illustrator Craig Thompson are "nostalgic for Orientalism—they know it's a dream, a vision in a bottle, but they just can't bear to put the bottle down." Understanding the different ways that Gaiman's works have perpetuated and resisted these tendencies is vital to understanding the legacy of the current *Sandman* television series, and can offer guides for future adaptations of his work.[1]

Orientalism, as defined by Edward Said in his book of the same name, is a style of thought that differentiates the East, or the Orient, from the West, or the Occident (Said 1978, 10). It is a series of ideas and fantasies about the East placed upon these cultures and people to differentiate them from the West, and in this differentiation, to justify and drive colonialism and empire. As a result of this mode of thinking, "a very large mass of writers … have accepted the basic distinction between East and West as the starting point for elaborate theories, epics, novels, social descriptions, and political accounts concerning the Orient, its people, customs, 'mind,' destiny, and so on" (11). This thinking impacts not only political policy decisions but also common tropes in popular culture. Therefore, by analyzing the work of modern acclaimed writers like Neil Gaiman, we can investigate how pervasive Orientalist tropes are even in a supposedly post-colonial landscape. As adaptations of Gaiman's works become more and more mainstream, their impact on American culture is increasing. Three of his most popular works, *Stardust* (adapted in 2008), *The Graveyard Book* (currently in early adaptation stages), and *Sandman* (2023–current) show the nuances in the ways these texts engage with Orientalism, and with study, can serve as important guides for the adaptations to follow.

Orientalism in Gaiman's Fiction

Before delving into the recent television adaptation of *Sandman*, this essay will provide an overview of the variety of ways that Orientalism has emerged in Gaiman's fiction. In *Stardust* (1998), *The Graveyard Book* (2008), and *Sandman* (comics 1989–1996, television series 2023–), Neil Gaiman builds on existing tropes, stories, and mythology, developing his own themes on top of them. Often, the common frameworks of Western literature contain inbuilt Orientalist tropes that writers may inadvertently replicate if they are not careful to address these themes. It is no secret that J.K. Rowling has been raked over the coals, and justifiably so, for her awkward and token attempts at "diversifying via revisionism" in the Harry Potter universe (Sims 2022, 106). These tropes delegate a strict binary between the East and the West, showcasing that while "the Oriental is irrational, depraved (fallen), childlike, 'different'; thus the European is rational, virtuous, mature, 'normal'" (Said 1978, 48). The Orient and its people are depicted as both evil or malicious and irrational or childlike, and in both ways deemed undeserving of the ability to rule themselves. This way, there was a justification for colonization of the East and a dismissal of the dissatisfaction of the native population. The Orient itself was depicted as a land of abundance, fantastical and unknowable, and poorly governed by the native people, ripe for exploitation by a colonizing entity.

These tropes are most clear in Victorian writing, the point of development for many tropes of literature about the East. Most of the best-known Victorian works deal with colonialism or the empire, even if just as a plot device or backdrop to their stories (Banerjee 2019, 86). Many of these works chose to depict India under the British Raj, and through these stories "Indians were cast with irredeemable difference," never on equal footing to their Western colonizers, and never given agency as characters with free will within the framework of the story (91). As a Victorian writer, Rudyard Kipling, who was well known for his short story collection *The*

Jungle Book, remained a "firm defender of empire" through the themes of his work (Bivona 2019, 103).

Even in stories that do not directly address the East or take place in a fantastic world where the East or the West do not exist, there is an overlaying of these dichotomies over fantasy peoples and nations. While fantasy may, at first glance, seem free from real-life political inequalities, fantasy stories are "socially embedded, and draw upon pre-existing cultural discourses" (Balfe 2004, 76). In the traditional fantasy adventure story, there is an encounter between the "us" and the outsiders, "them," and the "conflation of 'us' and 'good' often appears to confirm feelings of moral and cultural superiority when 'we' encounter 'them' in Fantasy narratives" (76). By placing the constructed ideal of the West as the "us" and the typical depictions of the East on the encountered outsider "them" in the world of a fantasy story, these Orientalist tropes are reconstructed within the fantasy framework.

Because of the perversity of these tropes, it can often be difficult to escape emulating them, even for modern writers who are hoping to subvert or reinterpret these commonly accepted dichotomies of the world. As Sims (2022) notes about the reimagining of the snake Nagini in *The Crimes of Grindelwald*, "Rather than the much-needed nuanced representation of Asian women, Nagini is nothing more than a 're-presentation' of a centuries-old Orientalist construct." Often by deliberately finding and subverting these tropes, writers can engage and grapple with their political and cultural implications. Gaiman, as a modern writer engaging with genres that typically contain Orientalist tropes, attempts to be in dialogue with these tropes to subvert them. But, like the creators of *Crimes of Grindelwald*, he instead "re-presents" them. While Gaiman nonetheless replicates these tropes by the conclusion of *Stardust*, ten years later, he successfully delivers distinct and opposing final themes in *The Graveyard Book*, showing that there must be careful consideration of themes and tropes within modern narratives to stop the perpetuation of Orientalist rhetoric. In *Sandman*, however, Gaiman's themes invite questioning of Orientalist rhetoric, while the frameworks may exacerbate colonial stereotypes.

Women of the East as Sexually Exotic Others: Stardust

The exotic othering of women that occurs in *Sandman* had a precursor in Gaiman's novel *Stardust*. In this book, Gaiman begins with the framework of a typical fantasy adventure story. According to Myles Balfe, often fantasy fiction parallels Orientalist tropes, and "Western heroes in these narratives have to voyage to the 'Fantastic East' for various reasons" (Balfe 2004, 79). In *Stardust*, this "Fantastic East" is Faerie, which Tristran voyages into in order to collect the star, Yvaine. Faerie and the East are framed in parallel ways, making the connection between the Orient and Faerie apparent. When Tristran is speaking with Victoria Forester, "the wind blew from Faerie and the East," giving him the courage to ask her to marry him (Gaiman 1998, 58). In declaring his love, he states, "I would go to India for you, Victoria Forester, and bring you the tusks of elephants, and pearls as big as your thumb, and rubies the size of wren's eggs" (61). Tristran initially offers the treasures of the actual East to Victoria to convince her to marry him, and in the end his actual quest involves collecting a treasure of Faerie as a sign of his devotion. The East and Faerie are framed in the same way through these parallels—as exotic and other.

Having established that Faerie is the parallel of the East, it is very easy to fall into common tropes of Western fantasy adventure books. The Western protagonist ventures into the East, and the hero is depicted in contrast to people of the East. The East cannot rule itself, and requires the assistance of the West in order to improve itself. In the colonial dichotomy, the East exists as a resource to be exploited, and those in the East are incapable of governing their own resources or caring for the treasures they have dominion over. The East and the West are distinct communities, which cannot be blurred. While Gaiman initially subverts some of these tropes, the actions of Tristran and the conclusion of the novel end up playing into these Orientalist frameworks.

Initially when Tristran encounters the star, Yvaine yells insults at him, which Alice Curry deems "testament to the text's emerging anti-imperialistic counter-discourse" by giving voice to the representative of the colonized (Curry 2010, 25). However, rather than being the symbol of "Gaiman's quiet mockery" of Orientalist tropes as Curry posits, in the overall framing of the book this does not have an impact on the Orientalist themes (23). This moment of agency granted to Yvaine does not change the fact that Tristran sees her as an object, a means to fulfill his quest. As he spends more time with Yvaine, he thinks:

> It was with this *and* that Tristran closed his mouth. For he could no longer reconcile his old idea of giving the star to Victoria Forester with his current notion that the star was not a thing to be passed from hand to hand, but a true person in all respects and no kind of thing at all. And yet, Victoria Forester *was* the woman he loved [Gaiman 1998, 279].

Despite the realization that Yvaine is not an object, Tristran still does not change his direction. He is still set on taking Yvaine with him all the way to Wall, even if he claims he wants to help her get back to her home after all that. Yvaine's freedom is not yet worth more than Victoria Forester's regard. As Yvaine is a magical Other, different from Tristran, and representative of Faerie, this goes to indicate that Tristran sees Faerie as something to be used for his own gains, as a means to an end. Even if he is not entering Faerie with malicious or colonial intent, this perspective of the East and its people contributes to a colonial framework of exploitation.

Orientalist thinking came with the justification of colonization through framing the East as infantile and weak-minded, people in possession of great treasures that they are incapable of wielding or caring for. This idea justified exploitation of resources and wealth by colonizing countries. This trope can be seen in the framing for the main villains of the story, Lord Septimus of Stormhold and the Witch-Queen. Both these characters are portrayed as evil in their quest to find Yvaine and use her for their own ends. The Witch-Queen is domineering, using her magic to hurt those who get in her way. It is clearly undesirable that these two capture Yvaine, as they see her as purely an object. However, Tristran begins the story with a very similar mindset, and it takes him much for the story to begin to change his mind. By the end of the story, the once terrifying Witch-Queen has become an old and frail woman, and "Yvaine realized that she felt nothing but pity for the creature who had wanted her dead" (Gaiman 1998, 322). The Witch-Queen squandered her youth in a chase for the star's heart and now will never claim it, as it belongs to Tristran. The two people from Faerie who come the closest to possessing the star are portrayed as unequivocally evil and dangerous. In contrast, Tristran, an outsider, is portrayed as well intentioned and generally a good person.

At the end of the novel, Tristran ascends to the throne of Stormhold, after he travels Faerie with Yvaine. His reign is portrayed as positive, and he is a just and wise leader, one who "made as few decisions as possible, but those he made were wise ones, even if the wisdom was not always apparent at the time" (Gaiman 1998, 330). This wise, level-headed ruling contrasts with the Lords of Stormhold, particularly Septimus, who is described as crafty and murderous, having killed many of his brothers on the way to the throne. The Lords of Stormhold are archaic, strict in their traditions, and it can be inferred that they would not have made good or wise rulers the way Tristran does. The idea that the East is wild, uncivilized, and thus incapable of governing itself, can be seen here.

One subversion of Orientalism comes in Tristran's origin, as he is half from Faerie and half from Wall. This allows for blurring of lines between the East and the West. However, Tristran is restricted to being one or the other for the duration of the story—despite his dual origin, he can only engage with one aspect at a time, and must eventually choose between them. Despite growing up in Wall, and having his family still residing in

Wall, when he gazes at the village at the end of the novel, "oil lamps and gas lamps and candles glowed in the windows of the houses of the village. To Tristran, then, they seemed as distant and unknowable as the world of the Arabian Nights" (Gaiman 1988, 324). Once again, there is a comparison to the East that emphasizes its distinctness from the West—the world of the Arabian Nights is used as a representation of the strange and unknowable. This comparison draws attention to the strict distinction between Faerie and Wall, even for someone ostensibly of both worlds like Tristran, who through becoming a part of Faerie has given up his understanding of and belonging in Wall.

At the end of the story, Tristran chooses to stay in Faerie with Yvaine. However, this option is only available to him if he cuts himself off from the West:

> He looked upon the lights of Wall for what he knew (it came to him then with certainty) was the last time. He stared at them for some time and said nothing, the fallen star by his side. And then he turned away, and together they began to walk toward the East [Gaiman 1998, 326].

There is once again a division, a choice Tristran must make. Despite his very existence being evidence of the mingling between the East and the West, the ending of the story closes the door on the potential of blurring these strict dichotomies, upholding the idea of "us" versus "them" that formed the basis of Orientalist thinking.

Resisting and Reversing the Binary: The Graveyard Book

Despite the replication of Orientalist tropes through the lens of the adventure story in *Stardust*, when dealing with explicit inspiration from a work steeped in Victorian era Orientalist thinking, the themes Gaiman considers work to subvert their Orientalist inspirations. *The Graveyard Book* is a novel explicitly inspired by *The Jungle Book*, a collection of short stories by Rudyard Kipling. *The Jungle Book* and *The Graveyard Book* each follow the story of a young orphaned boy who survives through adoption into a society very different from his own, by the jungle animals in *The Jungle Book*, and by the ghosts and monsters of the graveyard in *The Graveyard Book*. Kipling was born in British occupied India and wrote many works that reflected an Orientalist perspective of India and its people. In *The Jungle Book*, the clearest trope in use is the strict delineation of the Other, crafting a very binary sense of good versus evil. According to Robertson (2011), "the animals who break the Jungle Law are characterized as being evil, while those who remain obedient to the Law are commended for being good" (169). The tiger Shere Khan "is evil because he carries the shame of the First of the Tigers, who broke the law by becoming the first animal to kill in the jungle" (169). The main villain is marked as evil from the start, because of the actions of the tigers before him. There is no blurring of the distinctions between good and evil, as virtue and villainy are depicted as inherent properties of a group. The strict binary of good and helpful versus evil and incompetent reflects Orientalist tropes in fantasy.

Unlike in *Stardust*, in *The Graveyard Book*, Gaiman blurs these lines, indicating that the Other is often very similar to ourselves, and that the distinction between good and evil is not nearly as simple as it seems. This is evident in the section where Bod has been captured by ghouls and is hoping to be rescued. There is a figure behind him that looks like a monstrous dog, and he thinks, "I'm between the ghouls and the monster" (Gaiman 2008, 91). However, it is later revealed that the supposed monster is Miss Lupescu, his teacher, who is a Hound of God. According to Miss Lupescu,

> Those that men call Werewolves or Lycanthropes call themselves Hounds of God, as they claim their transformation is a gift from their creators and they will repay the gift with their tenacity, for they will pursue an evildoer to the very gates of Hell [97].

Through this depiction, Gaiman forces the audience to change their perspective of Bod's predicament multiple times. Despite being outwardly frightening and monstrous, Miss Lupescu reveals herself to be righteous, referred to in a way that makes her connected to and in the service of God. Rather than portraying outward difference as a sign of "Otherness," there is a reversal, showing us that our initial perceptions of those different from ourselves are not always reliable, and that the definitions of good and evil are not so black and white.

The main villain of the novel is the man Jack, a methodical killer who murdered Bod's family and is the reason he was stranded in the graveyard as a baby. When he is looking for Bod again, the man Jack (in disguise as Mr. Frost) attempts to find him through getting close to Bod's friend Scarlett. While being Mr. Frost, he is wholly human, and very kind to Scarlett and her mother. Only once he is able to meet Bod and get him away from Scarlett does he bring out his knife and reveal himself as the man Jack, "as if Mr. Frost has been a coat or hat the man had been wearing, that he had now discarded" (Gaiman 2008, 255). This easy switch between harmless human and dangerous killer emphasizes how initial impressions can be deceiving. It shows that the man Jack is not suspicious if he puts on an affable exterior, easily able to present himself as a kind and helpful person. His name, the man Jack, also continually serves as a reminder, that he is as far as the reader knows a living human man, not some monstrous creature. The major villain of the story being human and alive, just like Bod, makes it more difficult to dismiss him as purely monstrous or Other. This concept is further compounded by the scene where the man Jack wakes up and seems to know he has a lead to find Bod. When he walks downstairs, he greets his grandmother, who is cooking. This villain, who so far has been portrayed only as monstrous and as a threat to Bod's life, has a family and people who care about him and cook for him. It is a reminder that he is human, and a person with a family. Rather than the strange or supernatural being the villain, the main danger for Bod in the novel comes from a fellow living human, not so different from Bod himself.

Silas is Bod's guardian, and thus is a key figure of comfort and safety for Bod. In fact, Bod's capture by the ghouls occurs at a period where Silas is not present. However, when Bod indicates that Silas did the right thing by eliminating the Jacks, and that they deserved it because "they were terrible. They were monsters," his division of the world into the people he cares about versus monsters is yet again challenged (Gaiman 2008, 303). Silas responds by telling Bod, "When I was younger.... I did worse things than Jack. Worse than any of them. I was the monster then, Bod, and worse than any monster" (303). Silas represents the ability to grow and change, and to reflect. If there is a strict binary between those that are evil and those that are good, or as Bod presents it, between good people and monsters, there is no way that someone who was formerly a monster could be a good person, because being a monster is inherently part of them and their "Other-ness." Instead, through Silas, who is continually a reliable, comforting, and good character, we see that being a good person or a monster is a result of actions and choices, rather than any inherent qualities of a certain group.

Even Bod, the protagonist of the story, lives in morally gray areas. After Bod defeats the man Jack, his friend Scarlett beings to see him differently, and is now scared of him. She says, "You aren't a person. People don't behave like you. You're as bad as [the man Jack] was. You're a monster" (Gaiman 2008, 287). Bod is unhappy with this confrontation by his friend, and claims that "after everything he had been through that night, after everything that had happened, this was somehow the hardest thing to take" (286). Within the story, Bod is not absolved of this moral dilemma. Silas takes Scarlett away and erases her memory of Bod and his actions, and she walks away from him, not looking back. Bod's actions against the man Jack and his allies are not easily justified as the actions of a purely morally good and righteous character. Instead, while Bod was simply acting in order to defend himself and his friends, he must still face the consequences of his actions and contemplate his own moral standing.

Gaiman presents a complex and nonbinary sense of morality through this part of the novel. Rather than setting up an "us" versus "them" story with strict binaries of goodness and evil, it challenges our ingrained perceptions of who is considered justified and righteous in their actions. Bod is not absolved of his seemingly dangerous or violent actions, even if he was simply attempting to protect the people he cares about. Even Silas, who is a positive and comforting presence for Bod throughout the story, does not absolve him of this guilt. When Bod asks, "But why? I saved her life. I'm not a bad person. And I'm just like her. I'm alive too," he gets no answer from Silas (Gaiman 2008, 289). Bod seems to realize that there is no answer that Silas can give him that will be any different from his own conclusions and moves on to the next point in the conversation. He realizes that being the same as someone does not mean they will inevitably understand you, or that you will have similar values and ideas to them. Just because he is alive does not mean Scarlett will immediately understand him, any more than growing up in the graveyard will mean that the ghosts will immediately understand him.

The construction of these themes goes directly against Orientalist frameworks, which impose themselves on strict binaries of good and evil and hard lines between "us" and "them." In *The Graveyard Book*, nothing is as black and white as it might at first seem. Nearly all characters extend beyond the categories they "should" belong to. The dead are lively, the living boy converses with the dead, and the Sleer, an ominous entity that ultimately kills, isn't *evil*, it just acts according to its nature. Even Bod the hero makes choices that lead to another character's death (and horrify one of his only living friends). In *The Graveyard Book*, there is very little emphasis on othering the enemy and valorizing the protagonist. Rather, Gaiman emphasizes that one's initial impression can be deceiving, and touches on the capacity for both good and evil found in all people, regardless of the in-group they align themselves with. People can grow and change, and goodness is a choice, not a birthright.

Looking Backwards but Also Ahead: Sandman

The comic series *Sandman*, written by Gaiman and illustrated by several artists over its seventy-five issues and later spinoffs, covers a wide variety of fantasy genre tropes, with the main character Dream sliding in and out of different mythologies as the story progresses. When reflecting on themes of Orientalism in stories like "Calliope," Gaiman subverts these tropes and shows the depth of monstrosity concealed in the desire to control the Orient. However, in *Sandman* stories set more overtly in the East, among Othered people and their mythologies, there is less care to ensure the dignity of those cultures still suffering under the shadow of colonialism.

One issue of particular interest is issue #20, "Façade," which depicts a woman who is turned into a twisted elemental superhero after invading an architectural site from ancient Egypt. The story features the ancient Egyptian sun god Ra, and features an appearance of the fan favorite character Death. This issue focuses on the popular trope of ancient Egyptian grave sites or religious sites containing curses or other supernatural traps, a trope that bases itself on the common desecration and looting of Egyptian cultural artifacts and treasures by Western explorers. Egypt, which was under semicolonial rule by British forces until the 1950s, had at this time become a source of fascination in the West (Bryce 2007). The long history of Egypt and the artifacts that came with it were appropriated by Western archeologists and scholars, as "intellectual colonialism sought to extricate Egypt from its past glories and future potentials in service of the ruling empire" (Meskell 2006, 150). Continually depicting Egyptian archeological sites and Egyptian history as not only accessible but entitled to Western scholars reinforces that "Egypt and its riches are still seen as a global resource" (150). Popular media often only serves to reinforce that the legacy of Egyptian society belongs to the West, famously so in the Indiana Jones films, where the titular hero often repeats that the objects he finds "belong in a museum"—far away from their countries of origin. In "Façade" the protagonist Urania enters an archeological site seeking superpowers on the behest of her employers, but is given a lonely, lifeless existence as a metamorph by the sun god Ra. She gains the ability to transform her body into any element, but ends up living disfigured and abandoned by society and the company she worked for, and unable to die. While the story seems to warn against the grave-robbing common in fantastic depictions of Egypt, there is little to keep Egypt and its heritage from being deemed irrational or childlike. The sun god Ra continues to make metamorphs despite Death's assurance that the Serpent he wishes to fight is long dead. Ra is implied to be both irrational and dangerous, but also childlike, unable to understand what Urania wishes without Death's intervention. Through this depiction of Egypt, there is a reinforcing of Orientalist stereotypes and a co-opting of an already commonly co-opted history.

In contrast to "Façade," issue #50, "Ramadan," straddles the line between portrayal of Orientalist tropes and subversion. It sets a story in medieval Baghdad, depicted as it often is in Western imaginations. Baghdad is commonly associated with the fantastical depictions of the Arab world, a city easy to overwrite with fantasy depictions that ignore its modern cultural and political positions. The story depicts a king putting his beautiful, fantastical city into dreams, just as Baghdad exists in the collective consciousness of today—a mystical, magical city that will never die, so long as people still dream of it. The final pages of the story shift abruptly to a modern setting, likely meant to evoke modern Baghdad, as it existed during the War in Iraq—a ruined place, full of people who are deeply removed from the prosperity of the fantasy of its past. This is a very different Iraq, "ravaged by sanctions, brutally impoverished, and generally a gigantic mess" (Berlatsky 2011). This story reflects an awareness of the contrast of Baghdad in the collective imagination, and the reality for those who lived there, a subversion of Orientalism by addressing the gap between Western fantasy and Eastern reality head on.

However, when addressing this contrast, there is a lack of engagement with the dynamics that created this contrast—the Western Orientalist expectation of the East that generates the Western exploitation and invasion of these countries in the modern day. Dream's visual representation as a white man, and the exchanges between himself and the king, such as the admonishment for not keeping to fasting during the month of Ramadan, are at odds with a message that acknowledges the modern impact of Orientalism on the Middle East.

The opening panels speak of the king of Baghdad's harem, who made his palace "a palace of pleasure." From the start, there is an overly sexualized depiction of the East, of Eastern women in particular as sexualized objects. This continues in the fantasy of the harem, exacerbated by nineteenth-century "harem paintings," creating a sense of the East as exoticized and depraved, and this depiction sets the tone for the portrayal of Baghdad later in the comic. Orientalist depictions of the East depict Eastern women as objects "of a male power fantasy. They express unlimited sexuality, they are more or less stupid, and above all they are willing" (Said 1978, 207). The European fantasy of harems were of unrestrained sexual spaces, and "the lack of access to harems served only to further perpetuate erroneous stereotypes about the Orient which quickly became ingrained in the collective imagination of Europeans" (Herath 2016, 32). The emphasis in the art on "Ramadan" on the sexuality of the harem, evoking European harem paintings that "centered much of their artwork around the allure of beautiful, nude odalisques" reinforced ahistorical, European fantasies about harem life that removed agency and personhood from the women they depicted (32). Berlatsky (2011) particularly takes Gaiman to task for his "Ramadan" harem: "At his worst, he sounds like a sweatily clueless slam poet: there's just no excuse for dialogue like 'I can smooth away the darkness in your soul between my thighs.'"

"Ramadan" depicts the city of Baghdad as filled with innumerable exotic treasures and filled with magic, ripe for the taking by enterprising Western adventurers. By showing the preservation of the city in dreams, the comic does not acknowledge that the version of Baghdad being saved for eternity in dreams is a Western fantasy version of the city. The literalizing of the idea of Baghdad that lives forever in dreams ignores that the dreams it lives in are Western dreams that contributed to the justification of colonialism that contributed to the current situation in the Middle East. "[W]hose is this dream of Orientalism, exactly? Well, it's the Iraqi boy's, as I said, and before his, it was Haroun al Raschid's. But really, of course, it isn't theirs at all. It's Gaiman and Russell's," Berlatsky (2011) points out.

Despite these depictions, when focusing specifically on the implications of Orientalist tropes and the entitlement of one group to the resources and wealth of another, there are also explicit anti–Orientalist frameworks present in *Sandman*. In particular, issue #17, "Calliope," which was collected in *Dream Country* alongside "Façade," can be easily placed into these frameworks. The themes of the story focus on the direct exploitation of an Othered person, who is treated explicitly as an object by the two British men who trade ownership of her. While they prosper, she is abused, raped, and left to suffer, a situation that easily mirrors Western colonial exploitation of people around the world. Through this story, there is forcible reflection on the justification of horrific acts for personal gratification that could easily be applied to historical and ongoing colonial exploitation. (For more in-depth analysis of the power dynamics in "Calliope," see the essay by Pinky Chung-Man Lui in this collection.)

Now that the Orientalist impulses in these early texts have been examined, the next part of this essay will examine what happened to these impulses once the texts were adapted to the screen. While this examination will reveal a gradual improvement, it will also be a call to action for future televisual adaptations to do more.

Widening Audience Through Adaptations

Often, the adaptation of a work into a movie or television show is a hallmark of how popular the work is, and the adaptation of a story drives more interest towards the original. Because of this phenomenon, when choosing to adapt a story, creators must take care to ensure that the new work is not reiterating any unintended harmful tropes or ideas from the source material (or even worse, adding new negative tropes).

Gaiman has been known to take a strong interest in the adaptation of his work, and recently has been particularly heavily involved in the production of the television adaptations of *Good Omens, Sandman,* and

Anansi Boys. Yet the collaborative nature of film and television adaptation, along with the financial ties to production and distribution companies, mean that no single person, including Gaiman, has complete control over all artistic choices.

The film version of *Stardust*, released in 2007, has several noticeable changes from the original novel, both small (the protagonist Tristran becomes Tristan) and large (the addition of the character Captain Shakespeare and changes to the story's ending). While many aspects remain the same, and indeed the Orientalist storyline of a struggle between the East and West remains, many of the changes serve not to reduce Orientalist messaging but in fact, to reinforce it. At the end of the novel, Tristran rules Stormhold for the rest of his life alongside Yvaine, but after his death she lives on, watching the stars in the sky wistfully knowing she can never return to them. As Prescott-Johnson (2022) summarizes:

> He ages and dies. But Yvaine doesn't and won't. The story ends with her and it's so sad and beautiful […] and the text has prepared us for it, because there have been multiple times throughout the story where she talks about the existence of being a star … being alone and being independent and separate. And she's comfortable with that. She was comfortable with it before she [was] brought to earth. And she's comfortable with it at the end.

As this shows, the novel's ending is bittersweet, lonely, and beautiful, like Yvaine herself. And the story ends with her, not Tristan (and in fact, the story's title is one indication that the real star of this tale isn't the man). Perhaps under pressure for a happy ending, the film presents both Tristan and Yvaine as rulers, and when the time comes Yvaine returns to the stars, with Tristan tagging along. This change was likely meant to leave the audience with happy closure, yet nonetheless serves to reinforce *Stardust*'s Orientalist tropes. Tristan, in the film, is even further rewarded for his venturing into the East. He is given access not just to the land of Stormhold, to which he does have at least an ancestral claim, but also to Yvaine's homeland. While the film attempts to smooth over the violence of Yvaine's exploitation, allowing her to return to her home, Tristan being able to return with her and be rewarded furthers Orientalist tropes that mimic the justification of and reward for colonial exploitation.

If *Stardust* were adapted today (as it may be, given the enormous success of *Good Omens* and *Sandman*), obviously it would look very different. The most recent adaptations of Gaiman's work show an awareness of and response to the major social and cultural changes that have emerged over the last decade. And nowhere is this more evident than in the *Sandman* television adaptation, which stands out for its clear choice to introduce diversity through its cast (as discussed by Alexis Brooks de Vita and Novella Brooks de Vita in the previous essay). Whereas the original comics protagonists were almost exclusively white, the television version introduces several actors of color to play major roles like Cain and Abel and Death, and shifts some exclusively male-presenting roles to female and nonbinary actors. The diverse cast also introduces new dimensions to racial dynamics and tropes conveyed in the story. For example, in the adaptation of "Calliope," Amanita Suman play Nora, a medical student whose admiration of Richard Madoc leads her to steal a bezoar for him that he eventually trades for control of Calliope. The basis for Nora's character in the comic was originally an unnamed young man. But once this character is brought to life by an actress of South Asian descent, her interactions with Madoc now throw racial and gender power dynamics into higher relief. In the television version, there is now an even stronger allegory of colonial exploitation implied in Madoc's treatment of Calliope. Although their initial encounter occurs off-screen, it is implied that Madoc has used his power and status as an older, established male professor to coerce a young female grad student to break rules for him, and will do so again by the episode's end. The exploitive dynamic between Madoc and his grad student, thrown into further relief due to the history of colonial exploitation between the British Empire and South Asia, is setting the stage for Madoc's escalating acts of oppression and horror. By the end of the story, Nora is the one who finds the book where Calliope had been kept, bringing her connection to Calliope, whom she has never met, full circle. The casting change for the student who procures the bezoar may seem minor, but it amplifies the anti–Orientalist message of "Calliope" by connecting the story more explicitly to the dynamics of British colonial exploitation.

While it has not yet been adapted for the television series, if "Façade" (which appears in the same *Dream Country* collection as "Calliope") is adapted with this new cast, it will experience a shift in the racial dynamics as well, due to the portrayal of Death by Kirby Howell-Baptiste. While Death still represents a Western voice of reason within the story, the depiction of a Black woman as the reasonable, kind force changes the dynamics of colonialism inherent in the conclusion of the issue. In this way, a diverse cast can enhance the anti–Orientalist messages in certain stories, and can help navigate these tropes in a way that makes the adaptation still faithful to the original comic issues, while deliberately making choices that mitigate the damage of previously Orientalist tropes or storylines.

Netflix's response to adult audience demands for diversity is evident in its production of *Sandman*. What we have yet to see is how an even bigger entertainment corporation will handle similar adaptation challenges with one of Gaiman's books geared for children. The Walt Disney Company was in the process of adapting *The Graveyard Book*, which has curious genealogical ties to Disney's *The Jungle Book*, as both use Kipling's source as inspirational source material. Disney is no stranger to controversies around racist material from the past being repackaged and sold for modern audiences. It has tried several actions to grapple with the sins of its past, including suppressing material (*Song of the South*), revising content (racist jokes on the *Jungle Cruise* ride), and leaving problematic works intact but adding content advisories. (Films like *Lady and the Tramp* now feature a notice proclaiming, "This program includes negative depictions and/or mistreatment of people or cultures. These stereotypes were wrong then and are wrong now. Rather than remove this content, we want to acknowledge its harmful impact, learn from it and spark conversation to create a more inclusive future together.") It is unclear how invested this studio, which was responsible for the well-known animated adaptation of *The Jungle Book*, is in preserving *Graveyard Book*'s anti–Orientalist messages of unity and blurring the dichotomy of good versus evil and us versus them. Will they follow the common pitfall of simplifying the story with the excuse of making it easier for children to understand, even as Gaiman himself argues that children are able to handle much more complex ideas than many adults give them credit for? Will *The Graveyard Book*'s nods to its source material be removed? Will this complex story of loss and maturation become "Disneyfied"? Will the project collapse, like so many other projected adaptations of Gaiman's work, under the weight of these choices and conflicts between stakeholders? Only time will tell. But if Disney does successfully translate *Graveyard Book* into a new medium, it will likely widen the audience for the book tremendously.

The Shadow of Orientalism

Stardust, published in 1998, was described by Gaiman (2007) himself as a "fairytale for adults." It parodies many fairy tale tropes deliberately, as Gaiman explains, and thus is likely intended to subvert audience expectations. However, through the strict dichotomy of "us" versus "them" and the parallels to justifications of colonial entitlement, the established Orientalist tropes are not addressed or subverted by the end of the story.

The Graveyard Book, published ten years later in 2008, pulls many situations and characters straight from Kipling's Victorian era short stories. Despite this direct inspiration, in contrast to *Stardust*, Gaiman turns many of Kipling's originally Orientalist themes on their head by teaching the young audience about a more complex view of good and evil, and allows the audience to reflect on themselves and their own propensity for being good or being evil. By the end of the novel, the readers will understand that a person is defined by their actions, not by their belonging to one group or the other. By forcing young readers to see themselves reflected in the Other, boundaries can be broken down, and we can begin to unlearn some of these harmful tropes. As Said (1978) explains, we can begin to "stimulate a new kind of dealing with the Orient … eliminate the 'Orient' and 'Occident' altogether" (36).

Sandman, due to the nature of serialized comic books, depicts many different storylines, all engaging differently with the Orient and colonial tropes. Because it is in the process of being adapted, season by season, there is a strong incentive to examine the relationship of these stories to colonial tropes, and to use the opportunity of adaptation to bring a more critical eye to the times when the comic series depicted Orientalist notions and when it went out of its way to dispel them. As an adaptation of a work brings it further into the public eye, there is value in ensuring that the positions taken by the work reflect the intent of the author (both when it was written and now) rather than replicating tropes that may diminish the overall message. As Sims (2022) notes, "The rush to defend white writers when they perpetuate dangerous narratives about people of color affirms that many people continue to assume that the Western viewpoint, no matter how wrong or harmful, should be unquestioningly accepted and celebrated" (113).

Of Gaiman's many works, *Stardust*, *The Graveyard Book*, and *Sandman* have some of the most direct associations with Orientalist works—*Stardust* because it is set during the Victorian era and replicates the boys' adventure story of that time period, *The Graveyard Book* because of its direct parallels with a Victorian era fantasy story, and *Sandman* due to various issues that intersect with common perceptions about the East. Regardless, these stories were published in modern times, in settings not likely to evoke conscious ideas about imperialism for the average reader. However, the analysis of the effects of Orientalism in these works proves that far beyond the Victorian era, even in the modern, supposedly postcolonial era, the effects of Orientalist thinking still make their way into the stories we read and enjoy.

As Said (1978) explained, "Orientalism [is] a Western style for dominating restructuring, and having authority over the Orient," and that it was a series of ideas that colored every possible view of the East. There was no way to envision or think about the East without evoking the Orientalist tropes about the East, as "because of Orientalism the Orient was not (and is not) a free subject of thought or action" (11). These ideas impact the way people from the East are portrayed in the West, which goes on to impact both domestic and international political policy. The dichotomy between the East and the West set up by Orientalist tropes continues to impact people's lives to this day.

Fantasy fiction, despite being fictional, still has a very real impact on the world it exists in. And that is why it is essential for creators that are adapting fantasy fiction to screen to take harmful tendencies like Orientalism into account during their process. Fiction can both reflect the accepted views of the times as well as sustain modes of thinking further through reestablishing or normalizing certain tropes in the minds of readers. *Stardust*, *The Graveyard Book*, and *Sandman* are all works with high critical acclaim and wide readerships, which further expanded in their screen adaptations, reflecting the large readership of Gaiman's work and the respect it is given. Writers like Gaiman have far-reaching impact, from the wide readership of their original works to the adaptations that stem from them, and to the writers who are then further inspired by those works. If writers start to reflect more carefully on the tropes and themes they choose to write, the world of Western literature and popular culture can slowly begin to escape from the persistent shadow of Orientalism, and begin to mitigate some of its harm.

Note

1. Other planned adaptations of Gaiman's work that would particularly benefit from a careful analysis of Orientalist themes include Disney's adaptation of *The Graveyard Book* and Graphic India's adaptation of *Cinnamon*, which began as a short story by Gaiman and was released as a children's book with illustrations by Divya Srinivasan in 2017.

References

Balfe, Myles. 2004. "Incredible Geographies? Orientalism and Genre Fantasy." *Social and Cultural Geography* 5, no. 1 (March): 75–90. https://doi.org/10.1080/1464936042000181326.
Banerjee, Sukanya. 2019. "The Victorians: Empire and the East." In *Orientalism and Literature*, edited by Geoffrey P. Nash, 82–100. Cambridge Core. Cambridge University Press. https://doi.org/10.1017/9781108614672.005.
Berlatsky, Noah. 2011. "Just a Thing in Our Dream." *The Hooded Utilitarian*. https://www.hoodedutilitarian.com.
Bivona, Daniel. 2019. "Orientalism and Victorian Fiction." In *Orientalism and Literature*, edited by Geoffrey P. Nash, 101–16. Cambridge Core. Cambridge University Press. https://doi.org/10.1017/9781108614672.006.
Bryce, Derek. 2007. "Repackaging Orientalism: Discourses on Egypt and Turkey in British Outbound Tourism." *Tourist Studies* 7, no. 2 (August): 165–91. https://doi.org/10.1177/1468797607083502.
Curry, Alice. 2010. "'The Pale Trees Shook, Although No Wind Blew, and It Seemed to Tristran That They Shook in Anger': 'Blind Space' and Ecofeminism in a Post-colonial Reading of Neil Gaiman and Charles Vess's Graphic Novel *Stardust* (1998)." *Barnboken* 33, no. 2: 19. https://doi.org/10.14811/clr.v33i2.16.
Gaiman, Neil. 1998. *Stardust*. Harper Perennial.
———. 2007. "Happily Ever After." *Guardian*, October 12. https://www.theguardian.com/books/2007/oct/13/film.fiction.

———. 2008. *The Graveyard Book*. HarperCollins.
Gaiman, Neil (w), Kelley Jones (a), and Malcolm Jones III (i). 1990a. "Calliope." *Sandman* #17. DC Comics. July 1990.
Gaiman, Neil (w), Colleen Doran (p), and Malcolm Jones III (i). 1990b. "Façade." *Sandman* #20. DC Comics. Oct 1990.
———. 1993. "Ramadan." *Sandman*. DC Comics/Vertigo.
Gaiman, Neil, David S. Goyer, and Allan Heinberg, creators. 2022. *Sandman*. Season 1. Netflix.
Herath, Thisaranie. 2016. "Women and Orientalism: 19th Century Representations of the Harem by European Female Travellers and Ottoman Women." *Constellations* 7, no. 1: 31–40. https://doi.org/10.29173/cons27054.
Krieger, Lee Toland, dir. 2024. *Dead Boy Detectives*. Season 1, episode 1, "The Case of Crystal Palace." April 25. Netflix.
Meskell, Lynn. 2006. "The Practice and Politics of Archaeology in Egypt." *Annals of the New York Academy of Sciences* 925, no. 1 (January): 146–69. https://doi.org/10.1111/j.1749-6632.2000.tb05588.x.
Prescott-Johnson, Tara. 2022. "Catch a Falling Star and Put It in Your Pocket: *Stardust* in Context." Saint Louis University Campus Read Book Talk. YouTube. https://www.youtube.com/watch?v=5F-TpmgkvRI.
Robertson, Christine. 2011. "'I Want to Be Like You': Riffs on Kipling in Neil Gaiman's *The Graveyard Book*." *Children's Literature Association Quarterly* 36, no. 2: 164–89. https://doi.org/10.1353/chq.2011.0021.
Said, Edward W. 1978. *Orientalism*. Pantheon.
Sims, Jennifer Patrice. 2022. "When the Subaltern Speak Parseltongue: Orientalism, Racial Re-Presentation, and Claudia Kim as Nagini." *Harry Potter and the Other: Race, Justice, and Difference in the Wizarding World*, edited by Sarah Park Dahlen and Ebony Elizabeth Thomas, 105–18. UP of Mississippi.
Vaughn, Matthew, dir. 2007. *Stardust*. Paramount.

The Mythopoetic Memorial
Creating and Recreating Myth and Sites of Memory

ANGELA CARMELA UY FANTONE

Mythology forms part of a literary and cultural tradition that has shaped humanity's collective memory. Many scholars and historians consider myths to be the first forms of literature as they shifted from oral traditions to written texts. And these myths continue to shift, particularly in the fantasy genre, which often borrows from, reuses, and recreates myths as part of worldbuilding. Worldbuilding is a narrative strategy that helps audiences connect with the conditions in which the story will unfold. Mythopoetics, or mythmaking in fantasy literature, also builds on collective memory to connect to readers. Neil Gaiman's *Sandman*, in its comics, audiobook, and televised forms, is celebrated for how it borrows from mythology and recreates myths in ways that establish a new lore specific to his narrative. *Sandman*'s unique form of worldbuilding creates mythic sites of memory that reference familiar myths and the mythmaking process and recreates them in ways that make mythic references, mytho-historical time, liminal spaces, and characters function as sites of memory within the narrative.

This essay will first briefly lay out the theoretical framework behind sites of memory and then use this concept to establish what will be called "the pillars of the mythopoetic memorial" within the *Sandman* lore or the different ways sites of memory work in narrative worldbuilding. I will then tie these concepts together to solidify what the mythopoetic memorial is, how it builds the comics' and show's overall mythos, and how it can become a technique in fantasy and imaginative genres.

Sites of Memory

Memory studies was founded on many phenomenological definitions of memory and its various applications. To understand the function of mythopoetic sites of memory, one must first define the theories behind the concept of sites of memory and how mythology and literature fit that concept. The French historian Pierre Nora first coined the term "sites of memory," or *les lieux de mémoire*. According to Nora, memory is a remnant of experiences and traditions from the past. Therefore, anything built to remember the past is a site of memory. He wrote, "These *lieux de mémoire* are fundamentally remains, the ultimate embodiments of a memorial consciousness that has barely survived in a historical age that calls out for memory because it has abandoned it" (Nora 1989, 12). Sites of memory are created to preserve what society has deemed necessary enough to remember. Examples of sites of memory, according to Nora's definition, include places such as museums, shrines, war memorials, and more. Investment in and interpretations of remembering and commemoration build sites of memory.

However, Nora's presentation of sites of memory is limited in that it is bound to the concept of nation-state and historicism. His theories only present tangible places and markers, such as war memorials, museums, and national artifacts, as *lieux de mémoire*. They are also inextricably tied to the location or locations they are built in. By Nora's definition alone, myths would not function as sites of memory because they are not tangible and because myths tend to cross cultures and eras. However, as memory studies began to expand as a field, scholars have highlighted the contradictions and limitations in Nora's theories, and more recent memory studies research frequently intersects with the concept of sites of memory. Jeffrey Olick (2016) points out that memory studies now "has embraced concepts of travel, trade, and transmission across contexts, persons, borders, epochs, and entities, and has shown that memory transits these in ciphered as well as manifest ways, back and forth, again and again" (50). As memory studies research evolves to better integrate other fields of study, Olick's claim redefines sites of memory, not just as physical markers tied to nation-state and historicism, but as markers of memory that move and shift across time, space, and media. Memory scholars now take into consideration the temporal nature of memory itself and the various ways different disciplines perceive and preserve memory. With this in mind, even intangible literary concepts found in *Sandman* can function as sites of memory. Within *Sandman*'s texts (including the original comics, the spin-off stories, the audiobook, the new television series, and more), mythic references, mytho-historical time, mythic spaces, and mythic beings are different sites of memory that build the pillars of the mythopoetic memorial. In fact, now that most readers are unable to access the original floppy comics issues, the trade paperbacks and newer collections have become the new *Sandman*. In many ways, the new television show itself has become a site of memory for the *Sandman* comics and may eventually become the "definitive" version itself.

Mythic Reference

The first pillar of the mythopoetic memorial is mythic reference. It is the building block of *Sandman*'s narrative. Gaiman's use and renewal of existing mythology from different sources and cultures to fit his storytelling turn *Sandman* into a memorial of those myths. Thus, the stories commemorate myths that the reader might be familiar with and memorialize the mythic thought process that created mythology in the first place.

Myths become intangible sites of memory because societies once used them to explain and preserve history and culture. Myths can function as markers of remembering the fantastic and supernatural. In the modern sense, they are signifiers of memories of ancient thought. They are sites of memory created by ancient religious, cultural, and narrative traditions. As intangible sites of memory, myths carry that sense of historicism that existed in their original contexts. However, because myths no longer exist to explain and preserve history, their role as sites of memory shifts within the bounds of literary tradition. Thus, intangible concepts that amass cultural knowledge and customs must be considered sites of memory.

Investing in remembering is what makes a site of memory, which is one way in which myths can function as *lieux de memoire* (Nora 1989, 19). Gaiman's imaginative investment comes from mythic exploration and looking at myths not as they are but as they could be. His mythic explorations (including *Sandman, American Gods, Anansi Boys, Odd and the Frost Giants,* and *Norse Mythology*) come from taking mythic concepts and then redefining them. Additionally, the mythopoetics within *Sandman* function like a mosaic because Gaiman borrows from various points of world mythology and folklore to build the narrative. In other words, mythic references come from cultural memories of mythology. Jan Assmann and John Czaplicka (1995) coined the term "cultural memory" to describe that which "preserves the store of knowledge from which a group derives an awareness of its unity and peculiarity" (130). Thus, myths are intangible memorials of the cultures and societies that created those myths.

The concept of sites of memory connects to mythopoesis or myth-making because borrowing myths in worldbuilding takes not only a knowledge of these lores within their original contexts but also the images and thought processes that created myths as sites of memory in the first place. In an essay on mythic adaptation, Sándor Klapcsik (2008) notes, "Direct transformation preserves the theme, characters, and so on, of the source text, but places them into another setting, genre, or context" (320). In his research on mythopoetic thought, Leo Heirman (1978) found that "myths and fairytales are spoken expressions of medieval thought processes. For us to understand them means translating into modern abstract reasoning, what in tribal times had been clad in a picture language" (58). The language of myth involves invoking the divinity and supernaturalism that created mythology as they are recreated in this new narrative.

In "Reflections on Myth," Gaiman (1999) wrote, "*Sandman* was, in many ways, an attempt to create a new mythology—or rather, to find what it was that I responded to in ancient pantheons and then to try and create a fictive structure in which I could believe as I wrote it. Something that felt right, in the way that myths feel right" (77). When existing myths become references in *Sandman*, they become recreated sites of memory as they shift into new myths within the author's text. Each mythic reference Gaiman borrows from belongs to a different time and place, and many readers enjoy tracing the origins of the mythic references in *Sandman*. Gaiman's mythic references stem from Greco-Roman mythology, European folklore, and Judeo-Christian religious traditions. For example, *Sandman*'s protagonist, Dream, is a combination of several preexisting entities, including Morpheus, the Roman god of sleep and dreams, and the Sandman, a figure from European folklore who provides dreams through his dream sand. A new mythic personage arose from the combination of these two mythical figures, among others.

The *Sandman* TV episodes, like the comics they are based on, function as the passing on of myths. They exist as memories because someone is still telling those stories, and they become stamped as the lore's reality. As the titular character, Morpheus presides over the dreamers who narrate myths and memories of myths, fables, and histories. For example, *Sandman* issue #9, "Tales in the Sand" (Gaiman et al. 1990b), is narrated by a member of a tribe known as the First People who are recounting the history of Nada, a queen of their tribe and one of Morpheus's former lovers. Although this is considered part of their history, the First People pass her story down as a lore that invokes an imaginative investment in how they tell the story. Issue #50, "Ramadan" (Gaiman et al. 1993), is a story told to a young boy about how Baghdad was once a splendid dream city until it was preserved in a bottle according to the king's wishes. The story is told as a memory from one generation to the next. Because of how this cultural knowledge was passed on, it became a myth instead of an actual history. The story "The Song of Orpheus" (Gaiman et al. 1993) retells the myth of Orpheus and Eurydice but fits it into *Sandman*'s lore. In this case, Orpheus is the son of the muse Calliope and the Dream King, Morpheus. These stories and the references behind them are reframed as signifiers of the narrators' and characters' memories. Hence, these are examples of commemorating the mythic thought process that Gaiman executes.

Additionally, these comic issues function as sites of memory because they turn the stories into narrative spaces where readers and characters go in and out as though passing through doors. The TV adaptation of *Sandman* functions as a similar narrative space that also memorializes the original comics. The form of comics and television further demonstrate how *Sandman* is made up of narrative spaces. Comics are composed of panels and television episodes are composed of scenes. Each is like its own room; characters and readers enter and exit as the story progresses. Combined with cultural memory, *Sandman*, both as a volume of comics and as two seasons of television episodes, becomes a set of rooms that contain cultural memories of mythology and mythic thought processes. Assmann and Czaplicka (1995) wrote, "The communicative memory offers no fixed point which would bind it to the ever expanding past in the passing of time" (127). Treating *Sandman* volumes, panels, and episodes like rooms also puts these mythic references in locations that are not fixed or bound to time.

Mythic reference as a site of memory makes the text a holder of the different borrowed myths and the cultural memory and mythic thought processes that made it. These borrowings turn the text into liminal spaces where characters and readers experience memories. They are also spaces where myth is renewed to build the foundations of the texts' fantastic world.

Mytho-Historical Time

The reconstruction of these myths in *Sandman* (and reconstructed again in the television series) creates a specific way memory works in the story. The volumes function as texts of liminal fantasy where the real and fantastical are blurred together, so they are inseparable. This merge creates a mytho-historical time that functions as a site of memory within the lore. Thus, the fantastical elements of *Sandman*'s mythos create history and memory.

Like the mythic references that built the original comics, mythic occurrences explain, affect, and create historical events and timelines. They also commemorate those historical events and people contained within the narratives. Mytho-historical time shapes the remembering of these events. Because history is also a reference that Gaiman adheres to in writing this series, the events of the lore are manifestations of what was fated to be. Kristine Larsen, a professor of physics and astronomy, has examined the comics' aspects of creation and time. She notes:

> every event in the series occurs precisely at the time and order that it is meant to. Some larger, overarching figure organizes without undermining the plurality of times, places, and time-places onto which *The Sandman* is mapped, setting into place the various flows, contraflows, and excursions that simultaneously fracture and unify *The Sandman's* multiple temporalities [Larsen 2019, 36].

Additionally, Atkins (2015) writes, "Thus we as readers see Gaiman experimenting with a narrative that holds that revertible and non-revertible characteristic of myth by creating a narrative that exists in all times and places throughout real and imaginative history" (22). These intersections turn into signifiers where all the events in the comics happen. These events stored in these time-bound signifiers manifest remembrances. Mytho-historical time functions as a site of memory because it contains the memories of events that have shaped humanity and the people and physical markers of these events.

The phenomenon of mytho-historical time in *Sandman* "exists in all times and places throughout real and imagined history" (Atkins 2015, 22). Thus, it is structured to carry infinite interpretations of memory. Mytho-historical time is the architecture of *Sandman's* reality. Monsters, gods, and powerful beings exist in the world. Many of the actions of these powerful beings even create history. For example, *Sandman* begins with the capture and imprisonment of Morpheus. His absence from his realm is said to have caused the Sleeping Sickness of 1916, a real pandemic that lasted almost a decade (Gaiman et al. 1990). Some of the historical figures who make appearances in the comics include William Shakespeare (Gaiman et al. 1990), to whom Morpheus extends his patronage to create plays, Marco Polo (Gaiman et al. 1993) whom Morpheus guides through the desert during his explorations, and even Joshua Norton (Gaiman et al. 1993), who famously declared himself Emperor of the United States when Despair intervened in his life. It is the correlation between myth and history that creates these unique timelines.

Much like memory, historical events referenced in *Sandman* do not necessarily have a chronological order. Mytho-historical time becomes a crystalized moment in the spectrum of the universe. It's almost as though the readers receive a string of beads. The string represents the lore, while the beads represent historical events and figures. With this analogy in mind, the lore as the string connects them all. M.I. Finley (1965) believes that "memory leaps instantaneously to the desired point and it then dates by association" (293). Mytho-historical time is crystalized enough within the lore that, like a bead on a string, historical events are situated where they are designed to be in the narrative.

Mythic Beings

In defining what can contain and become a marker of memory, it would be safe to argue that certain characters function as living sites of memory, especially the Endless, the pantheon that oversees liminal time and space in *Sandman*. These characters function as living sites of memory because they are extensions of liminal spaces where memories are created. Because these mythic beings function as sites of memory, it is through them that other characters and the readers experience recall of what has passed in this metauniverse. In her definition of liminality within the fantasy genre, Farah Mendlesohn (2022) states, "we sit on the protagonist's shoulders and while we have access to their eyes and ears, we are not provided with an explanatory narrative" (175). The Endless, as protagonists of the narrative, are the eyes and ears of the universe as they manifest different aspects of reality. They are the access that everyone else around them has to memory.

The concept of deification works its way into how memory works in *Sandman*'s lore. In her dissertation on Neil Gaiman's application of mythology, Lenka Koudelková (2015) states, "In *The Sandman*, Gaiman put aside the deities commonly encountered in world mythologies, and developed a whole new pantheon of The Endless, a dysfunctional family of seven god-like beings, each representing and ruling one aspect of the world/ human life—and thus becoming a personification of the aspect. These are Death, Dream (The Sandman), Despair, Destiny, Delirium, Destruction, and Desire" (26–27). Gaiman didn't write the Endless to become gods but rather as manifestations of cosmic concepts that shape reality. The Endless are pillars of the universe's existence and their senses shape what other characters experience. Their interactions shape and create mytho-historical time.

These mythic beings are living sites of memory because they are physical memories of important cosmic concepts. Looking at the different roles of the Endless would aid in looking at how they become sites of memory. Morpheus as Dream of the Endless is the physical manifestation of dreams. He arguably has the most frequent interaction with humankind (although he doesn't truly *see* people for what they are until Death teaches him to), because people enter his realm every night in their sleep. Dreams come from human experience and memory. Morpheus exists because of dreams, and dreams exist because of him. He contains the memories that create dreams and the memories of every dream that has come to pass.

Desire and Despair are the physical manifestations of what humanity longs for and dreads. They are twins in the Endless family because one cannot exist without the other, and neither do the concepts they represent. According to the comics, "Never a possession, always a possessor.... Desire is everything you have ever wanted. Whoever you are. Whatever you are. Everything" (Gaiman et al. 1991). Their twin, Despair, has eyes "the colour of sky, on the grey, wet days, that leach the world of colour and meaning" (Gaiman et al. 1991). They hold the memories of every desire and despair that humans have experienced and will experience. Destiny, the eldest of the Endless, is the physical manifestation of what is to be and what has already been in the universe. He has a large book chained to him that contains all of history as well as everything yet to come. The comics establish that Destiny "sees the fine traceries the galaxies make as they spiral through the void, that he watches the intricate patterns living things make on their journey through time" (Gaiman et al. 1991). As of the first season of Netflix's *Sandman,* we have yet to see Destiny or Destruction, two members of the Endless that fans are eagerly awaiting. Destruction of the Endless manifests the end and the beginning of everything. Thus, he represents the cycle of creation; things must be destroyed before they can be remade. Destruction is often called "The Prodigal" because he leaves his family and disappears (he doesn't appear until towards the end of *Sandman*). In the volume *Brief Lives*, he tells Morpheus:

> I filled my role more than adequately for over ten billion years. A two-sided coin: Destruction is needed. Nothing new can exist without destroying the old. Things are created. They last for some little while, and then they are gone. Empires, cities, poems and people. Atoms and worlds. One cannot begin a new dream without abandoning the last, eh, Brother? Our sister defines life, just as Despair defines hope, or Desire defines hatred, or as Destiny defines freedom [Gaiman et al. 1994].

He is also the member of the family who is most aware of the interconnectedness of their roles and why the Endless exist in the first place. Thus, Destruction can point out the kind of investment in memories of cosmic reality, creation, and ruin that create and blend them together.

Delirium, the youngest in the family of the Endless, is the one who is the most changing. According to the comics, "Her appearance is the most variable of all the Endless, who, at best, are ideas cloaked in the semblance of flesh. Her shadow's shape and outline has no relationship to that of any body she wears, and it is tangible, like old velvet" (Gaiman et al. 1991). She was once known as Delight and was the physical manifestation of joy and contentment. We never learn how Delight became Delirium. She is now the physical manifestation of madness and insanity when something becomes too much to feel. As the only Endless to have changed so much that her name has changed, she is also representative of how perceptions of memory change. Kathryn Hume's (2013) research on *Sandman* states that while the Endless have a sort of eternal nature, "eternal need not signify unchanging" (350). Delirium carries the duality of her cosmic concept and proves that memory, even sites of memory, is not stagnant. Death, the sibling closest to Dream, is the last face that people see as they pass on to the next realm. Describing her role in the family, Death says, "When the first living thing existed, I was there, waiting. When the last living thing dies, my job will be finished. I'll put the chairs on the tables, turn out the lights and lock the universe behind me when I leave" (Gaiman et al. 1991). Death is, perhaps, the most aware of her purpose and how the Endless memorialize and deify cosmic reality.

As the Endless shape the cosmic experiences of humankind, they also symbolize how people perceive reality. Erica McCrystal (2019) states that "the series embodies them as physical figures that can be seen and heard. However, their embodiments are not concrete, and they shift appearances to meet the demands of the person viewing them" (187). This is another way the Endless as mythical beings become sites of memory. They are interpreted as the people interacting with them understand them and commemorate these ideals. In Morpheus's own words, "we exist because they know, deep in their hearts, that we exist ... we do not manipulate them. If anything, they manipulate us" (Gaiman et al. 1990). Because Gaiman made the Endless the pillars of the universe's reality, these core concepts are re-deified into a pantheon that is a mimesis of the mythic thought process and imagination of deifying the pillars of cosmic reality. Lee Atkins's (2015) essay on the structure of myth in Gaiman's works states, "Characters and events in his stories possess the gravity of the past and yet their modern appropriations give them grounding in the present and foreshadow of the future" (15). Thus, the Endless serve as memorials of the search for higher beings who have power over the domains of the universe's architecture. They are all together, past, present, and future.

Another way the Endless serve as living sites of memory is because they bear the duty to observe and remember. Patrick Hutton recounts the discussions of Pierre Nora and his contemporary, Paul Ricœur, regarding the differences between the "work of remembering" and "the duty to remember" (Nora 1989, 36). Nora himself states that "the form of memory comes ... from the outside" (14), which makes memory an individual phenomenon as much as it is a social one. Thus, those who are tasked with remembering pass on memory. Morpheus and the rest of the Endless become sites of memory, not only because they hold within themselves memories but also because they pass them on to others to carry forward.

Mythic Locations

Location is one of the aspects that Nora emphasized in the framework of his concept. In the older spectrum of memory studies, location was tied to the historicist view of memory. Thus, a location was only considered a site of memory if it marked where historical events occurred. However, in applying the idea of location to literature, Elzbieta Rybicka (2012) considers literary places or settings as sites of memory because of symbolism (137). This applies to the realms or kingdoms of the seven Endless siblings.

The realms of the Endless are also physical manifestations of cosmic ideals. They are the extensions of their rulers. Each of the Endless' realms are also built out of commemorations of what the Endless represent. For example, Destiny's realm is a garden of mazes. It is a place where the end and the beginning are so intertwined that they cannot be told apart. His realm is perhaps the one most attached to historical and universal memory because each path in Destiny's labyrinth takes whoever walks there to a different point in time. Destiny's garden is also a commemoration of the phenomenon of time. It is a location where "where the potential becomes the actual" (Gaiman et al. 1991). Even what is fated to happen eventually becomes a memory and the building block of Destiny's realm. The realms of the Endless are constructed from cosmic and historical memory while functioning as memories of their rulers. The Endless shape their realms according to their dictates and experiences, and even if they are replaced by another (as happens to Dream), their realms still serve as their memorials. They get to pass on to any successors a location that commemorates who they are and what they did.

Locations in literature are what Rybicka calls (2012) "the places hollowed out by memory" (133). However, as extensions of their rulers, they each shape where memories are stored and how they are commemorated. That is the symbolic function of the realms of Endless. Desire's realm, the Threshold, is the Endless realm that is closest to the human body, signifying that desire comes from within. In the television series, it is one of the most striking set pieces, a nude glowing structure built like a human form on the outside, with the main living space inside the chambers of the body's heart, with every surface a deep, glossy oxblood. The description of Desire's realm states, "The Threshold is a portrait of Desire, complete in all details built from the fancy of Desire out of blood and flesh, and bone, and skin" (Gaiman et al. 1990). Because the Threshold mimics the human body, their realm commemorates the fact that pleasure and desire are obtained through the physical body and the heart. As a replica of Desire's body, it also contains the memories of every desire ever felt and will be felt. The symbolic memorial functions of the Endless' realms also commemorate how cosmic concepts are deified and where they are thought to be situated.

In addition to being built out of cosmic memory and human reality, the realms of the Endless are also places where characters can see memory. Jay Winter (2010) describes sites of memory as "sites of second-order memory, places where people remember the memories of others" (313). This is especially true in Dream's realm because those who visit the Dreaming and directly interact with Morpheus can view other characters' memories. These liminal, mythic locations and spaces are also places where the readers experience the dreams and memories of the characters visually. As the most visited realm, the Dreaming shifts, not just with Morpheus's power over it, but also with the dreams and memories of those who visit it. Many of the characters who visit the Dreaming participate in building the location based on their memories. For example, Barbie enters the Dreaming and calls it "The Land," where she is heir to it, and beloved figures from her past imagination exist there. Barbie even sees a house that resembles where she lived as a child. When she sees the house, she says, "This isn't any citadel of the cuckoo. This is where I grew up. This is our old house. It's just like I remember it, only smaller …" (Gaiman et al. 1993). The other characters and readers get a glimpse of her past as she projects them into the Dreaming. The ability to project memories that others can also see signifies that the Dreaming allows memories to manifest in ways that characters can interact with them. Barbie can enter her house again and speak with the figments of her childhood imagination. Each Endless realm a character visits becomes a stage where memories are seen and sorted out, and new memories can be formed and kept.

Mythic location shows how sites of memory, as fantasy fiction creates them, dictate how narratives use memory. They can shape how characters experience memory and dictate what magical system is present. They even shape how the story is told because mythic sites of memory form the core of the narrative. In the case of *Sandman*, memory is not simply tied to having happened at a specific location but also to where memories can be (literally) stored and lived through.

The Mythopoetic Memorial

The mythopoetic language of *Sandman* is expressed through memory. *Sandman* becomes a grand mythopoetic memorial by making mythic references, mytho-historical time, liminal spaces, and characters function as sites of memory. The mythopoetic memorial is a work of fantasy or imaginative literature that creates or recreates existing sites of memory in its mythic world-building.

The series contains a multitude of mnemonic signifiers and places, and the narratives of these comics are architectured by memory. Mythic references, mytho-historical time, mythic beings, and mythic spaces are sites of memory within the lore of *Sandman* because they commemorate the contexts and the imaginative processes that created myths, and they serve as memorials of how cosmic ideals are interpreted and deified. Seeing what could function as a site of memory in mythic and fantasy literature and how they function as sites of memory is one way to branch out the dynamics of mythopoetics.

Sandman as a literary work also exists in a realm that "explicitly delimits the space between the created world, art's world, and the shared empirical reality of the readers" (Easterbrook 2012, 201) while also becoming a memorial phenomenon. Thus, literature itself is a site of memory. *Sandman* is very tied to memory, and in the metaphysical sense, its form is meant to capture memory. Gaiman chose a very visual format for the original *Sandman* that guides the reader to what they must visualize. Each panel containing every setting and plot also functions as a liminal site of memory where the images of these events are stained onto the pages for keeping. Thus, these literary texts become liminal, narrative spaces of memory that readers come in and out of.

Sandman is the kind of work that allows readers to become participants in memory. Skopljanac Lovro (2012) stated, "Literature is a prime example of a cultural activity that is dependent on both individual and cultural memory; it almost always depends on an individual memory in the writer's act of creation … and the single reader's act of re-creation" (211). Mythic literature built on concepts of memory allows characters and readers to become participants of memory as they interpret the memories presented to them, the mythic references used by the author, and even the author's memories that inspire the narrative. It is one of the most participative sites of memory available.

As an emerging concept, the mythopoetic memorial as an intersection between memory studies and fantasy literature has much potential to be applied and expanded. This concept might offer a blueprint or pattern for Gaiman's other mythic works or even become a blueprint or pattern for the works of other authors within the same genre. The mythopoetic memorial can even look at subgenres within fantasy and imaginative writing. But one interesting sublayer to the creation of mythopoetic memorials is transmedia adaptation. Transmedia adaptation adds another layer to the concept of the mythopoetic memorial as works of fantasy literature get adapted into films and TV series like *Sandman* did in 2022. This possible route might even open the doors to how memory ties in with fandom behavior when a work like *Sandman* amasses a larger readership and viewership founded by memorial interpretations and investments as those readers and fans interact with the texts as sites of memory (a topic that Adrienne E. Raw enthusiastically explores in "A Dreaming of Our Own: How Fandom Adapts Multiple Canons to Create a New Fanon," at the end of this collection).

Mythopoetic Memorials and Transmedia Adaptation

The emerging concept of the mythopoetic memorial applies to transmedia adaptations of fantasy literature. As one treats mythic fantasy literature as a site of memory, transmedia adaptation becomes another memorialization of the original work and the mythic blueprint which built the work's structure. This kind of adaptation adheres to the imagistic nature of memory and how investment in memory shifts over time. The 2022 adaptation of *Sandman* on Netflix has truly awakened and reawakened interest in the story, amassing a viewership of 328 million hours within the first month of its release (Perry 2022).

Netflix's adaptation of *Sandman* memorializes Gaiman's original volume of comics by using the plots, characters, and dialogue from the original work. The adaptation transfers the story from one narrative space (comics/graphic novels) to another (television series). The unique phenomenon that the transmedia adaptation of *Sandman* creates is that it recreates the visual aspects of the comics as it moves to the screen. Those who have already read *Sandman* are guided by the original art as they see how characters look and the locations they are placed in. The art of the comics shapes how readers remember the narrative. When the Netflix series came out, the overall look of the narrative changed as the producers and creative teams behind the series used their own memories and aesthetics to retell the story.

Both the comics and the Netflix series harness the imagistic nature of memory in building the *Sandman* universe. Paul Ricœur (2014), one of the foundational theorists in memory studies, pointed out that memory is associated with image and imagination (5). The visual aspects of the story seep into the readers' individual memories, which then create the collective cultural memory of the community or "fandom." Thus, in the case of *Sandman*, the images from the comics shape the imaginative and memorial investments of the community this literary work built. This becomes the building block of transferring the narrative of *Sandman* into a new medium. Melanie Schiller's (2018) research on transmedia adaptation states that adapting a work into a new medium "marks a cultural shift from a spectatorial culture of 'passive' media consumption to a more active, *participatory* culture" (98). The images and art of the comics defined the collective imagination of the people who read the comics first. Hence, the work is a site of memory of the fans' first interactions with *Sandman*. As the Netflix series references the art of the comics and adjusts it to create the standard aesthetic of the show, it invokes the collective memory of those who have previous interactions with the text and then shapes the collective memory of those who interact with *Sandman* for the first time through the show. The readers or fans of *Sandman* become indirect builders of a new mythopoetic memorial because they are the biggest target audience.

Transmedia adaptation creates the phenomenon of memorializing the original comics while changing certain parts of the story in order to fit a new mode of storytelling. Quoting media theorist Henry Jenkins, Schiller (2018) notes that while an adaptation of a previous text or work references the original source, the adaptation itself must be able to stand on its own so that no prior experience with the original source would be needed to appreciate it (100). With this in mind, the Netflix adaptation of *Sandman* becomes a secondary mythopoetic memorial that must be able to stand next to its mythopoetic memorial ancestor, while opening the doors for new fans and audiences to project their own imaginative memorial investments onto it. Mythopoetic memorials are created because of this level of investment in mythic fantasy literature and adaptations. Therefore, the term is one way to explain and observe the communities and "fandoms" that these works create. Nicolle Lamerichs (2018) defines a "fan" as someone "who is excessively affected by existing material and engages with popular culture" (19–20). I suggest that memory is the cause of such affection and engagement. Thus, the mythical texts become sites of their individual memories with the story and sites of collective memories when mutual love for *Sandman* is shared.

Additionally, when *Sandman* became a Netflix series, the same mythic references, mytho-historical time, mythic beings, and mythic locations that built Gaiman's work as a mythopoetic memorial now become a bridge for all narrative elements to cross over to their new medium. There may be shifts in the narrative elements, such as changing dialogue and adjusting the plot, but the foundation does not change. This is something audiences were eager to see in the second season, which continued to expand the *Sandman* universe.

Thus, mythopoetic memorials are sites of memory built from other sites of memory. They challenge previous notions in memory studies that sites of memory are simply tangible and static. Writers create mythopoetic memorials in their literary texts and adapters memorialize these stories in new mythopoetic memorials that are both distinct from and coexist the work they are adapting. Mythopoetic memorials are also narrative cycles where myth is commemorated in fantasy texts and fantasy texts are commemorated in transmedia adaptations. They memorialize individual and collective memories and investments of the story. While much more research could be done to intertwine memorial investments and "fandom" cultures, it can be concluded that mythopoetic memorials function to create communities and cultures based on those shared and reawakened memories. They are what the audiences come back to.

The creation of modern mythic fantasy texts is an act of memory itself. Memory is strange. We often treat it as factual, but it seeps into the fantastic, demands to be noticed, and often maintains its ties to myth. Memory is not linear. It shifts and is reused and recreated. Using *Sandman* as a referential text to build this concept is especially apt because *Sandman* is both a volume of comics and an ongoing television series that recognizes how it is built from liminal sites of memory while functioning as a site of memory that is as fantastical and memorable as dreams.

REFERENCES

Assmann, Jan, and John Czaplicka. 1995. "Collective Memory and Cultural Identity." *New German Critique* 65: 125–33. https://doi.org/10.2307/488538.

Atkins, Lee. 2015. "A Structural Study of Myth in Neil Gaiman's Adult Novels and Graphic Compositions: Relating Claude Lévi-Strauss to Contemporary Fiction." PhD diss., Millersville University of Pennsylvania.

Easterbrook, Neil. 2012. "The Shamelessly Fictive: Mimesis and Metafantasy." *Hungarian Journal of English and American Studies* 18 (1/2): 193–211. http://www.jstor.org/stable/43488469.

Finley, M.I. 1965. "Myth, Memory, and History." *History and Theory* 4 (3): 281–302. https://doi.org/10.2307/2504346.

Gaiman, Neil. 1999. "Reflections on Myth." *Columbia: A Journal of Literature and Art* 31: 75–84. http://www.jstor.org/stable/41807920.

Gaiman, Neil (w), et al. 1990–1994. *Sandman*. Trade paperback Vols. 1–10. DC Comics/Vertigo.

Gaiman, Neil, David S. Goyer, and Allan Heinberg, creators. 2022. *Sandman*. Season 1. Netflix.

Heirman, Leo. 1978. "The Nature of Mythopoetic Thinking." *Classical Outlook* 55 (3): 54–59. http://www.jstor.org/stable/43933929.

Hume, Kathryn. 2013. "Neil Gaiman's Sandman as Mythic Romance." *Genre: Forms of Discourse and Culture* 3: 345–65.

Hutton, Patrick. 2016. "Pierre Nora's Les Lieux de Mémoire Thirty Years After." In Tota and Hagen 2016.

Klapcsik, Sándor. 2008. "Neil Gaiman's Irony, Liminal Fantasies, and Fairy Tale Adaptations." *Hungarian Journal of English and American Studies (HJEAS)* 14 (2): 317–34. http://www.jstor.org/stable/41274433.

Koudelková, Lenka. 2015. "Neil Gaiman: Myths in Postmodern Literature." PhD diss., Masaryk University.

Lamerichs, Nicolle. 2018. "Shared Narratives: Intermediality in Fandom." In *Productive Fandom: Intermediality and Affective Reception in Fan Cultures*, 11–34. Amsterdam University Press. https://doi.org/10.2307/j.ctv65svxz.4.

Larsen, Kristine. 2019. "Dreaming the Universe: *The Sandman: Overture*, Creation Myths, and the Ultimate Observer." In *The Artistry of Neil Gaiman: Finding Light in the Shadows*, edited by Joseph Michael Sommers and Kyle Eveleth, 35–50. University Press of Mississippi.

Lovro, Skopljanac. 2012. "Literature through Recall: Ways of Connecting Literary Studies and Memory Studies." *Interdisciplinary Literary Studies* 14 (2): 197–212. https://doi.org/10.5325/intelitestud.14.2.0197.

McCrystal, Erica. 2019. "Liminality and the Gothic Sublime of *The Sandman*." In *The Artistry of Neil Gaiman: Finding Light in the Shadows*, edited by Joseph Michael Sommers and Kyle Eveleth, 185–203. University Press of Mississippi.

Mendlesohn, Farah. 2002. "Toward A Taxonomy of Fantasy." *Journal of the Fantastic in the Arts* 13, no. 2 (50): 169–83. http://www.jstor.org/stable/43308579.

Nora, Pierre. 1989. "Between Memory and History: Les Lieux de Mémoire." *Representations* 26: 7–24. https://doi.org/10.2307/2928520.

Olick, Jeffrey. 2016. "Sites of Memory Studies (Lieux des études de mémoire)." In Tota and Hagen.

Perry, Spencer. 2022. "Netflix's *The Sandman* Crosses Major Milestone." Accessed December 13. 2022. https://comicbook.com/dc/news/netflixs-the-sandman-crosses-major-milestone.

Ricoeur, Paul. 2004. *History, Memory, Forgetting*, translated by Kathleen Blamey and David Pellauer. University of Chicago Press.

Rybicka, Elżbieta. 2012. "Place, Memory, Literature (From the Perspective of Geopoetics)." *Teksty Drugie* 2:126–39.

Schiller, Melanie. 2018. "Transmedia Storytelling: New Practices and Audiences." In *Stories*, edited by Ian Christie and Annie van den Oever, 97–108. Amsterdam University Press. https://doi.org/10.2307/j.ctv5rf6vf.10.

Tota, Anna Lisa, and Traver Hagen, eds. 2016. *Routledge International Handbook of Memory Studies*. Routledge.

Winter, Jay. 2010. "Sites of Memory." In *Memory: Histories, Theories, Debates*, edited by Susannah Radstone and Bill Schwarz, 312–24. Fordham University Press. http://www.jstor.org/stable/j.ctt1c999bq.25.

"You're as bad ... as Desire! Or worse!"

Examining the Abject Nature of Death and Desire

Melisa Maryann Goveas
and Naveen Kelvin Dalmeida

The scholarship surrounding Neil Gaiman's works, particularly *Sandman*, has focused on viewing intertextuality and mythic aspects within his oeuvre as well as the elements of classical feminism and postmodernism as depicted in the graphic novels (Klapcsik 2008, 319). However, *Sandman*, particularly in its new televised form, has yet to be subjected to a poststructuralist reading using Julia Kristeva's tool of abjection (Dalmeida 2021, 6). In this regard, David Rudd, Dominik Becher, and Sándor Klapcsik have utilized tools of abjection, subversion of death, and the theme of the liminal respectively within Gaiman's works, albeit limiting their research to his novels (Dalmeida 2021, 8). The abject nature of the Endless has yet to be explored, especially the physical materialization of Death and Desire, whose portrayal in the Netflix series is of great interest.

Abjection could be defined as being the human reaction to anything that can result in the threatened breakdown of meaning, caused by the destruction of the psyche's conventional and secure boundaries. The nature of the abject is to fascinate and yet it challenges the carefully constructed, and then proceeds to collapse the boundaries that humanity builds around itself. This paradoxical double nature of pleasure and horror is what invariably draws us to it. For Kristeva, death is not just an abject, it is the ultimate abject. The materialization of this abstract reality into an anthropomorphic being makes death an abject. The further manifestation of death as a woman heightens the abject nature of Death, as Kristeva (1982) devotes an entire chapter on women as abject entities (157). Death as a character now highlights the double nature of the abject, as death and as woman. Desire too exhibits this characteristic of the double abject. As a genderless being, they destroy the boundary of the patriarchal expectations of gender and sex. At the same time, they manifest desire, a human emotion that can at once be joyful and repulsive.

This essay aims to unpack the following ideas. In the *Sandman* universe, there appears to be an inversion of the traditional abject, first in the comics and now in the television series as well. Despite being viewed as abject, Death also appears "calm" and "soothes" the humans she counters. This is classic subversion, a feat also visible in Gaiman's "ghost children," according to Becher (2016, 97). Desire, too, posits the possibility of the abject inverted. However, to what degree do the two embody this abjection and how precisely can the nuances in their subversion in the show be brought out? To further the scope of abjection as a relevant reading, it is interesting to see the fans on social media who were unhappy with the casting of Kirby Howell-Baptiste, a woman of color, as Death in the Netflix series. In the same regard, one can position such a casting choice as in keeping with the counterculture depiction of death as a goth girl in the comics. Likewise, the casting of Mason Alexander Park, a nonbinary person, as Desire, carries the same theme forward. The hate targeted toward these casting decisions could stem from the abjection that some fans embody. Therefore, the inclusive decision to cast a diverse group of actors could be viewed as an exercise in inverting the abject.

Scholarship applying abjection to the works of Neil Gaiman is scarce. The same can be said of most poststructuralist treatments of his works. David Rudd (2008) forays into applying abjection when he applies the psychoanalytic perspective as posited by Julia Kristeva in "An Eye for an I: Neil Gaiman's *Coraline* and Questions of Identity" (167). Likewise, in "Neil Gaiman's Irony, Liminal Fantasies, and Fairy Tale Adaptations," Sándor Klapcsik (2008) emphasizes the role of liminal spaces in Gaiman's work, but falls shy of employing abjection as a tool to best examine the role of boundaries in these works (320). The application of abjections can be seen to a great extent in Naveen Kelvin Dalmeida's (2021) *Reading Abjection in the Select Works of Neil Gaiman*, albeit with an emphasis placed on Gaiman's children's novels (45–46). We hope to help fill the gap in the research by offering an abject reading of the first season of Netflix's *Sandman*.

In her seminal work, *Powers of Horror: An Essay on Abjection* (1982), Kristeva highlights her concept of abject and abjection. The primary example that Kristeva gives is a person's reaction to a corpse. This reaction can suggest the state of rejection and is used pejoratively to describe the state of marginalized groups, "like homosexuals, criminals, transgender, orphans, poor or physically challenged people" (4). The abject is thus like the marginalized groups who question the idea of boundaries. It attempts to draw the human psyche to a meaningless place, leading to the breakdown of the carefully built, yet fragile, boundaries. This in turn can cause feelings of horror, disgust, repression, and nausea within the individual—besides leading to a complete collapse of the person's distinct personality.

Abjection can be described as the state of one's mind when confronted with what Kristeva describes as the abject. These reactions can be physical like nausea. However, Kristeva also discusses the concept of the abject as a "state of mind" that is present in all humans. Like the object, the abject is created during the psychosexual development of an infant. It is created when the infant realizes that the mother is not a part of itself and jettisons the mother. It is a "violent, clumsy breaking away" (13) and since it's the mother that has been jettisoned, the infant cannot completely let go of the abject and it will forever hover around the border of the psyche. This is the reason why as humans we are both fascinated and repulsed by the abject. In moments of vulnerability (like death) or disturbing scenes (like blood, pus, the graphic visuals of childbirth) the abject can raise its head and draw an individual where the borders of one's psyche can collapse. In this sense, it can be deployed both as a noun and a verb—as the thing that evokes dread and the dread it evokes as well.

Kristeva uses this idea of the abject to discuss the anti–Semitic rhetoric in the writings of Louis-Ferdinand Céline. It has to be emphasized that she is in no way justifying his racist nature but tries to offer an alternate theory to his thought and work. For Celine, the Jews become abject because of both his fascination and "hatred" of them. Similarly, members of the "marginalized" communities, especially those who question the stereotypical dialectical nature of society, like the LGBTQIA+ community or "strong and independent women" can become abject for individuals who cannot see beyond the binary nature of society. It should be noted that abjection is in no way to be used as a means to justify acts of racism, homophobia, or misogyny. Thus, Kristeva sees the abject as something as old as humanity. When we examine *Sandman*, we can observe that all members of the Endless are abject by nature. This is especially true of the physical materialization of Death. Unlike the classical image of the Grim Reaper prevalent in Western art and literature, this materialization of the abstract concept of death as an anthropomorphic being highlights the abject nature of Death. In issue #8, "The Sound of Her Wings," Dream accompanies his sister on her "rounds." As they move from dying person to dying person, Dream notices the varied reactions to his sister's approach and muses, "As we pass them, people shiver and look away, mutter to each other ... they fear her, dread her, feebly attempt to placate her" (Gaiman et al. 1989).

Kristeva (1982) notes that "one does not know [the abject], one does not desire it, one joys in it, violently, painfully. A passion" (9). The nature of the abject is thus twofold as it simultaneously fascinates and yet challenges the carefully constructed, and then proceeds to collapse the boundaries that humanity builds upon itself. The persona of Death in *Sandman* is aware of the attitude that people have toward her. In issue #20, "Façade," Death tells a troubled woman named Rainie, "For some folks, Death is a release, for others it is an abomination, a terrible thing" (Gaiman et al. 1990b). It is this dual attitude that humanity has toward the abject, the repulsion and yet at the same time fascination, that the characters in the Netflix adaptation now embody, perhaps picking up from where the comics left off.

In this regard, it is the double nature or the dual aspects of the abject that can be seen in the portrayal of the Endless. As anthropomorphic representations of abstract human realities and emotions, the Endless are abject. Death especially highlights this, when ironically she is depicted as a woman rather than the fearsome skeletal visage that usually accompanies death. For Kristeva (1982), "the two things that most threaten the socio-symbolic [are] -death and the feminine ... [and the feminine is] the second extreme of abjection and cause of uncanny strangeness" (72).

Further, Kristeva examines these women who destroy the notion of "woman," whom she describes as the "females who can wreck the infinite" (157–73). Examining in detail the writings of Céline, she prepares a list of those women who question the conventions of "femininity." Within this grouping, Kristeva establishes a subcategory of "capable woman." According to Kristeva, this intellectual "does not escape being grotesque ... she is fated to prove the absurdity of reason (a masculine element) when it is sheltered in a body that is feminine to boot. Such is the woman inventor, the railroad company attendant, an unusual person" (parentheses original) (169). *Sandman*'s Death embodies these characteristics of the capable woman. Her atypical physical presentation in the form of a woman who firmly but gently leads individuals to the next chapter may be bewildering to some dying people who wonder if this kind female in front of them truly is Death.

The Endless siblings often discuss their eldest sister's unique position. Death is, to put it bluntly, the beginning and the end, the Alpha and the Omega. The siblings understand this aspect to be the very embodiment of her nature and Death takes this role in stride. These qualities make Death the "strong capable woman." For Death, helping people cross over to the Sunless Lands is simply her job. As she bluntly puts it in issue #20, "Façade," "I'm not blessed or merciful. I'm just me. I've got a job to do, and I do it…. When the first living thing existed, I was there waiting. When the last living thing dies, my job will be finished. I'll put the chairs on the tables, turn out the lights and lock the universe behind me when I leave" (Gaiman et al. 1990b).

As the anthropomorphic representation of one of human beings' most complex emotions, Desire also exhibits this characteristic of the doubly abject. They are also represented as a genderless/nonbinary being that destroys the dichotomous boundaries of gender and sex. This dual nature becomes more interesting as the very nature of Desire, both as an emotion and as a living being, is at best ambivalent. As Kristeva (1982) emphasizes, the abject is "what disturbs identity, system, order. What does not respect borders, positions, rules. The in-between, the ambiguous, the composite. The traitor, the liar, the criminal with a good conscience" (4). The persona of Desire occupies this position in the *Sandman* series. They are "the traitor, the liar," and serve as one of Dream's primary antagonists. Desire is manipulative and vindictive toward Dream and does everything in their power to antagonize him. The "real" reason for Desire's antagonistic behavior is never really specified in the comics, including the prequel *Sandman: Overture* (Gaiman et al. 2013), where Desire in fact actually aids Dream. As Desire muses after Morpheus departs from the Threshold in "Lost Hearts," "Human beings are the creatures of Desire. They twist and bend as I desire it" (Gaiman et al. 1990a).

Desire's manipulative and ambiguous personality can be seen throughout the comics. In this regard, it is interesting to see how the screen adaptation may course-correct the character's portrayal and motivations. First, an in-depth appreciation of the numerous instances of the possible abject in the comics will lend light to the research question. In issue #41, Delirium breaks down in a club, desperately crying, "I want my sister!" and mistaking a Goth woman for Death (Gaiman et al. 1992, 10–11). Hearing Delirium's cries "from two continents away," Desire arrives. When a patron of the club asks, "And who are you?" Desire explains, "Well … sometimes…. I'm her sister" (11). At first, Desire seems annoyed at Delirium's "pathetic" behavior. Their exchange is interrupted by another clubgoer who propositions Desire. Desire turns her down, but uses the opportunity to manipulate the woman into embarking upon a toxic relationship with someone else. As Desire smirks, the reader observes an almost immediate shift in change in Desire's behavior toward Delirium— where before Desire seemed inconvenienced by Delirium, or downplaying their own efforts in coming to help, now Desire reaches gently for Delirium's hand in order to escort her away. It is very possible that in addition to both embodying and representing the abject, the Endless also invert it on occasions. Inversion can be defined as the absence to horror that is experienced via an interaction with what would have been seen as abject.

In order for inversion of abjection to take place in the universe, an entity which was previously identified as abject would then be required to "comfort" or "soothe." This is a contradiction of the abjection they embody, thereby inverting it. Death is a fitting example of the abject inverted. While Death is abject (and in fact, doubly so), within the *Sandman* universe there are ample illustrations of Death as soothing or calming. For any entity to be capable of having a soothing or calming effect, it must push aside any abjection it held in the first place. This can be viewed with respect to Death in the comics story arc "The Kindly Ones." Incidentally, it is Death herself who arguably spells out in "The Sound of Her Wings" the possibility of abjection being contradicted across the Endless when she accuses Dream of being "as bad … as Desire! Or worse!" (Gaiman et al. 1989).

On a more impactful level, the inverted abject of Death is more pronounced in the end of the universe, as depicted in "The Kindly Ones." In this story arc, Dream specifically asks for Death. This surprising turn of events is best captured by Matthew the Raven, who states, "He wants you to go to him" (Gaiman et al. 1995, 24). The implied last meeting of the two siblings is one where Dream functionally escaped the abject reality of what is happening to his realm as a result of his actions. When Death tells Dream, "give me your hand" (11), there is an end to Dream's pronounced "tiredness." The not-so-weary Death poses only the threat of probably hitting her brother with a piece of bread and is not the source of the traditional abject that actual-death would provide.

The obvious contradiction is that Death is full of life, in all of her iterations, including the cheery drawings in the comics, the chirpy tones of Kat Dennings in the *Sandman* audiobook, and the warm, smiling personal of Kirby Howell-Baptiste in Netflix show. Explorations of her contradictory, almost paradoxical nature, continue in "The Sound of Her Wings," where Death is presented as both abject as well as abject inverted. This state is expanded elaborately by the time the events in "The Kindly Ones" are realized in their full scope. None of Kristeva's traditional reactions toward the abject is seen once the initial contact and moment of realization has transpired. In this respect, the Endless' status as immortal (with perhaps the exception of Dream) is a key reason governing their inverted abject nature. By virtue of being incapable of coming to an end, they defy the source of the original ultimate abject in mortals: death. Whether it's a corpse or a mangled image of a loved one, the abject reminds the mortal of the inevitability of their own end. This is what gives rise to the horror. However, Death's calming, soothing actions, as in case of the end of "The Kindly Ones," result in the abject being violently inverted instead of "jettisoned" as Kristeva envisioned it.

This is further emphasized in Desire's eulogy for Dream as presented in issue #72, "In Which We Wake." The tone of the eulogy is subtle and mischievous, demonstrating Desire's frustration with their brother, and yet there is also sorrow in their words. As Desire so eloquently puts it, "The bonds of family bind both ways. They bind us up, support us, help us. And they are also a bond from which it is difficult, perhaps impossible to extricate oneself. My late brother being a case in point" (Gaiman et al. 1995c, 9). The tongue-in-cheek eulogy does not help in hiding Desire's sorrow over their brother's passing while it also heightens the nature of the inverted abject.

Desire's mischievousness can be viewed as another example of their contradicted abject nature, but there ae some rare instances when Desire in fact does show a softer side. In "Brief Lives," when Despair brings news of Dream's son Orpheus' death, we do not observe Desire as triumphant. They comment quite sadly, "So, the child is dead" (Gaiman et al. 1993, 19). When Despair inquires if Desire is happy that Dream has finally shed the blood of his own family, they reply, "No, I'm scared" (Gaiman et al. 1993, 10). Although Desire is almost always presented as eminently selfish, this is one of several instances that show an introspective Desire that thinks of others. Another example is when they visit Rose Walker in "The Kindly Ones," addressing the young woman as "Granddaughter" and having a heart-to-heart talk with her. Desire even leaves behind their heart-shaped cigarette lighter for Rose (Gaiman et al. 1994, 5–9). This isn't the first time Desire has given a personal object to comfort a human—they also clad the naked Tiffany with their coat and comforted her after she fled the burning nightclub (Gaiman et al. 1993, 25).

In "Neil Gaiman's Ghost Children," Dominik Becher notes that *Sandman*, like Gaiman's other stories that delve into the supernatural, exhibits a "positive approach toward death [that] subverts the horror genre" (Becher 2016, 103). While Becher focuses on *The Graveyard Book* and its depiction of the undead, within the *Sandman* universe Death takes on a far greater possibility of subverting horror. In this respect, the scope of the inversion of the abject in Gaiman's novels *The Graveyard Book*, *Coraline*, and *The Ocean at the End of the Lane* can be defined as moments "where there is no fear posed by the source of traditional abjection and further, the inversion is performed by fulfilling a positive function, that of nurturement" (Dalmeida 2021, 37). While nurturement cannot be evaluated within the scope of this essay, there is a likely leap of logic that Death is a source of some positivity, as envisioned by Becher, as a "comfort in the certainty of a sublime and beautiful death—an observation that all too often goes unnoticed in our modern society, which most of the time embraces a lifestyle and adolescent attitude toward death, pretending that we are all immortal" (2016, 103).

Most of these examples from the original comics have yet to be adapted for the television series, and reader-viewers may wonder in what way the show will differ in its approach to these scenes. The hint of abjection within Dream (Tom Sturridge) appears during his meeting with the three Fates in the second episode, "Imperfect Hosts." The three Fates appear in the form of the Mother (Nina Wadia), Maiden (Dinita Gohil), and Crone (Souad Faress) and greet Dream as if he were an old friend. Dream is reverential toward them, giving them a nuanced bow, and treating them with great respect. The Fates represented the gift of life, the measure of how long it exists, and cutting that life off at its end. But are they abject? The fear that the Fates evoke can be seen after Dream expresses his desire to summon them and Lucienne (Vivienne Acheampong) is clearly anxious, suggesting that he request help from a sibling instead. This fear could be abject as the Fates hold clear, destructive power over Dream.

Then there are the gifts that Dream procures for the Fates, including a live snake that slithers from Dream directly into the Fates' mouth. Dream's subtle expressions show the viewers that he is both fascinated and horrified by the Fates. Despite the fact that he himself is a mighty being, he acts with deference toward the three women, posing his questions politely, and is forced to accept the "riddle answers" that they offer. Thus, everything about the three Fates screams abject—they are women (and at least one of is beyond childbearing age, perhaps abject in another way), they are supernatural beings, and they live and occupy a space which even Dream of the Endless cannot touch. Therefore, the abject when represented as a woman takes on this monstrous form of the Fates. Incidentally, in *The Monstrous Feminine*, Creed discusses this very concept of the abject as something horrifying and its representation in films through the image of the abject woman.

In episode 6, "The Sound of Her Wings," the audience is repeatedly shown that even though death is not something that one would normally wish to experience, there is almost always a sense of relief or calm when Death (Kirby Howell-Baptiste) in fact arrives. In one example, Death appears to guide the person she is taking to, "walking along" with them, almost as a companion. Given that the *Sandman* version of Death is a departure from the traditional depictions of the male Grim Reaper or the skeletal leader of the Danse Macabre, it is quite telling that she does not elicit fear, but instead, an unlikely comfort. None of the individuals she "takes" in this collage of her duties offers sustained resistance. Harry the violin player (Jon Rumney) does try to bargain for more time, which she grants, so that he can recite the Shema prayer. He is obviously not ready to die just yet, but he makes peace with the reality of the matter pretty quickly. The same is true for the comedian who only appears in the comics, who Death asks to "come here, honey" (Gaiman et al. 1989) and again with the baby who presumably dies of SIDS (in this case, we have death as abject as well as the baby, for dying so unnaturally young). In the comics, the baby protests when Death arrives, questioning whether the tiny amount of life they have experienced is all that life has to offer, but in the series, we only get Death gently telling the baby that that is all there is.

The abject has been described in many ways, including being something that draws a person to a place wherein "meaning collapses" (Kristeva 1982, 2). In the series, we observe a number of places where we can find this collapse of meaning, but for the present purpose, we will focus on the Threshold and the Dreaming. The Threshold is the realm of Desire, best shown in episode 10, "Lost Hearts." The Threshold appears as a colossal statue of Desire's body with their red beating heart at its center. The Threshold is a monochromatic blood red; and the only other color is from the gallery where the sigils for the other Endless are lit up. This vibrant, angry, bold red suggests Desire's dangerous, enthralling nature: more blood than heart, more fatal passion than love. It is here than Desire forms their plan against Dream and where Dream finally confronts them. In this sense, the Threshold (like all realms of the Endless) can be seen as abject because its existence relies on the Endless it is tied to. Without their respective Endless, each realm collapses in on itself, as is evidenced by the collapse of the Dreaming during Dream's imprisonment. The realms are also abject because their Endless are physical representations of various abject human experiences / conditions and in situ will pass onto the realms. Lastly, both desire and death are manifested in the horrors of the diner scene in episode 5, "24/7."

Clearly, Desire is abject, but they also invert this status. In the scene where Dream confronts Desire, in both the comics and the show, Desire appears in the attire of a cat. Their tail makes swishing movements throughout the scene, a tell revealing Desire's feelings of triumph as they realize that they have succeeded in annoying Dream. With the mischievous look and swish of their tail, Desire both embodies and inverts the abject.

Abjection can also be extended beyond the theoretical framework and observed in one real-world reaction to the series itself: fan backlash. It is interesting to note that the criticism hurled at the show is usually from fans of the original comics (Rouner 2021). In this respect, the manner in which a subset of fans reacted with uproar over the casting of Dream and Desire, in particular, can be examined, as can the positive reactions of other fans. At its core though, both the backlash and the defense or celebration of these changes comes from a fan, an insider. The abject, as identified by Kristeva, emerges from within, and therefore the fan who feels "wronged" by casting choices which (according to them) deviated from the source material can be considered abject. Interestingly, Gaiman issued a pretty strong statement about this "backlash" via his Twitter feed, saying, "I give all the fucks about the work. I spent 30 years successfully battling bad movies of Sandman. I give zero fucks about people who don't understand / haven't read Sandman whining about a non-binary Desire or that Death isn't white enough. Watch the show, make up your own minds" (@neilhimself, May 29, 2021). This provides scope for further research, perhaps even within the realm of reader-response theory.

Given the relatively small sample size of these reactions, it can be argued that the negative reactions to inclusive casting stem more from racism and pre-conceived stereotypes than from a strictly critical analysis of the work, and this attitude itself can be seen as abject. It is important to note that this abjection can also be inverted and contradicted, which the first season has certainly done. By casting a diverse group of actors, particularly a woman of color as Death and a nonbinary artist as Desire, the Netflix series has made a vital course correction, absolving the comics from being a "product of their times" and leading the whole *Sandman* universe into the more inclusive space of the 2020s. The casting itself can be seen as an exercise in inverting the abject. The promise of the first season has left many hungry to see what else the series has in store, but based on the episodes so far, we can expect to see further explorations of abjection, inversion, and contradiction.

REFERENCES

Becher, Dominik. 2016. "Neil Gaiman's Ghost Children." In *Ghosts—or the (Nearly) Invisible: Spectral Phenomena in Literature and the Media*, edited by Maria Fleischhack and Elmar Schenkel, 91–106. Peter Lang AG.
Creed, Barbara. 1993. *The Monstrous-Feminine*. Routledge.
Dalmeida, Naveen Kelvin. 2021. *Reading Abjection in the Select Works of Neil Gaiman*. Mangalore: St. Aloysius Deemed to Be University (thesis).
Gaiman, Neil. 2002. *Coraline*. Bloomsbury.
_____. 2008. *The Graveyard Book*. Bloomsbury.
_____. 2014. *The Ocean at the End of the Lane*. Headline.
_____. 2020. *Sandman: Act I*. Adapted and directed by Dirk Maggs. Audible audio.
_____. 2021. *Sandman: Act II*. Adapted and directed by Dirk Maggs. Audible audio.
_____. 2022. *Sandman: Act III*. Adapted and directed by Dirk Maggs. Audible audio.
Gaiman, Neil, David S. Goyer, and Allan Heinberg, creators. 2022. *Sandman*. Season 1. Netflix.
Gaiman, Neil (w), Mike Dringenberg (a), and Malcolm Jones III (i). 1989. "The Sound of Her Wings." *Sandman* #8. DC Comics. August.
Gaiman, Neil (w), Mike Dringenberg (a), and Malcolm Jones III (i). 1990a. "The Doll's House: Part 7—Lost Hearts." *Sandman* #16. DC Comics. June.
Gaiman, Neil (w), Colleen Doran (p), and Malcolm Jones III (i). 1990b. "Façade." *Sandman* #20. DC Comics. Oct.

Gaiman, Neil (w), Jill Thompson (p), and Vince Locke (i). 1992. "Brief Lives: Part 1." *Sandman* #41. DC Comics. Sept.
Gaiman, Neil (w), Jill Thompson (a), and Vince Locke (i). 1993a. "Brief Lives: Part 5." *Sandman* #45. DC Comics. Jan.
Gaiman, Neil (w), Jill Thompson (a), and Vince Locke (i). 1993b. "Brief Lives: Part 9." *Sandman* #49. DC Comics/Vertigo. May.
Gaiman, Neil (w), Marc Hempel (a), and Richard Case (p). 1995a. "The Kindly Ones: Part 12." *Sandman* #68. DC Comics/Vertigo. May.
Gaiman, Neil (w), Marc Hempel (a), and Daniel Vozzo (c). 1995b. "The Kindly Ones: Part 13." *Sandman* #69. DC Comics. July.
Gaiman, Neil (w), Michael Zulli (a), and Daniel Vozzo (c) 1995c. "Chapter Three: In Which We Wake." *Sandman* #72. DC Comics. Nov.
Gaiman, Neil (w), J.H. Williams III (a), and Dave Stewart (c). 2013. *Sandman: Overture*. Vertigo.
Gaiman, Neil. (@neilhimself). 2021. "I give all the fucks about the work. I spent 30 years successfully battling bad movies of Sandman. I give zero fucks about people who don't understand / haven't read Sandman whining about non-binary Desire or that Death isn't white enough. Watch the show, make up your minds. https://t.co/KcNzap8Kt4." Twitter, May 29. https://twitter.com/neilhimself/status/1398500390912413698.
Klapcsik, Sándor. 2008. "Neil Gaiman's Irony, Liminal Fantasies, and Fairy Tale Adaptations." *Hungarian Journal of English and American Studies* 14 (2): 317–34.
Kristeva, Julia. 1982. *Powers of Horror*. Columbia University Press.
Rouner, Jef. 2021. "Racist Backlash about Netflix's *Sandman* Casting Gets Its Own Backlash." *Houston Press*, June 7.
Rudd, David. 2008. "An Eye for an I: Neil Gaiman's *Coraline* and Questions of Identity." *Children's Literature in Education* 39 (3): 159–68.

Superheroes Can Be Children in Footie Pajamas

The Sensible Revisions of Netflix's Sandman as Participating Within the Larger Project of DC's Sandmen

Joseph Michael Sommers

> "In my head, [adaptation of my work] is a lot closer to going to and seeing a play based on one of my stories. You know that it's not the story; you know that it's somebody's interpretation; and you know that the thing you saw that night will never happen again [...] it'll be completely different."
> —Neil Gaiman

Impossible as it might seem, it took Neil Gaiman and his fanbase *over thirty years* for a proper (read: good) adaptation of his comics magnum opus *Sandman* (1989–1996) to be realized. As Gaiman announced, "After three decades of stopping bad 'Sandman' adaptations from happening. By hook or by crook, by fair means or foul, I blocked and stopped so many bad 'Sandman' movies [because] if it's going to happen, why not make it good?" (Mass 2022). *Sandman* the narrative has evolved over time— not unlike Sandman the character, who was once a 1930s lesser-known gas-masked crimefighter named Wesley Dodds before Gaiman morphed him into Dream of the Endless, a gothic touchstone of the late 1980s.[1] The heart of the character has always evolved to fit different audiences, time periods, and mediums. While absence may indeed make the heart grow fonder, reuniting with something once loved in a particular manner and form in a new way can be a contentious if not mysteriously vexing affair when one discovers that, as a thing ages, it may change with the times.

So it went with Gaiman's critically triumphant and, occasionally, popularly challenged live-action adaptation of *Sandman*, a thing that everyone had wanted since the late eighties and, once the fandom got it, that a sizeable segment immediately complained about. The author and executive producer of the show obviously made changes in order to keep the story and characters as contemporaneous with today as it was when it first came out three decades prior. And in so doing, they bothered a small but vocal contingent. This was especially evident on the gaping maw of unpoliced-opinion-parroting-as-discourse-social-media-site formerly known as Twitter. As Matthew Jackson (2021) noted for *SYFY Wire*,

> Kirby Howell-Baptiste, who is Black, will be playing Dream's witty and wise sister Death, who was depicted in the *Sandman* comics as white. When some readers took to Twitter to complain about this change for the Netflix series, Gaiman pointed out both that the Endless are not human, and that while he helped create Death's comics look, he never felt her white-ness was somehow essential to her character.

The commentators who fixated on Death's pallor howled *before anyone had seen the adaptation* and their complaints were equal parts banal and ad hominem toward the writer of the comic who helped cast the role. Jackson reports one user, Asier3D, writing, "Death is black? Really? She was one of the most iconic characters." Another user, Herbert Watt, complained to Gaiman that "[Death's] design was pure brilliance in its simplicity and people love her and how she looks in the comic. As the creator you knew this. And that is the one design you went 'Screw all that' with? I hope the money was good."[2] Gaiman's response to these complaints, made by people who claimed to be fans and had not seen the show he adapted from his own work, was not defensive, but assuredly not polite either: "I give all the fucks about the work. I spent 30 years successfully battling bad movies of Sandman. I give zero fucks about people who don't understand/haven't read Sandman whining about a non-binary Desire or that Death isn't white enough. Watch the show, make up your minds" (tweet quoted in Jackson 2021).

In essence, a particularly disgruntled segment of *Sandman*'s fandom found voice from behind their keyboards and issued a peculiar display of dissatisfaction with a creator who finally acquired a measure of control over an adaptation of his work and did what he said he would always do. At the DC FanDome event in 2020, Gaiman stated,

> What we're doing with Netflix is saying "OK, it's still going to start in 1916, but the thing that happens in *Sandman* #1, the point that the story starts, is not 1988. It's *now*, and how does that change the story.... What does that give us? What does that make us have to look at that we wouldn't have to look at if we were setting it as a period piece? What is that going to do to the gender of characters? What's that gonna do to the nature of characters?" [quoted in Jackson 2020].

Or, as Jackson wrote, the show would be constructed with "a much more loose approach, and that means an updated timeline and a more modern feel." And, by almost any metric, that is simply good common sense by way of comics adaptation and its history.

Neil Gaiman knows his comics history. That history had early feelers in the culture of American serialized television such as *Batman*, the 1960s show starring Adam West that Gaiman watched as a young boy. Many of Gaiman's larger projects, including *American Gods*, *Stardust*, and *The Graveyard Book*, concern themselves with an acknowledgment and dutiful reenvisioning of the stories, myths, and narratives of his younger days, bringing them in line with the current moment's sociocultural mores. *Sandman*, like these other adaptations, is a tasteful update that acknowledges traditions and texts while also serving as a touchstone for a new audience in a new medium. What works in one medium in one time might not do as well in a different medium at a later time. Whereas the original, or pre-text[3] of something resonated with an audience of a certain time period, many of Gaiman's most well-received projects acknowledge such histories when he recrafts them for similar types of audiences in a *different* day and age. At the top of that list is *Sandman*, a critical darling, fan favorite, and one of the most influential comics of the contemporary era. Yet even such a thing did not make it timeless. To keep it from being a period piece, Gaiman would update his own work and do so in a way that allowed it to remain faithful to the original texts while resonating with a time period and medium that is significantly incongruent with the original day and age.

One of the most critical aspects stripped from the first season of the Netflix incarnation of *Sandman* was the outward connection with the larger DC universe that it was originally tethered to. In the original comics, Gaiman built the first story arc (*Preludes and Nocturnes*) into the existing DC universe by including a myriad of some of the company's most popular characters. Batman and his rogues, Martian Manhunter, and John Constantine all graced initial *Sandman* comic book pages only to quickly fall away as Gaiman's confidence in the story eliminated the need to rely upon connective tissue to established DC properties. Changes as a result of adaptation were made not only for the betterment of the show as an interpretation of his and his rotating cast of artists' work but also as historically consistent with the characters found in the *Sandman* comic. This self-reflexive reinvention and retelling might be best seen in the revision of Jack Kirby and Joe Simon's incarnation of the Sandman. As opposed to the original street level crime fighters, theirs was a yellow and red spandex-clad superhero occupying Morpheus's station while he was accidentally imprisoned by Roderick Burgess for a century. Gaiman adapts his own version of the character rather than practice absolute fidelity to Kirby and Simon's construction. Originally, they placed the station of Sandman on Hector Hall from *Infinity Inc*. Gaiman, instead, used a narrative loophole in order to place that silly suit upon a dream projection of young Jed Walker[4] in a dreamscape where it fits far more appropriately on a young child than a middle-aged, mostly dead, somewhat-super hero. The result of this change both acknowledges and participates in the history of comics legacy characters while also making a significant improvement to construction of the original character of Jed—a young boy suffering abuse from his foster parents who becomes an imaginary superhero to compensate for traumas he cannot confront otherwise. This change in the Netflix show both removes the need for the viewer to learn a maddeningly large corpus of preexisting comics texts (many of which are either out of print or so cost-prohibitive as to make access difficult for most readers) and revises and improves the narrative construct by making the show considerably more consistent with what the comic eventually became. Once the comic moved to the Vertigo imprint, it stopped being indebted to DC. Originally this move happened gradually across several issues, but could happen right from the start in the television series.

And while fans of the original comic may wonder why certain changes were made, Gaiman enacted these revisions as a corrective to a new but almost entirely faithful version of *Sandman* that knows what it wants and needs to be from the outset. In that, Gaiman has moved from being a writer to sitting at the editor's desk of his own work, remythologizing it for an entirely new audience while respectfully acknowledging his original audience *just as he did with the comics he originally based his comic on in the first place*. While the comic book *Sandman* is still plainly visible on the screen, the show now treats its story that arose from the late 1980s with a reverence for 2020s culture. And is still as timeless today as it was back then.

Adaptation and/or Retelling? And What Actually Is the Difference?

In "Weaving New Dreams from Old Cloth: Conceptual Blending and Hybrid Identities in Neil Gaiman's Fairy-Tale Retellings," Anna Katrina Gutierrez (2019) succinctly establishes the larger project of Gaiman's writings:

> Gaiman understands the power in traditional stories, or well-known and frequently retold tales that endure from one generation to the next.... He knows

that the most compelling modern tales have patterns from the old stories woven into them.... Like the most skillful weavers, Gaiman has the ability to [re-weave] them into a "third" narrative that is new yet old, strange yet familiar, and is ultimately unique and meaningful. Moreover, his contemporary retellings play with readers' expectations by disrupting standard patterns of scripts and schema, the effect which confronts readers with the validity of the [metanarrative] and its underpinning ideologies [217–18].

Here Gutierrez correctly identifies Gaiman as a reteller, a storymaker who works with old narrative to compose new narratives from similar DNA. And, as such, his stories participate within the greater fabric of storytelling contributing to the rich panoply of a larger cultural narrative; in this case, Gaiman's original work with his comic *Sandman* was a reinterpretation and progression of the Jack Kirby / Joe Simon reworking of the character from 1974[5]—which itself was a reinterpretation of the character, Wesley Dodds, who was a standard crimefighter in a mask and fedora created by Gardner Fox and Bert Christman in 1939 (Benton 1992). In adapting his own work for Netflix, Gaiman, again, participated in the act of reweaving his own cloth in order to streamline the narrative away from its DC Comics predecessors and offer a contemporary portrayal of his original work while removing the baggage of 80-plus years of comics reading. In doing so, he frees the new narrative from the shackles of the prior character's histories while also allowing the differing strata of his fanbase opportunities to realize the history he does give them while not hindering the narrative's progression with information that has become irrelevant in the new moment.

The results are both faithful and antagonistic to the fandom at the same time. Linda Hutcheon (2006) sees the entirety of the debate as a simultaneous matter of "familiarity" and "contempt" (2). Adaptation, she finds more often than not, is a matter where the source work is frequently, if not inherently, elevated over anything derived from it and retold in another medium. She writes, "In both academic criticism and journalistic reviewing, contemporary popular adaptations are most often put down as secondary, derivative, 'belated, middlebrow, or culturally inferior'" (2). It is, as another critic has put it, a movement to "a willfully inferior form of cognition" (quoted in Hutcheon 2006) where the adaptations are "haunted at all times by their adapted texts" regardless of their success, whatever who or what might define that, in translation from medium to medium (6). This matter of success, Hutcheon claims, arises from a history of criticism that ultimately evaluated a thing based on its "proximity or fidelity to the adapted text [and] should be the criterion of judgment or the focus of analysis" (6). From her vantage point, this fidelity criticism, as it is, becomes far more a hindrance than a thing of profundity or greater critical use. Instead, she argues one might consider the nature of adaptation itself from its first principles: "According to its dictionary meaning, 'to adapt' is to adjust, to alter, to make suitable. This can be done in any number of ways [and,] as a process of creation, the act of adaptation always involves both (re-)interpretation and then (re-)creation" (6–8). To those ends, she suggests that successful adaptation will be inherently "pamplisestuous," borrowing the term from Michael Alexander (6). By this reasoning, although Gaiman participates within the established history of the character and the comic from its situation within a larger DC Comics universe from which it hails and derives content, the novel joy of his work comes in the translation of the thing from one medium, printed comics, to another, filmic presentation.

If there *is* a problem, it likely resides in the ether between those media. It is a two-headed beast in that way; Hutcheon reminds us that adaptation is closer to art than a science. She writes, "As openly acknowledged and extended reworkings of particular other texts, adaptations are often compared to translations. Just as there is no such thing as a literal translation, there can be no literal adaptation" (16). Again, that "rhetoric of comparison has most often been that of faithfulness and equivalence" (16). Comics scholar Pascal Lefevre (2007) expands upon that notion to, possibly, get straight to the heart of the matter: the creators tend to desire an opportunity to change and develop their creation through a transmedia adaption while their fans would prefer a strict faithfulness to that which they first experienced (1). He writes,

> By contrast to the artists themselves, diehard fans of the original work rarely applaud such rewritings. [Some] comics fans tend to consecrate the original work and scrutinize a filmic adaptation for so called errors of misinterpretation. Almost every attempt of adaptation becomes in their eyes some kind of betrayal [5].

From Lefevre's perspective, fans such as these demand that the adaptation preserve the static reality of the comic under adaptation even though the entire premise of a medial shift is to inject a greater dynamism into the work. To do otherwise would be to render every adaptation a period piece. How time works in comics, especially ones that span several decades (even as characters age little), and how time works in film or television, is very different. Eliding the metatextual history would not only be an unsavory prospect but highly confusing to the story being told as well.[6]

Comics theorist and historian Jan Baetens (2018) proposes a caveat and a resolution to the dilemma at the heart of the contentions between artist and consumer of art that assumes a binary dialectical relationship. He states:

> We are all well aware of the great pitfall of classic studies on adaptation. It is not so much their attachment to the principle of fidelity that several recent studies have foregrounded, but rather their inability to break free from a certain *binary* approach. Adaptation implies a here and an elsewhere, as well as a before and an after, and the insistence on maintaining a similar gap between adapted and adapting remains one of the main elements hampering the development of adaptation studies [31, emphasis added].

In essence, Baetens argues that both artist and fan need to essentially get over themselves and remember that what is at the heart of the matter is the message of the piece, a thing that can change moment to moment and place to place. Anyone familiar with folk studies and folklore understands that what makes a lore of the *folk* is its itinerant nature. A certain pre-text, a tenor, of the message will travel and adorn itself with new clothes when taken up by different people, taking on its cultural tenets while maintaining the essentials of the message. And, even at the level of reading something, anything, including this paragraph itself, adaptation is at play—less translation, as others purport, and more "transformation." Baetens feels that "adaptation is not only that which 'reveals' the work retrospectively; it constitutes the work itself, which exists only as a chain or network of ceaseless transformations" (32). Further, as indicated earlier, over time and space, these adaptations will themselves likely be further adapted still.

As such, Baetens (2020) immediately dismisses one end of Hutcheon's concerns; the "fidelity framework comes down to a simple argument: a filmic adaptation of a literary text is always disappointing except when it manages to be faithful to the original, but absolute fidelity is nearly impossible" (611). It is impossible and *untenable* as the medial shift in adaptation does not allow for that which was held sacrosanct by the reader and fan to translate or be transformed by the very nature of the move between mediums. To subscribe to a perfect fidelity, the creator must negate the need or even urge to adapt one thing into another. If something is so perfect as it was originally, then why would anyone wish to see it transformed into something else when, by definition, a thing even perfectly faithful to the original will fail to live up to the original, as the original came first, always rendering subsequent efforts as inferior. Worse, by nature of this faulty orthodoxy, the scope of the audience for the original work cannot expand past the original fandom as it will make no sense to anyone unfamiliar with the time or place as no assimilation between what a new audience knows and comprehends and the old audience knows and understands will be possible. The texts and pre-texts best suited to survive are those fit to be adapted. Hutcheon (2006) reaches a very similar conclusion: "Adaptation is repetition, but repetition without replication. And there are manifestly many different possible intentions behind the act of adaptation: the urge to consume and erase the memory of the adapted text or to call it into question is as likely as the desire to pay tribute by copying.... Oedipally envious and worshipful at the same time" (7). In other words, the offspring will share DNA with their parents, but, even at the moment of birth, they will be fundamentally new and different while deriving veritably everything constituting their being whence they came.

From Sandman to Sandboy by Divisive Means

In the seventh episode of *Sandman*, "The Doll's House," the viewer begins the second arc of the first season where Morpheus (Tom Sturridge), having recovered his tools of office after over one hundred years of imprisonment away from the Dreaming, begins his search for a dream vortex, mentioned and (as the viewer comes to learn) made by Desire (Mason Alexander Park), which threatens reality itself due to its peculiar nature. The plot and subject matter of this arc is complex and part of Gaiman's long game for both the comic and the show. It exacerbates the sibling rivalry between Dream and Desire in what the viewer/reader will come to discover is Dream's fatal flaw: his awkwardness with humanity in all manners and measures will ultimately lead to his undoing. For my purposes, however, as opposed to discussing the numerous small changes to the path that leads *Sandman* to.... *Sandman*, I will focus on Gaiman's division of the character of the Jack Kirby / Joe Simon Sandman into two unique roles in the Netflix series with two explicitly different purposes.

Derived from the original source material of *Sandman* issues #10 and #11, Lucienne (Vivienne Acheampong), the reenvisioning of Lucien, chief librarian of the Dreaming, informs Morpheus that a select few major figures of the Dreaming have gone AWOL during his imprisonment. This includes Brute and Glob (Gaiman 2012, 278), two relatively minor arcana within the history of the comic and now utterly reimagined as the singular Gault (*Ann Ogbomo*), an "untrustworthy ... shape-changer" who, as the viewer will come to learn, never wished to be a nightmare, and, in Morpheus's absence seeks further reinvention through redemption. Within the original comic, Brute and Glob hearken back to their 1974 incarnations as associates of the Kirby/Simon Sandman who keeps them captive and summons them as needed in his role as a more superheroic version of the title character (Gaiman 2012, 295). Gaiman compounds the history of the Sandman and his major incarnations even more by presenting the Kirby-era Sandman,[7] garishly attired in orange and yellow tights with cape and collar, in an eight-panel presentation in the style of Windsor McKay, who also wrote and drew of dreams, a king named Morpheus, and so forth in his *Little Nemo in Slumberland* (Gaiman 2012, 294). Gaiman weaves his narrative with reworked cloth of different eras, drawing the name of his Sandman from McKay, the comics sensibilities of Kirby's "revamped" by Kirby's dynamic aesthetic and deep cuts within DCs universe (Hatfield 2012, 30), *Sandman*, and his own comics' darkness of Jed's abuse by his foster parents requiring a safe space, his dreams.

Jed's dreams are quite unique though. As Lucienne and Morpheus discover, the last noted connection Jed Walker (Eddie Karanja) had with the Dreaming was a nightmare Jed had of Gault (the compressed and reimagined version of Brute and Glob). This aligns with Brute and Glob's machinating use of Jed to hide from Morpheus from the comics: "They severed the child from the true Dreaming," Morpheus tells Lucien in *Sandman* #12, "They are living in his mind" (Gaiman 2012, 314). Further, as Lucienne informs Morpheus, Gault seemingly takes Jed in particular due to his filial bond to Rose Walker (Kyo Ra), the vortex—a being so powerful that she can actually manifest in Morpheus's throne room uninvited. After Lucienne briefs Morpheus on Rose's presence and his need to take action against her, the Sandman rebuts, stating, "the Endless are forbidden from taking action against any mortal *who is not an active threat*." Moreover, Morpheus hopes to use Rose's nature as a vortex to draw the missing arcana to her and then to him. As it happens though, Rose does as Morpheus hopes and a little more: she draws the dead to her. In this case, she draws Hector Hall, Lyta's husband and the character separated from the Kirby incarnation of Sandman.

Gaiman makes a fundamental alteration to the characters of Kirby's Sandman, Jed Walker, and Hector Hall, collapsing the comicsy discourses of the garishness of his visual design of the Sandman and placing them with exactly who they might make the most sense: young Jed. In the eighth episode of the show, "Playing House," we find Gault not using Jed to hide from Morpheus but rather guarding the boy's fragile mind in dreams when he is in physical danger by empowering him as Gaiman's new version of Kirby's Sandman. When danger arises, Jed reimagines himself as he sleeps, clad in the guise of a superhero with Gault heralding him into action. Jed slips into his own sustained dreamworld where he is its most powerful hero, the Sandman, called forth by Gault to stop "The Pied Piper" from attempting "to control all the area's children." And, adorned in a perfect facsimile of Kirby's spandexed superhero costume, Jed's youth allows the otherwise campy Halloween costume—or, as I see it, the sleeper's footie PJs, echoing something akin to Adam West's 1960s version of Batman—to appear as not a ridiculous thing to be mocked or derided but a thing filled with the power of childlike wonder. It's transformative as the audience reads Jed slipping into a place of control to offset the powerlessness of his situation. In this new version of the narrative, upon Sandman meeting Sandman, Morpheus is no longer angry with a dead Hector Hall slipping into his role but, instead, is incredulous with something mirroring bemusement and delight at seeing a small child, admittedly using powers without permission, but essentially playing pretend in order to survive being locked in a rat-infested cellar. Morpheus would be right and just to be angry, Gault has told Jed that he is "the King of Nightmares, and he has come to take me away from [Jed]." Both claims are true, but Gault withholds vital context from Jed who only wishes to save her. When he arrives to meet the real Sandman (who travels with Rose), he does so with considerable flourish: "Halt, King of Nightmares, or I'll send you both to Dreamland!" At the precocious pronouncement, Morpheus can barely contain his incredulity and giddiness; Jed exclaims: "I am the Guardian of Sleepers. I am the Lord of the Dream Domain. I am the Sandman." Morpheus chuckles out a response: "You are the Sandman?"

Morpheus directs his anger solely upon Gault. His feelings are mirrored by Rose but sadness, not anger, at Gault as the dream has chosen the form of the Walker siblings' mother in an effort to gain and keep Jed's trust (whether or not he is aware of it). However, where Brute and Glob's machinations were not entirely dissimilar in *Sandman* #12 (nor was Morpheus's "admiration" matched by his "anger"), their ultimate goal was to befuddle Hector Hall as Sandman in an effort to "make our own dream king. One *we'd* be running" (Gaiman 2012, 323–25). They burned through the Sandford Sandman (Hector's predecessor) and then the Hall Sandman in the process, and Morpheus banished them to the darkness for several thousand years as a result of their hubris and disdain for their creator and humanity (Gaiman 2012, 335). Gault, however, sought only a life better than a nightmare, and part and parcel to that, came to the aid of a little boy in fear of his uncle who threatens physical violence. Gault, knowing full well that her crimes are without explanation, still fights for the boy even as she, like Brute and Glob before her, faces banishment, if not outright destruction. Prior to this eventuality, Gault implores Morpheus: "Do you have any idea what [Jed's] life is like in the waking world? ... The boy is being abused. He's suffering." Morpheus parries her supposed concern stating that she abused his suffering "to *build a Dreaming you could rule*" (emphasis added). Here, Gaiman conflates Brute and Glob's intentions with Gault's actions; however, this new nightmare never sought a kingdom—she sought to fight her own nature and design as a nightmare in order to help someone in the only way she could in her aspiration to be a "Dream." The capitalization of "dream" from the teleplay is critical here in the sense that Gault *is* in fact indicating that she wants to be the good that Morpheus *could* be for Jed if he merely took greater interest in humanity as opposed to being the nightmare of abandoning Jed to his foster parents. This is a different hubris than Brute and Glob's offense while still being offensive in the sense that she rebukes her purpose and construction by Morpheus, Dream with a capital *D*, as well as wishing to do better than him.

Needless to say, Morpheus believes in a platonic fixedness to one's creation and responsibilities, which is his fatal flaw in both the comics and, likely, the show. Morpheus punishes her exactly as he does Brute and Glob, exiling her to darkness, for now. Gault's interaction with Jed and her explanation for her actions do compel Morpheus to act differently, to change—something he does not believe is within his station. However, this does not occur before Morpheus must rectify the other half of the equation of splitting the Kirby Sandman into Jed and Hector Hall (Lloyd Everitt), the ghost who was once the Sandman in comics but is now merely a ghost sucked in by Rose's vortex and residing in a dream with his wife Lyta (Razane Jammal). As in the comics, Morpheus feels bound by the rules of his station, and he has not yet engaged with the idea of change as Gault charged. The result of that is the immutable law that a "ghost cannot escape his fate by hiding in the Dreaming."[8] Here, the contention that the violation of the natural order is actually damaging the Dreaming itself; as such, Morpheus coldly executes Hall in front of his wife, with whom they have conceived a child within the Dreaming (which will become a major plot point later in the series), stating: "You belong with the dead. You must go to the place appointed for you." Morpheus then disintegrates Hall before callously explaining to Lyta, "Your husband died a long time ago. He was a ghost and this is a dream. The Baby is yours. For now…. The child was conceived in the Dreaming. It is mine. And one day, I will come for it. This dream is over." There is no element of Dream's declaration that is incorrect, in fact, the entirety of this situation was caused by the vortex that is Rose Walker. However, in his implacable demeanor and totalitarian mindset, his immutability and disgust with the violation of the natural order will ultimately lead to his own destruction. This is one important aspect of Morpheus's person that Gaiman preserves in the adaptation.

* * *

In a 2018 interview, I asked Gaiman whether any movement had been made on the long gestating adaptation of *Sandman*; he said, "It's a no-brainer…. Here's two and a half thousand pages of story. [It's] already there and it already exists, and all you have to do, really, is to tell these stories. And you're in business" (Sommers 2018, 204). What he did not say was *how* to tell these stories as, in truth, the sheer number of pages of his original written story does not translate to serialized programming, let alone original plans at shorter movies, well or effectively. While an unwavering fidelity to the original comics would possibly delight a small percentage of comics enthusiasts giddy to see the innumerable amounts of mythologizing and remythologizing of all points from the *Sandman* comic that Gaiman layered into even one character (the second incarnation of the Sandman) and his untimely destruction, the narrative itself would not lay out quite as clearly as sequential seven and nine panel pages did in *Sandman* #12. Not to mention the fact that in concluding *Sandman*'s first season, Gaiman might have been unwise to leave the audience with such an ugly reception of this new version of the Sandman who assigned Lyta Hall's husband to the land of the dead as well as laid claim to her child as if he was entitled to it (which he blanketly says he is). Granted, if the fidelity with which Gaiman translated his comic to a show as a writer and producer continues, these tethers to the narrative's larger arc will likely quickly be revisited in the second season.

However, in the penultimate episode of Season 1, "Lost Hearts,"[9] Morpheus reveals a somewhat altered ending. The original arc concluded with his ominous warning to Desire in their Threshold. Now, found on a beach crafting a new dream, Morpheus entrusts the remains of the first season's antagonist, the Corinthian, to Lucienne, while he finishes his work. Before she departs, Morpheus invited Lucienne to greet the new Dream, a rechristened and resplendent butterfly, Gault. Surprised by her new existence, Gault asks her creator, "What made you change your mind about me, sir?" Morpheus replies, "I had no right returning here after over a century expecting everything to be just as I left it. Lucienne tried to tell me that. So did you. I'm listening. Or trying to." This change is still consistent with Morpheus's general demeanor of being ardently resistant to change, but it also acknowledges that "New Dreams," again with a capital *D*, come with "a new age." The context and the subtext here are clear: Gault empowered Jed's Sandman to help him survive in a sanctuary of his Dreams—not to make a play for control of the Dreaming à la Brute and Glob. Whereas the comics' interpretation used Kirby and Simon's Sandman as a callback to acknowledge its history, the new incarnation *still* does that while also acting as the catalyst for the growth of Brute and Glob's replacement. It gives Gault an arc and dimensionality in her own right while also enabling dynamism, the possibility to change, for Morpheus. His struggles with his desperate adherence to his function and how it will cripple his connection to humanity over and over again is both consistent with Morpheus's comic history and also consistent with his errant treatment of Kirby's Sandman prior host Hector Hall. The Sandman will *try* change, but that doesn't mean he will always be successful, a subtextual message, perhaps, to the show's stricter fanbase.

Notes

1. Dodds was created by Gardener Fox and Bert Christman in 1939. *Sandman* and all of its characters was always a team effort, led by Gaiman, and space precludes me from including the veritable panoply of artists, inkers, letters, etc., who realized the comic together.

2. For the record, as Lanette Cadle states in "The Power of the Perky: The Feminist Rhetoric of Death," Gaiman's Death, aside from the color of Kirby's skin and texture of her, is virtually unchanged from her depiction in *Sandman* #8. Cadle (2012) writes, "Death is just a girl, after all. Just a perky, Goth-clad, ankh-wearing girl…. In appearance, her style is distinctive, yet easily recognizable to anyone who has a teenager—or has been a teenager—who embraced the fashion outlook called 'Goth.'"

3. A "pre-text," per Robyn McCallum and John Stephens, refers to the ur-text of a story or the master narrative where what follows from it "discloses . . . some aspect of the attitudes and ideologies pertaining at the cultural moment in which that retelling is produced" (1998, 4, ix).

4. For more on Jed and Jed's evolution in adaptation, readers should visit Alexis Brooks de Vita and Novella Brooks de Vita's essay in this volume, "Fresh-Faced: The Interpretive Impact of Race, Gender, and Ethnicity in the *Sandman* Series."

5. This, it should be noted, was a reworking by Simon and Kirby of their own reworking of the character, "a standard costumed superhero" (Gravett 2009), from the early 1940s. The history of *Sandman* is, itself, a history of retelling and adaptation.

6. By metatexual history, I mean the history surrounding the comic book as artifact—the actual world that the reader exists within that crafts the socio-cultural mores that influence the writing of the comic in question.

7. Without compounding this history too much further, it's important to note two vital points as regards Sandman's history: (1) The 1974 Sandman is a new Simon/ Kirby iteration of the version from 1941's *Adventure Comics* #69, "a standard costumed superhero, a fairly blatant imitation of Batman, complete with his own Robin, known as Sandy the Golden Boy" (Gravett 2009). As Gravett notes, it was a pale and blatant recapitulation of a standard super-powered crime-fighter and his sidekick á la Batman and Robin or Captain America and Bucky "quickly headed for the chop" (2). Gaiman's passion for the character came as result of Kirby and Simon's ability to take a character placed "into a yellow and purple skintight costume and gave him a kid sidekick, but they were the ones who made it work" ("Simon and Kirby," 2016, 278–79). In fact, Gaiman first encountered the 1974 version, a thing he saw as, "part cartoon, part caricature" (2016, 280), and entirely remythologized, which appealed to him as this was the project of the writers he admired most and wished to emulate in his own work.

8. In the "Collectors" episode, it's important to note that this statement by Netflix's Morpheus is somewhat untrue as Morpheus's ravens, most prominently Matthew (Cable), were once living beings who died, and have been given a new lease on their existence in service of Morpheus (Gaiman 2012, 299).

9. Originally, this episode *was* the conclusion to Season 1 until Netflix released the partitioned coda "Dream of a Thousand Cats / Calliope" two weeks after the original batch of ten episodes on August 19, 2022.

References

Baetens, Jan. 2018. "Adaptation: A Writerly Strategy?" In *Comics and Adaptation*, ed. Benoît Mitaine, David Roche, and Isabelle Schmitt-Pitiot, 31–46. University of Minnesota Press, 2018.

———. 2020. "Literary Adaptations in Comics and Graphic Novels." In *The Oxford Handbook of Comic Book Studies*, ed. Frederick Luis Aldama, 611–30. Oxford University Press.

Benton, Mike. 1992. *Superhero Comics of the Golden Age*. Taylor.

Cadle, Lanette. 2012. "The Power of the Perky: The Feminist Rhetoric of Death." *Feminism*

in the *Worlds of Neil Gaiman: Essays on the Comics, Poetry and Prose*, edited by Tara Prescott and Aaron Drucker, 32–46. McFarland.
Gaiman, Neil. 2012. *The Annotated Sandman: Sandman #1–20*. Vol. 1. Vertigo.
_____. 2016. "The Simon and Kirby Superheroes." In *The View from the Cheap Seats*, 278–281. HarperCollins.
Gaiman, Neil, David S. Goyer, and Allan Heinberg, creators. 2022. *Sandman*. Season 1. Netflix.
Gutierrez, Anna Katrina. 2019. "Weaving New Dreams from Old Cloth: Conceptual Blending and Hybrid Identifies in Neil Gaiman's Fairy-Tale Retellings." In *The Artistry of Neil Gaiman: Finding Light in the Shadows*, 217–33. University Press of Mississippi.
Hatfield, Charles. 2012. *Hand of Fire: The Comics Art of Jack Kirby*. University Press of Mississippi.
Hutcheon, Linda. 2006. *A Theory of Adaptation*. 2nd ed. Taylor & Francis.
Jackson, Matthew. 2020. "Neil Gaiman Teases Progress on Netflix's the Sandman Series at DC FanDome." SYFY. August 22. https://www.syfy.com/syfy-wire/neil-gaiman-update-sandman-netflix-dc-fandome.
Lefevre, Pascal. 2007. "Incompatible Visual Ontologies? The Problematic Adaptation of Drawn Images." In *Film and Comic Books*, ed. 1–12. University Press of Mississippi.
Maas, Jennifer. 2022. "How (and Why) Neil Gaiman Finally Adapted 'The Sandman' for TV 'after Three Decades of Stopping Bad' Versions." *Variety*. August 4. https://variety.com/2022/tv/features/the-sandman-premiere-preview-neil-gaiman-interview-1235328771/.
Paul, Gravett. 2009. "Simon & Kirby's The Sandman." Paul Gravett. September 6. https://www.paulgravett.com/articles/article/sandman.
"Sandman Author Neil Gaiman Responds to Complaints over Death, Desire Casting in Netflix Series." 2021. SYFY. June 1. https://www.syfy.com/syfy-wire/sandman-author-neil-gaiman-responds-to-trolls-death-desire-casting.
Sommers, Joseph Michael. 2018. *Conversations with Neil Gaiman*. University Press of Mississippi.
Sommers, Joseph Michael, and Kyle Eveleth. 2019. *The Artistry of Neil Gaiman: Finding Light in the Shadows*. University Press of Mississippi.
Stephens, John, and Robyn McCallum. 1998. *Retelling Stories, Framing Culture: Traditional Story and Metanarratives in Children's Literature*. Garland.

Turning Toward the Sound of Her Wings

The Sandman *Series as a Doorway to Grief Literacy*

Drea Letamendi

> "Transformation, you've learned,
> Is not a tender task.
> It's mostly ugly and disjointing,
> Before the turning out
> Of something beautiful."
> —Caroline Miskenack, "Metamorphosis"

What are the cultural messages and expectations associated with grief and loss? How are we taught to make meaning of death, whether of loved ones or of ourselves? And where do we situate that grief in our bodies? So much attention is given to the concept of "closure" surrounding personal loss that our journey toward finding meaning about and beyond our grief can be barricaded. Our contemporary Western, North American culture pressures us to seek the theoretical final stage or resolution called "acceptance" following tremendous pain, and to bypass, disavow, and avert our gaze from our internal, natural, and complex responses to the transformative event of loss. Social pressures often shame people in bereavement or in terminal illness about their feelings of pain and suffering. People who are perceived as "doing well" with their grief are considered "strong" and "in control." The person in grief receives indirect and direct suggestion to "buck up," "keep it together," or simply *power through* their turmoil—and they are rewarded when they deny, overcome, or numb themselves to the pain of the experience.

The sixth episode of the *Sandman* television series, "The Sound of Her Wings," mediates our psychological perceptions about death by inviting us to experience the concept with curiosity and wisdom, to open our attention to what arises within us when we do not avert our gaze, and to appreciate the emotional, internal process as a human phenomenon. This episode disrupts our current postpandemic climate of grief phobia by reengaging us to recognize, honor, and express our unresolved grief.

"The Sound of Her Wings" also attends to life losses as an unveiled medium, itself becoming a grief companion to us as we navigate our lived experiences during our collective tragedy. The episode is an invitation to experience grief from a different vantage point, to turn toward liminal spaces seen as forbidden, mystifying, and transgressive. The psychological processing of grief is itself a duality practice happening inside the threshold between the known and the unknown. Liminal spaces operate in horror, fantasy, and fairy tale works as textual gaps and oscillations between the real and the illusion, the protagonist and the reader, and in Gaiman's fiction, the hypertext and the hypotext (Klapcsik 2008), presuming that you need awareness of both sides of the gateway to appreciate the message.

A Gentle Guardian

> "When the last living thing dies, my job will be finished. I'll put the chairs on the tables, turn out the lights and lock the universe behind me when I leave."
> —Death, "Façade," *Sandman* #20

Death (Kirby Howell-Baptiste) is a member of the Endless, a family of seven physical, anthropomorphic representations of powerful cosmic forces. Death came into existence when the first life forms appeared in the universe, and she functions as the embodiment of the living world, a physical guardian of life until the end of existence. Death, like other mythical psychopomps, is a conveyor of the soul, but she does not guide people's souls to the afterlife; rather, she is a gateway or a steward for a person during their transition from life to death.

Death's form is not grotesque, ghostly, or cloaked like the Grim Reaper. Her appearance does not inspire mystery, horror, or dread, or any frightening or cryptic characteristic typically associated with psychopomps. In fact, Death of the Endless presents in a body that, in many ways, is unremarkable. In her human form, she can blend in as a spectator, a visitor, a passerby among humans during their everyday mundanity. Despite her uncanny role and potential for loneliness, Death is friendly, gentle, and sociable with humans. Imagine a Nazgûl strolling through a crowded park in a low-cut tank top! In defying our expectations about hooded wraiths and scythe bearers, Gaiman creates a new iconography (Cadle 2012), and with it, the availability of new ideas surrounding our reception of mortality. This is undefeatable, unsettling power delivered in a less desperate and less predatory form. Howell-Baptiste's translation leans into this self-confident feminine energy and could prove the Goth aesthetic as an everlasting fashion trend. As Alexis Brooks de Vita and Novella Brooks de Vita note in their essay at the start of this collection, Howell-Baptiste's incarnation of Death also does vital work in dismantling gender and racial tropes.

In "The Sound of Her Wings," Dream (Tom Sturridge) observes his older sister's demeanor—her sense of humor, lightheartedness, affection, and honesty among the mortals. Death's ability to notice slight glimmers of happiness, to be present and content in the smallest of moments and in the simplest of ways, confounds him. "How do you do it?" he asks her, somewhat repulsed by her incessant compassion for and patience with humans, the very beings who imprisoned him for over a hundred years. Noticing that Dream seems to have lost his purpose and grown disillusioned, Death insists that he accompany her during her "work errands." He witnesses her stewardship with people—young and old, frightened or at peace, suffering or stoic—as they approach the Sunless Lands. That we never see Death accompany her subjects to the Sunless Lands on screen is significant: the sound of her wings comforts us into a feeling of peace.

Death serves as a grief companion. Grief companioning is a service given by grief care workers or counselors supporting a person at the end of life or in process of grieving the anticipated death of a loved one. Grief companioning centers on being present to another's pain, not about eliminating the pain or explaining the afterlife. Death provides a relational container, a safe refuge for persons while she travels alongside them toward their next chapter. When Death approaches the humans who are near their end of life, she is caring, warm, and gentle. She is steady and matter-of-fact, but not apathetic in her attendance to grief. She is truly being hospitable to another person and their pain.

Though it is unavoidable, grief is the most widely and commonly avoided human experience. Even the most trained doctors, nurses, and mental health practitioners who are positioned to serve as stewards often lack thanatology training, the skills needed to instill effective and competent grief companionship during loss of life.

Grief companions do not metaphorize, reduce, or negotiate with suffering, but they can ease the burden of aloneness during the transition. They do not offer empty platitudes ("at least" statements that minimize the situation). Dream wonders how his sister tolerates constant loss and lifelessness, so she explains the importance of self-preservation. "I thought about giving up…. I got brittle," she tells him, about earlier centuries of her work. Humans "get upset and hurt and shaken when they die." Even powerful cosmic beings can experience compassion fatigue! Death learned, however, that her presence has a powerful impact, and that she must honor and preserve her own spirit. Aligning her values to sync with her professional identity was the answer: "At the end, I'm there with them. I'm holding their hand, and they're holding mine. I'm not alone." She explains that her service to humans has a worthwhile and lasting impact on her sense of being, her purpose, and her worldview. As Death says, "I realized I need them as much as they need me." Death does not allow the cumulative effects of vicarious suffering to impact her own sense of self. Like any end-of-life caregiver, counselor, or death doula, she tends to her own emotional well-being, so that she can be calm, present, and available to the people she serves. Death makes taking care of herself an ethical imperative.

Attending to Traumatic Grief through Continuing Bonds

> "Companioning is about listening with the heart; it is not about analyzing with the head."
> —Alan Wolfelt, *Tenets of Companioning the Bereaved*

Grief is our internal, natural, and involuntary response to a life loss. Grief is a layered phenomenological experience that includes reactions that are emotional (loneliness, anxiety, sorrow, anger), somatic (fatigue, restlessness, chest pain/tightness), social (withdrawal, isolation), cognitive ("grief fog," disbelief, negativity), and spiritual (worldview shift, faith-based questioning, hopelessness). Despite colloquial shortcuts such as "stages of grief" and widely held constructs that recovery is stepwise, bereavement is dimensional. Nonlinear. Continuous. Just because someone we love dies doesn't mean that our relationship with them ends. "The Sound of Her Wings" validates that grief itself is not a static event with a beginning and end; rather, it is an ongoing journey that continues well past the physical presence of a deceased person. "Continuing bonds" refers to the psychosocial experience that we remain connected in complicated ways with our loved ones lost, often for our entire lives. At the time of their death, we do not detach from them or leave them behind; we (intentionally) carry their memories, traits, and interrelationship with us throughout our own existence (Klass 1996). This "meaning making" is considered a transformative, healing, and continuous stage of grief and loss recovery (Kessler 2019).

Though social pressures encourage "moving on" and "closure," or a weakening of attachments, continuous bonds offer ongoing healing and healthy emotional growth well past the transition of death, especially if the death was sudden. The death of a loved one is considered traumatic if it occurs without warning, if it is untimely, involves violence, suffering, or bodily violation, or if the survivor regards the death as unfair and unjust. Post-traumatic stress disorder (PTSD) can occur after a person experiences losing someone close to them to an unexpected, early, nonlinear (e.g., younger sibling, offspring), or tragic death.

Post-traumatic growth describes the human ability to participate in continuing bonds. It is the positive, transformative psychological change resulting from a struggle with a highly challenging or traumatic life circumstance. *Sandman*'s Death is one of many comic book and fantasy figures representing a narrative of post-traumatic growth following traumatic grief and loss (e.g., Batman and criminal justice; The Punisher and vengeance; Spider-Man and prosocial responsibility; Black Panther and cultural preservation). *Sandman*'s Death demonstrates a full and holistic psychological resilience despite her exposure to endless tragedies, characterized by her personal strength, her ability to maintain close relationships, a greater appreciation for life, an openness to new possibilities, and a readjustment of spiritual purpose ("I need them as much as they need me"). Her continuing bonds include an attachment to the collective people she supports; she sees humanity as her ongoing connection that will go beyond the extinction of the human species.

But Dream has yet to experience an appreciation for humanity, and his trauma—his imprisonment—seemed to only worsen his outlook about being Lord of the Dreaming. Despite Dream's exceptional omniscience and cosmic power, being captured and imprisoned by humans took a toll on his spirit. He angrily tells Death, "When they captured me, I just had one thought: Vengeance." But, after being freed, he goes on to wonder, "I'm now more powerful than I've been in eons … and yet?" He feels purposeless and indifferent. Disappointed. *Empty*. The torture, exploitation, and deprivation of his physical body had a profoundly corrosive effect on his soul. After recently escaping 70 years of naked, solitary confinement, Dream is in "a unique position to sympathize with [human trauma]" (Prescott 2012). Dream accesses his anger and resentment with ease, but is not fully aware of the profound shame, numbness, depression, and anhedonia spreading throughout his being as a result of the trauma.

Counting Blessings versus Burdens: Dispositional Gratitude

> "Grief is neither a disorder nor a healing process. It is a sign of health itself, a whole and natural gesture of love….

> No matter how much it hurts—and it may be the greatest pain in life—grief can be an end in itself, a pure expression of love."
> —Gerald May, psychologist

> "I feel like ... nothing."
> —Dream, "The Sound of Her Wings," *Sandman* #8

Gratitude has been conceptualized as an emotion, a virtue, a moral sentiment, a motive, a coping response, a skill, and an attitude. Gratitude as a state of mind can be generally distilled into a two-step cognitive process: (1) "recognizing that one has obtained a positive outcome" and (2) "recognizing that there is an external source for this positive outcome" (Allen 2018). Gratitude blocks toxic emotions, such as envy, resentment, regret, and depression. Some have even described gratitude as "social glue" that fortifies relationships—between friends, family, and romantic partners—and serves as the backbone of human society.

Gratitude intervention, which requires therapy clients to engage regularly in brief activities designed to cultivate a sense of gratefulness, is an effective and common component of psychological treatments for mood disorders, post-traumatic stress disorder, anxiety conditions, and prolonged grief. Common examples of gratitude-inducing experiences include: "waking up this morning," "the generosity of friends," "to God for giving me determination," "for wonderful parents," and "to the Lord for just another day" (Emmons and McCullough 2003). Examples of hassles/irritants include situational experiences such as "hard to find parking," "messy kitchen no one will clean," "finances depleting quickly," "having a horrible test in psychology [class]," "stupid people driving," and so forth (Emmons and McCullough 2003). People who consciously focus on their blessings—and less on things that bother them—tend to exhibit heightened well-being, and emotional and interpersonal benefits. Death fundamentally understands that a grateful outlook—not necessarily a generic optimistic one—has a positive impact on psychological well-being. It is those sweet, small moments that Death savors. As she approaches Sam (Leemore Marrett, Jr.), a young man who is about to drown during his honeymoon, Death takes off her shoes to feel the warmth and texture of the lakeside shore beneath her bare feet. Similarly, she basks in the sunlight, enjoys classical music, and appreciates the hand of a friend. Death is the personification of fleeting, bittersweet, appreciation for life.

Dispositional gratitude is the stable lifelong characteristic of noticing and appreciating the positive in life. Gratitude at a dispositional trait level refers to our tendency to "recognize and respond with grateful emotion to the roles of other people's benevolence in the positive experiences and outcomes that one obtains" (McCullough, Emmons, and Tsang 2002). Because it tends to be a pleasant emotion, dispositional gratitude is associated with ongoing life satisfaction, greater eudaimonic well-being, less maladjustment, and less negative affect (Emmons and McCullough 2003; Wood, Froh, and Geraghty 2010).

Dream examines his sister's interactions, observing the mundaneness, the pointlessness, the fleeting nature of care and compassion in her work. What's the purpose of closeness if it goes away? Death asks her brother to consider his relationship with Hob Gadling (Ferdinand Kingsley), the man she made immortal in the 1300s as an experiment. Dream had wondered if Hob, or any human for that matter, would wish for eternal life. So Death allowed Hob to keep living so Dream could find out. Dream agrees to meet Hob every hundred years at the White Horse Pub, expecting to find him desperate for death after the first century. To Dream's surprise, living through many historical eras does not make Hob disillusioned or directionless. Instead, he is astounded. Exhilarated. Grateful. It does not matter if he is destitute or wealthy, in mourning or celebration, he is aflame with life. He excitedly shares his gratitude for the little things to take pleasure in, like the invention of chimneys, playing cards, and handkerchiefs. "Life is rich," he remarks to Dream, who stares at him, unmoved, unable to grasp his contentment. Hob's *joie de vivre* may also explain why he is such a fan favorite. To learn more about how fans incorporate Hob into their fanfic, see the last essay in this collection, "A Dreaming of Our Own: How Fandom Adapts Multiple Canons to Create a New Fanon" by Adrienne E. Raw.

After five hundred years of meeting at the tavern, Hob gains the courage to confront Dream about his ambivalence and detachment. "I think it's you that changed," he argues, when Dream insists his interest in the experiment centers around novelty. "It isn't because you think I'll seek death," Hob explains. "I think you're here for something else. Companionship. I think you're lonely." Dream, denying any emotional attachment to the mortal, takes great offense, and as proof that he needs no companionship, he cuts the visit short.

Dream, over the course of several hundred years, chooses to see the "pointlessness" of intimacy with Hob, and doesn't notice the cumulative effect of their meetings—friendship. But his sister's lessons spark a realization that the simplicities of their companionship, their shared adventures, the very things that do not last forever, are the unnamed exchanges of genuine compassion. He learns to appreciate the moments he has had with Hob. "See them on their terms instead of yours," Death advised. Like his sister who makes herself available for humans and their suffering, Dream begins to see what is being asked of the Endless is not so much about "doing" but instead about "being."

Improving Our Grief Literacy through Parasocial Relationships

> "I have always heard it was impolite to keep one's friends waiting."
> —Dream, "Men of Good Fortune," *Sandman* #13

Grief literacy does not only encompass the tragedy of losing life. *Sandman*'s Death represents dignity for all types of life transitions that may involve tremendous change, facing upsetting news, or experiencing a new chapter in life and letting go of an old one. Death shows us the virtues of an open heart, a willingness to partake in life in direct knowledge of these transitions. "The Sound of Her Wings" reminds us that unexpected hardships and losses befall us all, and this is something we cannot avoid as humans. As witnesses to her work, we can also choose to lean closer into our discomfort, to anticipate the disappointments, anguish, and loneliness of our setbacks, rather than give in to the impulse to emotionally armor up and take refuge.

The concept of parasocial relationships (also called mediated relationships) refers to the nondelusional one-sided connection, interest, and fondness a media user has toward a personality, character, or story. Mediated relationships can include animation and gaming characters, tabletop RPG characters, live-action film and television roles, and real-life personas such as social media hosts/influencers.

Viewers who interact with "The Sound of Her Wings" at the parasocial level may process difficult emotions such as grief, anger, anxiousness, hopelessness, and fear in a contained and psychologically safe way. As Death takes on a stewardship with the fictional people she supports, we as active viewers journey alongside with our own emotional processing. The medium allows us to approach feelings within ourselves through a healthy detachment called psychological distancing, where our uneasiness is met with the intimacy of Death's stewardship, her comfort, peace, contentment, and quietude. For some, we are reminded of our own unresolved pain, the tremendous grief we sustained during the pandemic, when and where we often did not have the spaces to process our losses due to the constant insistence of "returning to normal." As a collective, we lost out on fundamental parts of grief and mourning—to understand what happened, acknowledge the impact through shared expression, and re-orient ourselves to the aftermath for new and renewed meaning.

Sandman teaches us lessons in grieving mindfully. What do our bodies feel like when we attend to these feelings? What happens when we are open to the viscera of our experiences—the sights, sounds, scents, and feelings within and around us? We disrupt our indifference, our numbness, and passivity; we are fully available and open. This fuller embodied self-knowing is further explored later in this collection through the metaphorical "aperture of the heart" in Samara V. Serotkin's "The Therapeutic Value of Hope as Shining through the Lens of *Sandman*." The dark and unpleasant emotions need to be held in the same way happiness and joy need to be held—with respect and humility. *Sandman's* Death leans into each emotional experience that exists in the unspoken and obscure liminal spaces—sorrow, devastation, fear, pain, uncertainty, curiosity—to show us a fuller range of human presence.

Our grief does not experience space and time the way our heads do. Death is unexpected, out-of-order, ambiguous, and inexplicable. Instead of pushing away suffering or merely releasing the need to "fix" it, we are able to enter into it as it is.

"The Sound of Her Wings" is not meant to rewrite our entire belief systems. Nor does it frighten, guilt, or punish us. Its gentle touch, a container, a dimension for our growth, allows us to learn how to move through loss in a holistic and heart centered manner, creating the conditions for resilience, ensuring that we are not shaming ourselves into silence.

References

Allen, Summer. 2018. *The Science of Gratitude*. Working paper, University of California, Berkeley. https://ggsc.berkeley.edu/images/uploads/GGSC-JTF_White_Paper-Gratitude-FINAL.pdf.

Bell-Laroche, Dina. 2021. *Grief Unleashed: Moving from the Hole in Our Hearts to Whole-Hearted*. Self-published.

Byock, Ira. 1998. *Dying Well: Peace and Possibilities at the End of Life*. Riverhead Books.

Cadle, Lanette. 2012. "The Power of the Perky: The Feminist Rhetoric of Death." In *Feminism in the Worlds of Neil Gaiman: Essays on the Comics, Poetry and Prose*, edited by Tara Prescott and Aaron Drucker, 32–46. McFarland.

Emmons, Robert A., and Michael E. McCullough. 2003. "Counting Blessings versus Burdens: An Experimental Investigation of Gratitude and Subjective Well-Being in Daily Life." *Journal of Personality and Social Psychology* 84: 377–89.

Gaiman, Neil (w), Mike Dringenberg (a), and Malcolm Jones III (i). 1989. "The Sound of Her Wings." *Sandman* #8. DC Comics. August.

Gaiman, Neil (w), Mike Zulli (a), and Steve Parkhouse (i). 1990. "Men of Good Fortune." *Sandman* #13. DC Comics. February.

Gaiman, Neil (w), Colleen Doran (p), and Malcolm Jones III (i). 1990. "Façade." *Sandman* #20. DC Comics. October.

Gaiman, Neil, David S. Goyer, and Allan Heinberg, creators. 2022. *Sandman*. Season 1. Netflix.

Jenkinson, Stephen. 2015. *Die Wise: A Manifesto for Sanity and Soul*. North Atlantic Books.

Kessler, David. 2019. *Finding Meaning: The Sixth Stage of Grief*. Scribner.

Klapcsik, Sándor. 2008. "Neil Gaiman's Irony, Liminal Fantasies, and Fairy Tale Adaptations." *Hungarian Journal of English and American Studies* 14 (2): 317–34.

Klass, Dennis, Phyllis R. Silverman, and Steven L. Nickman, eds. 1996. *Continuing Bonds: New Understandings of Grief*. Routledge.

McCullough, Michael E., Robert A. Emmons, and Jo-Ann Tsang. 2002. "The Grateful Disposition: A Conceptual and Empirical Topography." *Journal of Personality and Social Psychology* 82: 112–27.
Miskenack, Caroline. 2021. *Shaping Pearls: A Collection of Poems*. Self-published.
Prescott, Tara. 2012. "It's Pretty Graphic: Sexual Violence and the Issue of 'Calliope.'" In *Feminism in the Worlds of Neil Gaiman: Essays on the Comics, Poetry and Prose*, edited by Tara Prescott and Aaron Drucker, 64–80. McFarland.
Wolfelt, Alan. 2004. *Understanding Your Grief: Ten Essential Touchstones for Finding Hope and Healing Your Heart*. Companion Press.
Wood, Alex M., Jeffrey J. Froh, and Adam W.A. Geraghty. 2010. "Gratitude and Well-Being: A Review and Theoretical Integration." *Clinical Psychology Review* 30: 890–905.

"Calliope"

How Off-Screen Sexual Violence Changes the Narrative

PINKY CHUNG-MAN LUI

For a story that centers around rape, the *Sandman* episode "Calliope" shows surprisingly little of it. In terms of sexual violence, it gets as visually graphic as a small scratch on a man's face, just enough to hint at a violent encounter with resistance. The scratched face belongs to Richard Madoc (Arthur Darvill), the antagonist in "Calliope," the second half of the eleventh "bonus" episode of Netflix's *Sandman* (2022). As with the first ten episodes of the series, "Calliope" is a close adaptation in which the plot, dialogue, and even camera angles highly resemble its source material: *Sandman* #17, released on May 29, 1990, and later collected in the trade paperback *Dream Country*. The story "Calliope" was first adapted in 2020 into audiobook form by Audible before its first televisual adaptation with Netflix. *Sandman* has been widely praised for its faithfulness to the original comics source, no doubt largely because of Gaiman's involvement as an executive producer. In *Radio Times* David Craig writes that the first season "is extremely faithful to the source material ... bringing the world of the esteemed comic book into live-action with appropriate visual flair." Caroline Framke (2002) concedes in *Variety* that while the show "errs toward a literal translation of the comics as often as possible," it also "finds a way to introduce new fans without completely confusing them." Other critics acknowledge the show's faithfulness while also questioning it; Daniel Joyaux notes that the show "is about as faithful an adaptation of the source material as could reasonably be imaged," and while it pleases fans who think "the only good adaptation is a verbatim one," others may just "grow weary of just how unimaginative—how sadly undreamt about—this series of dream really is." This essay will explore how one important episode in particular is adapted, in order to examine how some of the most important deviations from the source material turn out to be the most beneficial.

When the *Sandman* comic first came out in 1989, it was no less controversial than it is today. In an online journal entry from 2003, Gaiman writes that he "date[s] the success of *Sandman* to the letter from the American Family Association's 'Concerned Mothers of America.'" The letter, from 1992, criticizes the comic for "its excessive and needless emphasis on homosexuality, profanity and Christian bashing" and threatens to boycott the comics "unless you [Gaiman] stop glorifying homosexuality." Gaiman ignored those homophobic comments, and the Netflix adaptation, following the comics' original inclusion of LGBTQ romance, transgender characters, and antiracist commentary, ensures that *Sandman* stays politically engaged. This extends to its portrayal of gender politics, particularly in "Calliope," a horrific story of a muse goddess imprisoned and sexually assaulted for decades by mortal men. As the rest of the *Sandman* series does not shy away from adapting the graphic details from comics to screen, including bodily dismemberment (the Corinthian), child abuse (Fun Land, Jed Walker), and murder (John Dee), viewers might naturally presume that the violence of "Calliope" would also be depicted. Yet the series chooses a different method to portray, and consequently condemn, sexual violence. Without showing any nudity or violent acts, *Sandman* instead *suggests* the cruelty, leaving room for the audience to imagine (or not) the abuse that Calliope suffers. This is aligned with the general feminist approach of not only Netflix's adaptation but also the core spirit of the original comics. As Tara Prescott (2012) notes in "It's Pretty Graphic: Sexual Violence and the Issue of 'Calliope,'" "Gaiman insists on telling the stories of people who are traditionally marginalized, missing, or silenced in literature in general and in comics in particular," and this tendency to give voice to the dispossessed is not just adapted, but in fact amplified by the television series (64). The "Calliope" episode depicts sexual violence through silence, where cruelty is suggested but neither heard nor shown, in direct contrast to the original comics. By making these changes, the adaptation updates the story of Calliope for the 2020s, inviting its contemporary audience to be a part of the narrative and challenging them to sympathize and critique at the same time.

Sexual Violence in Films and Television

Sexual violence is not an unusual theme in storytelling. In fact, it happens excessively in the Greek mythologies from which "Calliope" draws from. Io, Philomela, Leda, and Persephone are well-known examples from mythology of vulnerable women sexually assaulted by powerful gods. But it is one matter to read and hear about such cruelty, and another matter to see it visualized—in art, paintings, photography, and, with the rise of film in the early twentieth century, in motion pictures.

Western television and films have long included representations of sexual violence to various degrees. Specifically in the American context, Vivian C. Sobchack (1977) suggests in *"No Lies:* Direct Cinema as Rape" that it has been "a cinematic subject since the beginnings of film" (13). She gives a list of films that feature rape, from as early as D.W. Griffith's *The Birth of a Nation* (1915) to Martha Coolidge's *Not a Pretty Picture* (1976), and suggests "the only major change in the visual treatment of rape in mainstream cinema has been in the area of explicitness" as "we can now see most of what used to be only suggested" (14). There were certainly efforts preventing the film industry from depicting graphic sexual violence, among other exploitative elements, although the definitions of what makes something unacceptable kept changing. Perhaps the most famous of these efforts was the Motion Picture Production Code, more commonly known as the Hays Code, which was a set of guidelines for self-censorship used from 1934 to 1968 to ensure the film industry as a whole (from filmmakers, actors, to the actual films) adhered to a certain moral standard. The film industry was instructed to eliminate explicit scenes that suggest sex and violence. Yet the Hays Code would occasionally turn a blind eye, such as "the Academy Award-winning rape of silent Jane Wyman in *Johnny Belinda* (1948)" directed by Jean Negulesco (Sobchack 1977, 13). With the rise of American television culture in the 1950s, the Hays Code was not as effective in censoring visual media as the film and television industries were at odds trying to garner more audience for themselves. The Hays Code was replaced in 1968 by the Motion Picture Association film rating system, which is still in use today. The television industry, on the other hand, has followed the TV Parental Guidelines since 1997.

As film censorship relaxed and competing forms of media had to go to greater and greater extremes to attract wider audiences, graphic content became a strategy to pique the audience's curiosity, and in the process, many shows turned sex and violence into a part of the entertainment. It is important to note that the awareness on the problematic nature of this strategy truly grew in the 2010s as a consequence of the #MeToo movement. There was a call for more oversight and examination for how the entertainment industry treats actors and actresses engaged in intimate scenes, as well as more scrutiny on the nature of the content being created. Several famous examples of problematic sex scenes from past decades were put under the spotlight again. In *Entertainment Weekly,* Jessica Wang (2023) writes about the infamous rape scene from a 1979 episode of the long-running American soap opera *General Hospital* (1963–). The scene featured Luke (Anthony Geary) and Laura (Genie Francis), "a supercouple beloved by viewers," whose relationship was built on the ground of sexual assault. Laura marries her rapist and "their wedding [became] a major TV event when it aired in 1981." The rape-into-love plot may have worked in the eighties, but it certainly screams Stockholm syndrome to audiences today. Genie Francis, the actress who portrayed Laura, notes that now, four decades since the rape scene aired, she cannot condone it as a love story anymore.

A similar situation also happened with *Buffy the Vampire Slayer*, a supernatural television drama popular with teenage audiences, in a 2002 episode where the vampire Spike (James Marsters) attempts to rape Buffy (Sarah Michelle Gellar) and later becomes a romantic prospect for her. James Marsters, the actor who played Spike, reflected on the controversial scene for the twentieth anniversary of the show's finale, stating that filming the scene "was the hardest day of [his] professional career" but he was "contracted to do anything that they said" and "was legally compelled to do that scene" (Griffin 2023). He explains that the rape scene, horrible in its context and its production, was deliberate in order to deter the audience from shipping Buffy and Spike as a couple and to highlight that love and consent between the characters would always be questionable. The problematic nature of this plotline was further thrown into relief in the 2000s, when several actors on the show spoke out about the abuse and sexual discrimination they experienced at the hands of the show's creator, Joss Whedon.

It is fair to say that in the early twenty-first century, sexual violence became even more frequent and explicit in visual media and understandably more attention is now paid to how film and television handle sexual elements on and off screen because of the Harvey Weinstein scandal, the #MeToo movement, and cultural conversations around the need for and definition of consent. In particular, viewers who care about the representation and treatment of women have maintained that a lot of sexual violence on screen is unnecessary. Especially for survivors of assault, these scenes can be traumatic, triggering, and dangerous (a topic that psychologist Samara V. Serotkin discusses in the next essay). When sexual violence becomes a part of the entertainment, regardless of the production's attitude toward the violence portrayed on screen, survivors find that their own trauma has been diminished into a plot device.

Besides being difficult to watch, sexual violence scenes are also challenging to film. It is only in recent years that intimacy coordinators have become part of film and television productions. In fact, SAG-AFTRA only issued the first industry Standards and Protocols for the Use of Intimacy

Coordinators in 2020, and didn't accept these coordinators for SAG-AFTRA membership until 2022. However there have been efforts to organize intimacy coordinators and establish them as a part of the entertainment industry. Today there are nine SAG-AFTRA-accredited international intimacy coordinator training programs. But the first one, named Intimacy Directors and Coordinators (IDC), was established in 2016 by the world's first intimacy coordinator, Alicia Rodis, and her cofounders Tonia Sina and Siobhan Richardson. According to IDC (2023), an intimacy coordinator "is a choreographer, an advocate for actors, and a liaison between actors and production for scenes that involve nudity/hyper exposed work, simulated sex acts, and intimate physical contact in tv or film." It is worth noting that Netflix's *Sandman* employed two intimacy coordinators, Enric Ortuno and Yarit Dor, both trained and certified by the IDC. Surely having an intimacy coordinator on set feels safer for both cast and crew to ensure the work environment is consensual and transparent. But even with these protections in place, the fundamental question remains: do we need rape scenes at all?

This has been a heated topic over the past decade with controversies around massively popular shows deploying rape as a plot device. Television networks and companies that require paid subscriptions have been historically behind the controversial shows, with the competition from streaming services upping the ante. Traditional premium cable networks such as HBO, Cinemax, and Showtime have transitioned into offering online streaming services, next to competing platforms such as Netflix, Disney+, and Amazon Prime Video. Online streaming services have more freedom in their content making because of larger budgets and relatively relaxed regulations compared to public broadcasting, which directly correlates with how many controversial sex scenes can be found on these platforms. One prime example is HBO's *Game of Thrones* (2011–2019), which, like *Sandman*, is an adaptation of a large-scale fantasy series: George R.R. Martin's A Song of Ice and Fire novel series (1991–). As one of HBO's most successful shows both in terms of viewership and critical ratings, *Game of Thrones* has also been heavily criticized for its unnecessarily brutal depictions of sexual violence. As Valerie Estelle Frankel notes in *Women in* Game of Thrones: *Power, Conformity and Resistance* (2014), while the "frequent rapes and attempted rapes [were] even more frequent in the books," the television series' decision to display graphic sexual violence "also generate[s] a great deal of controversy" (8). The main controversy is whether *Game of Thrones* "treat[s] rape as entertainment" or "as a violent, traumatic experience from which the victims must recover and discover the way to peace" (9). Most criticisms lean towards the first. After all, as Lorna Jowett suggests in "Rape, Power, Realism and the Fantastic on Television" (2009), "original programming from subscription channels like HBO attempts to distinguish itself by pushing televisual limits: 'It's not TV, it's HBO,' as the slogan goes" (218). In "Why Does *Game of Thrones* Feature So Much Sexual Violence?" Christopher Orr (2015) criticizes how showrunners David Benioff and D.B. Weiss "have gone out of their way, time and time again, to ramp up the sexual violence well beyond their source material" and that "[n]ew characters have been invented in order to become victims (or victimizers), and existing ones have had their sexual cruelty amplified." Orr concludes that the reasons behind the excessive sexual violence are a combination of "it's good for ratings" and the showrunners being "blasé and careless when it comes to the subject." In "*Game of Thrones*, Rape Culture and Feminist Fandom," Debra Ferreday (2015) discusses the ambivalent place of the show in feminist discourse, that the show's portrayal of rape "seems to invoke particularly polarized claims that it either *is* a feminist text, or that it is extremely anti-feminist and oppressive to women" based on whether one thinks the violence is "a realistic, if superficially fantastical, depiction of patriarchy" (24). It sparks the question for shows like *Game of Thrones*, whether rape is a useful or necessary tool to depict patriarchy once the shock factor of graphic sexual violence is removed. Or is there any way to justify having rape as a plot point without exploitation?

Although the most notorious rape in the show occurs to Sansa Stark (Sophie Turner) in Season 5, rape had been a plot point since the show's pilot. Toward the end of *Game of Thrones*' debut episode, Princess Daenerys Targaryen (Emilia Clarke) is forced to marry warlord Khal Drogo (Jason Momoa) to form a political alliance and thus also forced to consummate the marriage. First, viewers see a sobbing Daenerys undressed by Drogo. She quickly raises her arms to cover her bare breasts, but her arms are pried open, and Drogo bends her over his knees. It is a small mercy that the scene ends before the viewers see the actual assault. By Season 5, it is much worse. Sansa's rape scene happens on her wedding night with Ramsay Bolton (Iwan Rheon), who forces her adopted brother Theon (Alfie Allen) to watch the rape. Ramsay rips off her dress and pushes her on the bed. There is no nudity, yet the viewers can hear Sansa's grunts and whimpers as the camera zooms in on Theon, crying at the sight of the brutal scene. Sansa's rape is a completely unnecessary plot device; the viewers know (from many, many examples) that Ramsay is a cruel character—there is no need to show how he rapes Sansa or forces Theon to be a silent accomplice. Sansa's rape is an event that adds nothing to her character arc and is in fact a redundant display of cruelty used to further emasculate Theon. By focusing on Theon and using the male gaze, the rape scene is not about the victim or the rapist, but the helpless male bystander. Theon having to bear witness to Sansa's rape shifts the male gaze (however reluctant), making it about *Theon* rather than Sansa, further reducing her agency and further objectifying her. Despite being a key character in the show, Sansa is still stripped of her agency throughout the scene and further objectified through Theon as the unwilling spectator. She functions as an object. Ramsay demonstrates dominance over both Sansa and Theon, and he specifically targets Theon again later for further humiliation by castration in Season 3. It is important to note that the Ramsay scene is not the only rape scene involving Sansa: she has been fixed as the helpless, defenseless girl since the first season. Ferreday briefly discusses "Sansa's near-rape" in Season 1 when she is threatened by a violent mob, suggesting that "it is shown as the natural consequence of a high-born and beautiful woman who suddenly lacks the protection of a man" (30). This applies to the Ramsay scene which emphasizes the *lack* of male protection (in the form of Theon). Whether the audience perceives it as a small mercy that the brutality is not explicitly shown but clearly suggested, this controversial scene is merely one of many that involves sexual violence against women in *Game of Thrones*.

The scene faced massive backlash almost immediately after it aired, due to its excessive cruelty against a beloved heroine. Joanna Robinson (2015) wrote for *Vanity Fair* that "this rape scene undercuts all the agency that's been growing in Sansa" and questions whether "it really [has] to be rape that brought her low." Another critic from the *Washington Post* defended the show's choice, noting, "as a story about the consequences of rape and denial of sexual autonomy," Sansa's rape scene is appropriate in the context of the show (Rosenberg 2015). Similar to Marsters' reflection on Spike's rape scene in *Buffy*, Rheon also expressed his distaste for the making of the scene, stating, "nobody wants to do that, but if it's telling a story then you have to tell it truthfully" (Deen 2020). It once again begs the question of whether the scene is necessary, regardless of Rheon's claim that "they didn't sensationalise it" and "it's a horrible thing that happens, unfortunately, and it shouldn't be." Thankfully, all of the criticism and discussions around the use of the sexual violence in *Game of Thrones* made a difference in successive *GOT* properties. Miguel Spochnik and Ryan Condal, HBO's showrunners for *Games of Thrones*' prequel series *House of the Dragon* (2023–), state specifically that while the prequel acknowledges "violence against women is still very much part of the world," it would pull back on showing the violence explicitly on screen so as to not downplay or glorify sexual violence. So while brutal rape scenes are not present in the first season of *HOD*, violence against women is still present such as the brutal birth-giving scene of Queen Aemma where she is cut open in her deadly labor, since the King decides to sacrifice her to save the life of his potential male heir. The violation of women's bodies on screen sadly still produces enough shock factor that sells.

All of these discussions around the portrayal of sexual violence in films and television lead to two pivotal questions: Is it necessary to describe, mention, or depict rape in order to tell a story that includes it? And if it is necessary, is there a way to ethically represent rape without making it a spectacle? Netflix's *Sandman* is a feminist example that respects the viewers' ability to comprehend a story about rape without showing them the act, and proves that compelling storytelling can be powerful enough on its own merits.

"Calliope": A Feminist Story

The original *Sandman* comic can be regarded overall as a feminist narrative, or at least politically conscious of its representation of marginalized people. While characters make problematic choices, the narrative is conscious of these actions, and demonstrates how characters either grow or suffer from their choices. Netflix's *Sandman* certainly picks up on the comic's feminist stance concerning the representation of women. Characters such as Johanna Constantine (Jenna Coleman) in "Dream a Little Dream of Me," Death in "The Sound of Her Wings" (Kirby Howell-Baptiste), and Lucienne (Vivienne Acheampong)—a gender-swapped version of the librarian Lucien from the comics—are strong and intelligent women who are not only essential to the plot, but also unafraid to contradict and take a stand against the central power figure in the story, Dream (Tom Sturridge). The story of Calliope presents itself as one of the most feminist tales in the comic, and subsequently in the adaptation, condemns toxic masculinity and rape. The adaptation represents rape trauma without displaying it in graphic details and instead, demands the audience take part in the unravelling of the horror Calliope endures for decades. Louise Hooper, the director of the "Calliope" episode, emphasizes that she is telling "a story about a woman being victimized and abused" but that she aimed to "do it in a way that still has her strength and dignity" (Palmer 2022). Portrayed by Canadian and Greek actress Melissanthi Mahut, Calliope remains a composed and dignified goddess figure throughout the episode. While she is silenced and enslaved by mortal men, she preserves her dignity and self-possession, maintaining a strong stance against her abusers, in stark contrast to her comic counterpart.

Sexual violence is silent in Netflix's *Sandman*, but it does not mean it is absent. The word "rape" is never used in the series, which the audience may only realize in hindsight. It is important to note that sexual violence is not exclusive to the "Calliope" episode. In fact, the originating event that propels the events of the second half of the season (the *Doll's House* storyline) is a rape of an unconscious woman orchestrated by a member of the Endless. During Dream's imprisonment by Roderick Burgess (Charles Dance), a sleeping sickness plagued the human world and those affected were unable to stay awake. One victim of the sleeping sickness was Unity Kincaid (Sandra James-Young), ancestor of Rose Walker (Kyo Ra). In *Sandman* #1, "The Sleep of the Just," readers learn that Unity "was raped, seven years ago" and "gave birth to a baby girl" despite sleeping "through the whole thing." However, the Netflix adaptation is less transparent with the truth of what happened to Unity when she was asleep and unable to consent to anything. The audience sees Unity and Rose reunite in "The Doll's House," with Unity explaining how she lived "the most glorious life" in her dream which turns out to be real, including meeting "a man with golden eyes" and having a baby with him. Sidestepping the word "rape," Unity simply tells Rose that "they hushed it up," silenced the crime and sent her baby away for adoption. Both Rose and her friend Lyta (Razane Jammal) are shocked and confused at the revelation that Unity's baby became Rose's mother. Unity considers her dream life to be a blessing since she slept most of her life. Unity recounts her story two times, first in "The Doll's House" and then again in "Lost Hearts." She feels content about having had a baby, even though she had been unconscious through all of it. The man with golden eyes is later revealed to be Desire (Mason Alexander Park), one of Dream's younger siblings who constantly meddles with his realm out of spite. In impregnating Unity, Desire has set a trap for Dream: in order to fix the threat to the Dreaming, Dream will have to kill the vortex, and in the process, unknowingly spill family blood (and lead to his own demise).

Yet the fact that Unity displays such fondness over her experience with the man with the golden eyes distances the audience from the sexual violence that took place while she was unconscious. Unlike the comic, which clearly deploys the word "rape," the series is in danger of not only downplaying the severity of sexual violence but also romanticizing it. It is tragically real that unconscious female patients have been victims of sexual assault in the real world, probably even more than we are aware of due to the difficulties in the victims' ability to report the crimes. Some of the most recent high-profile cases have resulted in pregnancies and even deliveries, like Unity's (Haag). Unity's contentment with her dream life might be her way of coping with the fact that years of her life have been lost to the sleeping sickness. Desire uses Unity to achieve their own means. Unity thinks she lived a full life in dreams with the man with the golden eyes, but in truth she was horrifically abused. The show's glossing over of Desire's crime, however, is certainly a problematic decision, especially considering how sexual violence becomes a central theme in "Calliope."

Prescott (2012) calls attention to the "graphic" nature of the story in her essay, referring both to the drawn nature of the comics and the explicit nature of Calliope's trauma. Yet the creators of "Calliope" chose to make a different choice in adapting this story: they made the explicit violence implicit. The story focuses on Calliope, one of the nine muses from Greek mythology, who was captured, imprisoned, and repeatedly raped over eighty years of confinement, first by Erasmus Fry (Derek Jacobi) and later Richard Madoc, men who used her as their vehicle for successful writing careers. Without saying the word "rape" or actually showing any sexual violence in action, the audience understands what happens behind closed doors. This is in stark contrast to the source material. The title splash page of the "Calliope" issue features a naked woman kneeling in the dark, appearing sickly and vulnerable with exposed ribs and a hollow, empty gaze. Prescott (2012) observes that this image is "stark and terrifying" because "the reader now shares Madoc's and Fry's point of view," so "Calliope also cowers from the reader's gaze" (67). The comic shows Calliope naked most of the time, kneeling on all fours or struggling to hide her bare breasts with her arms, even when she is begging the Fates for help. Prescott notes that Calliope's nudity and vulnerability are related, as evidenced by Gaiman's notes to the illustrator, Kelley Jones, asking him to "avoid exploiting this moment, of at all sexualizing or romanticizing Calliope's rape" (68). Indeed, there is nothing sexual about Calliope in her naked comic portrayal, or her television counterpart, who wears a white silk gown throughout the episode. When the audience sees Calliope for the first time, she simply sits on the basement floor against a wall, defeated and frustrated by Fry's visit and what it usually entails. She states flatly, "Am I to perform for your amusement? Is this man to be our audience?" The irony in this statement is not lost: the television viewers are now bystanders to Calliope's suffering as well.

Richard Madoc and the Power Structures of Force

The television adaptation makes two critical departures in bringing the comic to the screen. The first is the more sympathetic, relatable portrayal of the villain, Richard Madoc. The comic begins directly with Madoc visiting Fry in order to give the old writer a bezoar in exchange for Calliope. After he takes Calliope home, the comic Madoc's "first action was to rape her, nervously" and he justifies to himself that "she's not even human" to lessen whatever guilt or hesitation he has. The television adaptation also starts from Madoc's point of view, giving more screen time to his thought process, and presenting the story through the perpetrator's eyes. The episode begins in August 2018 with Madoc delivering a lecture on storytelling in front of a bleak PowerPoint titled "Controlling the Narrative." Indeed, the story begins by discussing control, with Madoc having the authority and the voice to deliver it. Madoc tells his students, "You can't force your character to do something just because it's easier for you as a writer." The irony, of course, is that when this particular speaker gets the chance to take the "easy" route, he absolutely will use force to get what he wants.

The show cleverly adds the detail of Madoc giving an assignment to his students, asking them to write "the same event told from two characters' very different points of view," which foreshadows the structure of the episode. After giving his lecture and getting a bezoar sample from a medical student who is a fan of his debut novel, Madoc goes to Fry's house, just as he does in the comic. Madoc is more mellow in the adaptation; while the comic Madoc grows impatient with Fry talking for too long, the Madoc on screen simply listens timidly to Fry until the old man eventually takes him to get Calliope. Madoc looks visibly uncomfortable and shy when Fry tells Calliope that she's being given to the young writer, who seems to be avoiding eye contact with the prisoner. When they are leaving, Madoc says to Fry, "I don't know if I can do this." The camera immediately shifts to Calliope, who looks at Madoc with faint hope in her eyes, thinking perhaps that not all male writers are as bad as Fry, who lied about eventually freeing her. Fry goes on to advise Madoc how to use Calliope, that while "they say one ought to woo her kind," he has "found force most efficacious," hinting that he has chosen sexual violence to exploit Calliope's gift for as long as he has kept her prisoner. When Fry utters the word "force," signifying rape, Madoc looks at Fry with disbelief, passing silent judgement on the old man's cruelty. Sensing Madoc's shock, Fry reassures that Calliope is not human and that she was created to inspire men like them, justifying any perceived violation because they are her masters and she is their servant.

Both Calliope and the audience are led to hope that perhaps Madoc is a decent man, judging from his reaction to Fry's instructions. The scenes that follow before Madoc eventually rapes Calliope are all original to the adaptation. They show Madoc perplexed as to how he should proceed with keeping Calliope while still trying to write on his own. He takes Calliope home and installs a lock on her bedroom door, which is sadly an *upgrade* from Fry's basement. But even if the bars are gilded, a cage is still a cage. The Netflix series deliberately motivates all of the characters with hope; Madoc hopes Calliope will just do what he wants without force; Calliope hopes Madoc will do the right thing and release her; the audience hopes that they won't need to witness the cruelty played out. Of course, they are all disappointed. The audience is placed into a particularly precarious situation, forced to watch from Madoc's point of view, to sympathize with his increasing desperation as an author with bills to pay, under intense pressure from an already-missed deadline, and suffering crippling writer's block. As the Muse known for her beautiful voice, Calliope tries to persuade Madoc with reason, arguing that he must set her free because she is a goddess and "not a possession to be kept and used and traded." To do the right thing, Madoc only has to say the words, showing how important voice is in the narrative. Ironically Calliope the Beautiful Voice is silenced in her enslavement, while the writer controls the narrative by withholding the words, hoarding the ideas and the goddess that grants them for his private use. Madoc responds to Calliope's plea for freedom with a plea of his own, asking whether she will just help him with one novel. During this entreaty, he subtly puts one of his legs on the bed between them, attempting to initiate the process of taking inspiration. Madoc, unbeknownst to himself, is already repeating Fry's deception, telling Calliope that he swears to let her go after and that "not all" writers lie like her previous captor. This line echoes the horrific "not all men" rationale that frequently shows up in contemporary American society when a prominent male figure is called to task for misogynist statements or behavior. Rather than acknowledge the continuing harmful effects of patriarchy and sexism, a certain type of defensive male response involves deflecting attention away from the real problem, an attempt to diminish its importance as a perceived aberration rather than an example of a much larger pattern of harm. To resist acknowledging the harm that men do to women and instead focus attention on "not all men" is to deny responsibility, privilege, judgement, or even possible allyship. To echo this rhetorical defense tactic, not all writers are liars, but Fry and Madoc certainly are. When Calliope firmly states that the power to share her gift should remain hers, Madoc closes the door, followed by a shot of a key turning and the sound of bolting locks.

Madoc returns to his writing desk, where he sits motionless and devoid of ideas. As the camera zooms onto a blank page with a to-be-confirmed title and a blinking cursor, Madoc appears more anxious and panicked. The impotent writer fails to perform, which translates to a form of emasculation. The silence of the scene is heightened by the still keyboard and disturbed by Calliope's footsteps coming from the upstairs room. When Madoc eventually types, he is not writing but checking his own subreddit, Instagram, and Twitter accounts. The close-up on his computer screen reveals that whenever Madoc types in the address of a social media site, all the prompted suggestions are porn. It's more than just his search history—for Madoc, literature and sex have always been mingled. Keeping Calliope a prisoner and eventually raping her for inspiration are physical manifestations, albeit extreme, of what he normally does in his thoughts and online.

Frustrated by Calliope's rejection and the people online questioning where his next novel is, Madoc ends up sitting on the sofa, drinking and scrolling on a dating app while a television show plays in the background. The episode comes from HBO's *I May Destroy You* (2021), which is also a story about a struggling writer and sexual violence. Directed, written, and produced by Michaela Cole, who stars as Arabella, it is an autobiographical story of how a woman comes to write down her experience of sexual assault. While both Madoc and Arabella are writers, they obviously embody two very different positions. One is a man who sexually exploits a helpless woman for ideas, the other a woman and rape survivor who is grappling with narrating her rape trauma. The specific scene that is playing in the background (which of course Madoc completely ignores) gives a very specific message about toxic men; it is the opening scene of episode 8, "Line Spectrum Border," when Arabella attends a support group for sexual assault survivors and delivers a haunting monologue about the psychology of male predators. Arabella suggests that a male sexual predator tests the limits to locate "the line of being neither in one place or another," for the "grey area where nothing was quite clear, no one could be clear." Madoc finds his own gray area in Calliope's status as a goddess. After all, if Calliope is not human, she can't be raped. In "Line Spectrum Border," the woman is gaslit and speechless, incapable of pinpointing exactly the crime of a man who has taken advantage of a gray area to shrug off responsibility and guilt. Madoc completely ignores the television, but the audience clearly sees Madoc as one of the men Arabella is talking about, the predator in hiding who cowers in the gray area, strikes whenever he pleases, and plays clueless when he is caught.

Madoc makes one final plea before using force to get what he wants from Calliope. Returning to her room with gifts such as flowers, dresses, jewelry, and perfume, Madoc hopes perhaps he can woo her, as if she were a woman on a date instead of a prisoner in a cell. Calliope stands aloof with crossed arms, sarcastically questioning why he is wooing her with gifts when he clearly knows "how it is done." Calliope once again speaks up and tries to persuade Madoc to follow the rules, an artist should pray for the Muses' gift with vows of service and devotion. Sensing that Madoc is not as cruel and determined as Fry was, Calliope softens and shares the story of her original capture. But Madoc can only think of himself. He kneels in front of Calliope and begs for her help. It seems Calliope pities him, even after all she has been through. Perhaps, as the muse for artists, she cannot help herself. She does not flatly refuse, but instead, gently tells him to ask her again once she is free. The Muse simply wants to reclaim her agency to share her gifts on her own terms.

The scene swiftly returns to a close-up of the blinking cursor, followed by Madoc once again sitting in front of his computer in the throes of writer's block and Calliope's pacing footsteps echoing above. The audience then witnesses Madoc receiving a phone call from his agent, who warns that he will lose everything if the second book is not written soon. This ultimatum sends Madoc into despair, and finally, cruel determination. Fry's voice returns to fill the scene, repeating how Calliope is not human, suggesting that Madoc finally gives into Fry's words and the ease of the gray area. A desperate man such as Madoc eventually turns dangerous, despite Calliope and the audience holding out hope for a change of heart. The camera pans down to the blank page on Madoc's computer as he walks out of the shot. As the camera zooms into the blinking cursor once more, the suspenseful music is interrupted by a few knocks, Richard saying Calliope's name and unlocking the door. Then the screen turns to black.

Prescott (2012) suggests that the comic "Calliope" is "a story in which the reader does not want to identify with any of the main characters, and yet, by nature of the medium, must," since the readers are made to "supply the plot for what happens between panels" (69, 70). Like the readers of the comic, the television audience *knows* what Madoc is going to do after he knocks on Calliope's door. Even without seeing it or hearing it, the horror of the rape darkens the scene and creeps into the audience's imagination. And then the next scene shows a close-up on Madoc's fingers rapidly typing. The sound announces that he has *done it*. As the camera pans up to show Madoc's focused face, the audience sees a red scratch mark on his left cheek, a bloody sign of Calliope's futile defenses. The audience can imagine how she must have fought and struggled, in vain.

In desperation and grappling at eternal straws, Calliope implores the Fates to intercede on her behalf. They refuse—but remind her that her former lover Dream may be of help. The episode then takes a two-year time jump to a scene showing a successful Madoc at the launch party of his new book. The camera follows the smug writer moving between partygoers who have very different attitudes toward his book and fame, until Madoc eventually sits down on a couch to chat with a woman who praises him for his representation of "strong female characters." The entire conversation is nearly word-for-word identical to the original text from three decades ago, and yet is still horribly timely and relevant today. In some ways, Gaiman's feminist satiric portrayal of a hypocritical rapist is more poignant after #MeToo, but even more so after the publication of "There Is No Safe Word," the cover story of *Vulture* written by Lila Shapiro and published on January 13, 2025.

Shapiro points out the similarity between Gaiman and his faux-feminist writer character, how "Like Madoc, Gaiman has called himself a feminist [...] has racked up major awards [...] [and] has come to be seen as a figure who transcended, and transformed, the genres in which he first wrote: first comics, then fantasy and children's literature." Regardless of the future development stemming from Shapiro's article and other alleged accounts of Gaiman's misconduct, the disturbing similarities between Gaiman and Madoc now cannot be disregarded. The establishment of his public image as a feminist writer took years of work, yet no one knows, or can be sure, as in "Calliope," what acts authors are capable of behind closed doors. Madoc understands the importance of curating his image. When he receives praise for his protagonist Eileen, Madoc states that it is false when people say, "Only women can write authentically about the female experience." In truth he is lying; after all, it is Calliope's gift that becomes his novel, not his "talent." The Madoc speaking now is clearly a different man from two years ago; no longer timid and anxious, he has adopted the pretentious name "Ric" and is now an egotistic writer who utters possibly the most obnoxious and hypocritical sentence (taken directly from the comic), "I do tend to regard myself as a feminist writer." Just as Madoc knows how to manipulate the gray area, he also knows how to use performative feminism to his advantage. Later when Madoc talks to a film studio about adapting his novel, he deliberately stresses that they need to ensure that at least half of the cast and crew will be women and people of color; surely not because he cares about underrepresented groups, but because it plays well, and makes him look feminist and *good*. The hypocrisy of Madoc parading himself as both a feminist and a writer, considering he is a rapist who cannot write without Calliope's power, is astounding. Not only is he the opposite of everything he presents himself as, he is also silencing more women than just Calliope by suggesting that a man like him can replace women writers when it comes to writing about the female experience. When the young woman praising Madoc asks about the origin of his female voice in fiction, he unashamedly credits "the women" in his life, naturally omitting the fact that he has to rape a woman every time he wishes to write.

While sexual violence is silent in the adaptation, the Netflix Calliope has much more to say than she did in the comic. The episode jumps ahead two more years to August 2022, four years since Calliope was passed from Fry to Madoc. Calliope reads in a newspaper article about Unity awakening and realizes it means that Dream is now free. At the same time, Calliope is about to get trafficked to LA by Madoc to shoot the movie version of one of his novels. When Madoc tells her that "maybe we'll decide to stay in LA" Calliope repeats the sentence with an emphasis on the "we," pointing out the hypocrisy of pretending she has any say at all in what Madoc plans. The disillusioned Madoc still feels Calliope is simply being moody and refusing to enjoy "their" success. After all, Madoc feels Calliope is doing what muses were made for (despite Calliope stressing that muses were *born*, and not things to be possessed and used). Calliope, desperate to be freed, burns a piece of paper with the Greek "Oneiros" written on it, summoning Dream. The old lovers reunite in Calliope's bedroom-cell and empathize with each other's confinement. Yet Dream recognizes that Calliope's imprisonment and repeated rapes are way worse: "my suffering was nothing compared to yours." Calliope's torture was mental, physical, and sexual. But she quickly stops Dream from comparing their suffering because she recognizes it isn't a contest and there are no winners. She has larger, much more important goals in mind.

Finally, Dream becomes the first person with power to call out Madoc. He commands, "be quiet," and takes control of the situation, and the narrative. At first, Madoc denies the crime of keeping a woman hostage and ignores Dream's command to set her free. Getting in touch with his inner Karen, Madoc even threatens to call the police and suggests this strange man in his home does not *know who he is*. Yet when Dream sternly says he knows exactly who and what *Richard* Madoc is, using the name the writer has abandoned, the ego crumbles and Madoc reveals his insecure and guilty self, pleading that he cannot let Calliope go because he needs her to write. Once again, Dream silences Madoc as the mortal makes excuses for his selfish needs. Enraged, Dream stands up and blasts Madoc for thinking his needs are more important than the muse goddess, who "has been held captive for more than sixty years. Demeaned, abused, defiled." Without call it rape, Dream emphasizes how Calliope has been exploited in every way possible, including her body, spirit, dignity, and even her sacredness as a goddess. And then Dream gives Madoc a fitting punishment for his crimes: he'll have ideas, oh yes. Relentless, senseless, maddening ideas without end.

The audience follows Madoc back to his lecture hall where he is answering students' questions when the ideas come rushing in. Madoc quickly loses control and cannot stop expressing his ideas; suddenly noticing a dark ominous figure standing at the back of the auditorium, Madoc understands what has happened and panics, rushing out of the lecture hall. A few of his students find a deranged Madoc sitting in the stairway, still muttering endless ideas to himself, his fingertips all bloodied from writing his ideas on the wall. This is arguably the most graphic scene in the "Calliope" episode, with the bloody words dripping down the wall. Yet the physical and mental anguish that Madoc feels at this moment, finally getting all the ideas he could ever have or use, is nothing compared to the crimes he committed against Calliope. He begs his student Nora (Amita

Suman) to go to his house and free Calliope, not remembering that saying the words alone would suffice. But when Nora arrives at his house and unlocks the bedroom-cell, it's empty except for a copy of Fry's most treasured, out-of-print novel—*Here Comes a Candle*, about a writer's muse being the "slave of his lust."

The last time we see Madoc is in the hospital, no longer spilling ideas and now having trouble just thinking and remembering. With Calliope at last free, Madoc returns to his impotent old self, at last confessing that all the ideas and stories belonged to *her*. To his horror, he has no recollection of Calliope or Dream's name anymore. The false writer has no more ideas, and the man has no more words, no voice, suffocating in his own impotence and helplessness as his punishment.

Calliope: From Silent Victim to Empowered Survivor

The second feminist twist in the Netflix adaptation that greatly affects the narrative and updates it for the twenty-first-century audience is how Calliope reacts to her release. The adaptation extends the reunion between Calliope and Dream, allowing them to talk about punishment and recovery. When Dream first comes to Calliope's aid, he threatens to make Madoc free her and punish him. Yet Calliope rejects Dream's insistence on retribution because, in her words, "What punishment could be enough? Even his death would not bring back what he has taken from me. He's nothing. He's just a man." Instead of seeking revenge, Calliope simply wants to be freed and to move on, shattering the possibility of this episode turning into a standard rape and revenge story. Films and television often show female rape survivors going on a rampage for revenge, such as the classic film *I Spit on Your Grave* (1978). Madoc is right; popular media often rewards male writers for *imagining* what women's experiences are, rather than giving women the platforms to tell their experiences themselves. Michaela Coel's *I May Destroy You* and Emerald Fennell's *Promising Young Woman* (2020) are two examples of critically works acclaimed not only for their acting but also for their honest portrayal of sexual violence, and they were both made by women about women who seek to confront their rape trauma. Whereas Arabella writes her own story as a way of processing it and Cassie (Carey Mulligan) from *Promising Young Woman* sacrifices her life to expose the rapist of her best friend, Calliope simply erases herself from Madoc's memory and moves on. Her former lover Dream had put the son of his captor, Alex Burgess, into eternal sleep, but Calliope lets Madoc walk free. She later explains to Dream, "I will not forgive what he has done, but I must forgive the man" in order for her wounds to heal. As a goddess, she knows humanity is flawed and easily corrupted. While feminists may condemn how easily Madoc is forgiven, and clearly Dream thinks Madoc deserves more punishment, the episode emphasizes caring for the self and others rather than nurturing revenge.

Instead of unleashing her wrath, which would not be productive to her healing or useful to anyone else, Calliope chooses advocacy over violence. In the comic, after her traumatic imprisonment, Calliope understandably takes a relatively passive approach and simply decides to "return to the minds of humanity." The sense of Calliope's resignation, even after she has being freed, is profound. In comparison, the Netflix adaptation establishes a more assertive Calliope who sets herself into motion to make a difference. While both Calliopes return to their duty of inspiring mankind, the television Calliope has a goal in mind: she must "make sure that this never happens to anyone else ever again." This is a very feminist response, to move from the personal to the political: "By inspiring humanity to want better for themselves and each other. By rewriting the laws by which I was held. Laws that were written long ago in which my sisters and I had no say." The laws refer to the fact that Calliope is bound to whoever comes into possession of her scroll. It is not enough to be free if it means the same tragedy can befall others.

In "The Uses of Anger: Women Responding to Racism" (1981), Audre Lorde (2019) calls for the strategic use of anger as a tool to change the status quo: "I am not free while any woman is unfree, even when her shackles are very different from my own" (126). Calliope shares the same sense of responsibility for her fellow sisters and women, therefore, choosing to rewrite the laws is a constructive way of resolving her trauma. Her undefeated spirit that strives to improve the world also inspires Dream, who is suffering from his own unrecognized trauma. The major storyline after *Dream Country* (the collection which features "Calliope") is *Season of Mists*, which has Dream deciding to correct his mistake of sending his ex-lover Nada to Hell for ten thousand years simply because she rejected him. It's not hard to imagine that Calliope has also inspired Dream himself to act better.

While "Calliope" appears as a standalone story without much participation of the Sandman himself until the last fifteen minutes, it is a great example of how the creators translated and updated the feminist power of *Sandman* to television. Rape is clearly a difficult topic to discuss or depict, yet "Calliope" manages to do so without nudity or violence, or even using the word. In effect, the episode obeys the classic writing rule: show, don't tell. Through the blinking cursor, the bloody scratch, and the sound of footsteps and door locks, "Calliope" makes the audience part of the story, responsible for completing the action sequences in their minds. This approach of leaving the audience to their imagination is very much intrinsic to the *Sandman* worldview, which stresses our imaginations and dreams are powerful and life-shaping. As Prescott (2012) suggests, "the act of putting on the page the horrible logic of rape is part of what makes this work feminist" (77). Showing Madoc's hesitation, anxiety, and eventual cruelty gradually unfold, the episode is not simply about the capture and release of a Muse, but also about a man who chains himself to blind greed, success and validation. The sexual violence allegations against Gaiman may on the surface dampen the power of his writing, particularly a storyline like "Calliope" that presents itself as feminist and critical of sexual violence. It is particularly difficult to separate the art from the artist in this case. But the adaptation of "Calliope" offers one solution: we can invest in our power as readers/viewers to create meanings from narratives for ourselves. Netflix successfully brings the story into the 2020s and turns a damsel in distress into a feminist activist. The last scene of the episode shows Calliope returning to her element, signified by her reclaiming the traditional Greek chiton garment. At last, leaving Madoc's house, she smiles and breathes in the night air, illuminated by streetlamps, and walks free.

References

Coel, Michaela, and Sam Miller, dirs. 2020. *I May Destroy You*. Season 1, episode 8, "Line Spectrum Border." Written by Michaela Coel. June 30. BBC One and HBO.

Deen, Sarah. 2020. "Iwan Rheon says Game of Thrones Sansa Stark rape scene was 'worst day of my career.'" *Metro*. November 1. https://metro.co.uk/2020/11/01/game-of-thrones-iwan-rheon-rape-scene-worst-day-13517366/.

Ferreday, Debra. 2015. "Game of Thrones, Rape Culture, and Feminist Fandom." *Australian Feminist Studies*, vol. 30, no. 83, pp. 21–36, https://doi.org/10.1080/08164649.2014.998453.

Framke, Caroline. 2022. "Netflix's 'The Sandman' Keeps the Spirit of Neil Gaiman's Sweeping Comic Intact, Avoiding (Most of) the Usual Streaming Pitfalls: TV Review." *Variety*. August 5. https://variety.com/2022/tv/news/the-sandman-review-netflix-neil-gaiman-1235333550/.

Frankel, Valerie Estelle. 2014. *Women in* Game of Thrones: *Power, Conformity and Resistance*. McFarland.

Gaiman, Neil. 2003. "Remembering the Concerned Mothers of America." May 16. https://journal.neilgaiman.com/2003/05/remembering-concerned-mothers-of.asp.

Gaiman, Neil (w), et al. 2022. *Sandman Book One*. DC Comics.

Gaiman, Neil, David S. Goyer, and Allan Heinberg, creators. 2022. *Sandman*. Season 1. Netflix.

Griffin, Louise. 2023. "*Buffy*'s James Marsters: 'I Would Have Killed Spike Off in a Heartbeat.'" *Radio Times*. May 20. https://www.radiotimes.com/tv/fantasy/buffy-spike-james-marsters-rt-rewind/.

Haag, Nathan. 2019. "Nurse Charged with Sexual Assault of Woman in Vegetative State Who Gave Birth." *New York Times*. January 23. https://www.nytimes.com/2019/01/23/us/nathan-sutherland-vegetative-arizona.html.

Intimacy Directors and Coordinators. 2023. "TV/Film." Accessed August 12, 2023. www.idcprofessionals.com/for-tvfilm.

Jowett, Lorna. 2009. "Rape, Power, Realism and the Fantastic on Television." *Feminism, Literature and Rape Narrative: Violence and Violation*, pp. 217–32. Taylor & Francis. 2009.

Joyaux, Daniel. 2022. "The Sandman Fails to Live Up to Fan's Dreams." RogerEbert.com. August 5. https://www.rogerebert.com/streaming/the-sandman-tv-review.

Lorde, Audre. 2019. "The Use of Anger: Women Responding to Racism." In *Sister Outsider*, 117–128. Penguin.

Orr, Christopher. 2015. "Why Does *Games of Thrones* Feature So Much Sexual Violence?" *The Atlantic*. June 17. https://www.theatlantic.com/entertainment/archive/2015/06/game-of-thrones-sexual-violence/396191/.

Palmer, Katie. 2022. "*The Sandman* Star Explains Why Rape Scene Was Axed from Bonus Episode." *Express*. August 26. https://www.express.co.uk/showbiz/tv-radio/1660848/The-Sandman-rape-scene-axed-Calliope.

Prescott, Tara. 2012. "It's Pretty Graphic: Sexual Violence and the Issue of 'Calliope.'" In *Feminism in the Worlds of Neil Gaiman: Essays on the Comics, Poetry and Prose*, edited by Tara Prescott and Aaron Drucker, 64–80. McFarland.

Robinson, Joanna. 2015. "*Game of Thrones* Absolutely Does Not Need to Go There with Sansa Stark." *Vanity Fair*. May 17. https://www.vanityfair.com/hollywood/2015/05/game-of-thrones-rape-sansa-stark.

Rosenberg, Alyssa. 2015. "'Game of Thrones' Has Always Been a Show about Rape." *Washington Post*. May 19. https://www.washingtonpost.com/news/act-four/wp/2015/05/19/game-of-thrones-has-always-been-a-show-about-rape/.

Shapiro, Lila. 2025. "There is No Safe Word: How the best-selling fantasy author Neil Gaiman hid the darkest parts of himself for decades." *Vulture*, January 13. https://www.vulture.com/article/neil-gaiman-allegations-controversy-amanda-palmer-sandman-madoc.html.

Sobchack, Vivian C. 1977. "No Lies: Direct Cinema as Rape." *Journal of the University Film Association* 29 (4): 13–18.

Wang, Jessica. 2023. "*General Hospital* Star Genie Francis Will No Longer Defend Luke and Laura's Rape Scene: 'I Think That the Story Was Inappropriate.'" *Entertainment Weekly*. January 12. https://ew.com/tv/general-hospital-genie-francis-luke-laura-rape-scene/.

The Therapeutic Value of Hope Shining through the Lens of *Sandman*

SAMARA V. SEROTKIN

> Hope is never mere, even when it is meager.
> —Gil-galad, *The Lord of the Rings: The Rings of Power*

It's easy to underestimate the value of hope. This is especially true in my line of work as a therapist. Yet in challenging times hope can be the most valuable of resources. Once ignited, it can often be rekindled even in the darkest of moments. When my clients experience moments of hope in their hearts, we practice sitting with it mindfully to nurture it and help it grow. Darkness, as we know, is really just the space before the light. Sometimes we need to bring the light ourselves.

I am a mindfulness-based psychologist and life coach running a private practice in Seattle, Washington. I meet with an average of twenty-five clients each week. All of these sessions take place online or over the phone. I specialize in teaching clients how to use mindfulness meditation to help them live more authentically fulfilling lives, but this manifests quite differently for each person. Many of my clients are working on managing symptoms of depression and/or anxiety, while others come to me for help with changing habits, such as those required for healthy and sustainable weight loss. Others come to me for a renewed sense of purpose or to reclaim their creativity.

Many of my clients are fans of *Sandman*. The TV adaptation kindled powerful conversations that catalyzed meaningful and positive change in the lives of my clients. I would like to "amplify the signal" of the healing potential that can come from this series. My clients have given me permission to discuss some of the most meaningful themes that came up for them in the hopes that highlighting these themes will in some way help others.

At the start of a session, many of my clients ask me to lead them through a brief mindfulness meditation. Moments of silence are a natural part of our sessions. Sitting in silence together, especially when witnessing and experiencing strong emotions, can lead to some dizzying and deep discussions about mortality, purpose, and spiritual inquiry. I often experience moments of deep awe and wonder throughout my day as I marvel at my clients' experiences and actions.

Some days my job leaves me with a sense of whiplash. I meet with clients every hour, with a break in the middle of the day. Generally, I have no idea what each hour will bring. Some sessions feel full of lightness and energy as my client experiences progress and growth, while other sessions surprise me by taking us through terribly dark places neither my client nor myself expected to be talking about that day. Time seems especially relative as it stretches out to hold the enormity of the emotions we can experience in a session. Sometimes when I come out of my home office for lunch and join the rest of my family upstairs, it feels as if we've been on different planets all morning.

These deeper, more vulnerable discussions require a sense of connection and trust so my clients can feel safe to let me in. One way I forge this connection early on is by asking my clients about their reading life. In fact, one of the first questions on my intake form asks a new client to name any books that have had an important role in their life. Conversations about meaningful texts often lead us to important places of great value in our therapeutic and coaching work.

When I started asking new clients about books that have had the greatest impact on their lives, I saw them come alive in ways I rarely otherwise see in a first session. An initial session with a new therapist can sometimes be a bit anxiety provoking. Clients often come in with their guard up, which is understandable. I find that when I ask clients the book question, they often relax a bit and speak with more authenticity. Their eyes light up and they become more expressive.

In the 2011 *Doctor Who* episode "The Doctor's Wife" (written by Neil Gaiman, BBC One, May 14), the Doctor (Matt Smith) complains to the temporarily personified TARDIS (Suranne Jones) that she wasn't very reliable. The TARDIS responds by pointing out that while she hasn't always taken him where he *wanted* to go, she always took him to where he *needed* to go. While most of my clients didn't expect to be talking about the books they loved in a first session with me, those conversations always seemed to lead us exactly where we needed to go.

There are some titles that I have noticed come up frequently in these discussions, and many of those books fall into the science fiction and fantasy genres, including *The Lord of the Rings* and *Sandman*. Again and again,

I hear clients describe how important these books have been to them and the long-term impact the books have had on their lives.

The connection between storytelling and audiences has always been extremely powerful, tracing back to when the ancient Greeks invented "drama" as we know it. Back then, audience members attended the theater not just for entertainment, but also because it was considered important for their health. Both Plato and Aristotle wrote about the concept of "catharsis" as an important process of cleansing and purification. It was thought that when audience members witnessed tragic drama and had an emotional release of some sort, they experienced this catharsis as a kind of alchemy between the actors and the audience, producing something greater than the sum of its parts. In the field of psychology, the word catharsis has also been adopted to describe the process of healing from trauma by retelling the event while also allowing oneself to feel the emotions related to the event (Jackson 1994).

When I first encountered *Sandman*, it was being released one issue at a time, with a whole agonizing month between issues. In fact, a big motivator for me to get my driver's license was to drive to Comics Etc., the comic book store in my hometown located right next to the YMCA and across from the store that sold D&D supplies. I wanted to get down there each month as quickly as possible on the day a new issue was released. And all these years later, the series continues to be on top of my list of favorite and most meaningful pieces of literature I have ever encountered.

So you can imagine how nervous I was when I heard Netflix was going to produce it as a show. The stakes were high. I had been imagining my dream cast for the series since I was seventeen! But Gaiman's first novel to TV adaptation, *American Gods*, was disappointing. It's hard to put into words why I found it so off-putting, but I just couldn't connect to it in the same way I connected to the novel. It felt like it had lost some of its magic. I already knew that many of my clients were fans of the *Sandman* comics, and many were already talking about their hopes and fears about the upcoming TV adaptation in a way that had us kind of holding our breath. We all felt such a deep attachment to the comics that we were all feeling a bit anxious as the release date approached.

And seeing how *Sandman* has played such a valuable role for so many of my clients at pivotal moments in their lives, I knew we might need to process a lot of heavier material in therapy sessions as I made my way through the series. How were we going to get through the graphic violence and psychological horror in the diner scene from "24 Hours," for example? And would the show include "Calliope"? Because so many folks were likely to get triggered by the interaction between the depiction on the screen and their own personal experiences with trauma, I had many discussions with clients about how to prepare for such moments. We talked about meditations to practice, self-soothing techniques, and made sure everyone remembered that they had the power of pressing the pause button at any time.

For those who have experienced it, trauma can be easily retriggered by witnessing intense and dark scenes. Yet those moments also contain an opportunity to delve into the feeling and find healing from the trauma. It takes enormous courage to walk this path, and constant diligence to bring light into the darkest of places. For many, being in continued unsafe environments kept them from being able to do this healing work in the presence of others. Therefore, a private experience with a book or television show can offer enormous healing potential. Unfortunately, though, all too often this experience can be retraumatizing when encountering a character affected by a similar trauma that is not treated with dignity and respect. I was understandably concerned about how this was all going to go.

I was so relieved when the series finally dropped. Instead of being retriggered and retraumatized, many of my clients in fact felt hopeful after watching episodes, and discovered some newly found healing in their hearts. As I processed the episodes with my clients, I noticed some common themes emerging.

Hope was the core theme threaded throughout most, if not all, of the discussions we had after watching the series. While many of my clients spoke about hope, these conversations taught me that the experience of hope is not the same for everyone. The more we clarified what hope meant to them, the more I realized just how personal and important one's own experience of hope really is. I began to see the concept as similar to a beam of light shining through a prism. This prism splits the light, allowing us to discern all the bands within the spectrum.

My clients felt hope in so many different, but deeply important ways. One client who identifies as bisexual said she felt hope and healing through Jenna Coleman's portrayal of Johanna Constantine. In the original comic, this character was a straight man. In the Netflix version, Constantine is a woman with an ex-lover who is female, but this isn't depicted as a big deal or tokenized in any way. Another client who identifies as nonbinary spoke of how healing it was to watch *Sandman* and see nonbinary characters treated with the appropriate dignity and respect. Others described a healing experience through bracing for an awful thing from the comic that ultimately didn't happen in the show. For the most part, many of the most shocking and horrifying moments from the original comics that my clients were concerned about weren't depicted in the TV series. The felt sense of safety and relief where previous danger had been assumed is therapeutic gold.

In over twenty years of providing therapy, I have learned that for many people, the root of their suffering can be found in a desire to feel hope where none can be currently felt. This may be one reason why Despair and Desire are twins. I use the word "felt" intentionally here as hope isn't something that comes from our heads. Hope must be felt in our hearts and bodies for it to be believed in any real way. The human brain can do a lot of amazing things, but in matters of the heart it tends to have little authority or influence. Media can sometimes help us bridge the gap between our heads and our hearts.

As we watch the characters develop and interact in media, we have our own experiences with them. This process sometimes offers us hope: that things will get better, that things will become easier, that we can continue to learn and grow all the while being truly OK and loved just as we are. We hope that after our final breaths there will be something more to experience. Hope that we will learn more about what this mortal experience has all been about. That we will learn we did well, what we did mattered, and that there is more to come for us.

Emily Dickinson wrote, "'Hope' is the Thing with Feathers"—likening it to a bird calling through a storm. It is the light that guides through the darkness—a nonverbal felt sense that we all can orient to on a very deep and personal level. Hope is what we all deeply want to feel in a sustainable way. So as a therapist, when I see a flicker of authentic felt hope in a client, it's always worth exploring and nurturing. I'm so grateful for the hope that has shined through the lens of *Sandman* and the resulting conversations my clients and I have had.

Hope Through Expecting the Worst but Receiving the Best

As we neared the release of the TV series, my clients and I held our collective breath, worried about how certain scenes would play out, especially Calliope's rape and John Dee's murders. Trauma is much more prevalent than many people realize. As a therapist, I get more of the real picture. The past few years have brought so many difficult emotions into my therapy sessions as my clients have had old trauma responses retriggered by current events. Witnessing the media attention and conversation around the #MeToo movement, for example, can bring up a lot of difficult emotions for a sexual assault survivor. Clients have also been coping with the continuing incidents of racially-driven murders, the climate crisis, the Covid-19 pandemic, gun violence, and the wars in Ukraine and Gaza. And now the recent news articles about the sexual assault allegations against

Gaiman are especially triggering for survivors who have found comfort in his work.

It's become disconcertingly common for clients I have known for many years to suddenly recall traumatic events from their past that they are only just now realizing and acknowledging. As they witness emotionally difficult stories in the news and the media, they begin having huge reactions that they can't explain. Their hearts suddenly slam shut and their whole flight or fight system goes on full alert. They come to me asking for help figuring out what is happening.

In a way, their bodies are responding in the present moment to something that happened at a different place in their timeline. In other words, their bodies' felt memories of the past trauma are activated by association with something occurring here and now. Any feelings their psyche didn't let them experience back when the traumatic event occurred now come roaring back when triggered by association in the present moment. So suddenly there is felt crisis in the present moment, but their psyches aren't yet letting them access the whole story. They just feel their hearts slam shut in unexpected ways.

Sometimes I use the term "aperture of the heart" when we talk about this kind of experience. The aperture in a camera refers to the device in the lens that opens and closes for a given shot based on how much light the photographer needs to let in. If the photo is being taken in the evening, you generally want to open the aperture to let in more light in order to increase the exposure and pick up more detail. During the day, you usually want to create a smaller aperture to let in less light so the picture doesn't get washed out.

We have all had moments that, for some reason, make our hearts want to open up widely, letting in the full experience. We also have all felt things that make our hearts want to slam shut immediately and not let anyone or anything in. So much can be gained in understanding why these reactions happen and learning how to be more intentional about adjusting our heart's aperture more skillfully.

It feels like the intensity of the horror and violence depicted in movies, television, and in the news over the last decade has increased. The bar has been raised further and further when it comes to the kind of shock value producers need to elicit in an audience to stand out and make an impact. Producers and directors have been upping the ante, using more graphic depictions of traumatic events without really pausing to let the audience reflect and connect to the reality of what they are watching. This capitalistic mode of content production doesn't allow for catharsis or healing; rather it simply rapidly fires shocking material at the viewer. This frustrates me as a psychologist and as a member of common humanity. It is so far removed from what the Greeks had in mind when it comes to the role of drama and catharsis.

When strong, negative feelings from one's past are evoked in the present moment, it is felt as a crisis. But just like all crises, it's made up of both danger and opportunity. These moments hold deep opportunity for meaningful change. If we can meet them head-on with compassion and care, we can steward old wounds through our conscious mind, ultimately shifting our relationship with them in important and deeply healing ways.

Netflix's *Sandman* offered many of these healing moments for my clients, but two particular choices stand out. The first regards the adaptation of issue #6, "24 Hours." This issue follows John Dee, who has just escaped Arkham Asylum. He flags down a car and forces the driver, Rosemary, to take him to a storage facility where he has stashed Morpheus's missing (and incredibly powerful) Dreamstone. During the ride, Rosemary tries to make small talk and ask him about his life. She responds with honesty, kindness, empathy, and compassion. As the two converse, the tone of the story briefly softens and the conversation almost seems friendly.

When I first read this issue, I remember feeling a surge of hope for John, anticipating some kind of redemption for the character. These hopes were shattered when John gets out of the car and suddenly shoots and kills Rosemary. He then retrieves his stone and proceeds to go to a twenty-four-hour diner where he uses the stone to psychologically torture everyone in the diner and force them to do incredibly cruel, sadistic things to each other until they all die.

I found this story incredibly heartbreaking. As a therapist, I witness plenty of unnecessary cruelty, suffering, and trauma on a daily basis. So many of my clients are genuinely good people trying to do their best in a difficult world, just like Rosemary. All too often, I see hearts break when it seems like no matter how hard they try to make progress, they hit walls. There are bumps in the road that can be mistaken for mountains and risks dooming our goals if not handled with care. And sometimes when you try to engage in self-improvement, you become a target for other peoples' cruelty and judgment. No good deed goes unpunished, as the saying goes. But did Rosemary's kindness really not matter at all? That didn't feel right to me and it still doesn't.

However, when I watched "24/7," the episode based on this issue, there was a surprise twist: not only does John Dee let Rosemary live, but he also offers her the protection stone in gratitude for her assistance! This was a welcome departure from the awfulness I was bracing myself for. I don't know why the creators made that change, but I can say that many of my clients mentioned it in session. They were bracing for yet another reminder that bad things happen to good people, but were pleasantly surprised to see that Rosemary's kindness *did*, in fact, matter. And John Dee was no longer a one-dimensional "bad guy," but someone who could also show some growth and change. Change is possible, even for someone labeled a "villain," and kindness does, in fact, matter.

The second healing moment that stands out for me involves the powerful "Calliope" episode (the second half of the two-part bonus episode 11). Pinky Chung-Man Lui discusses this episode in more depth in the essay in this volume ("'Calliope': How Off-Screen Sexual Violence Changes the Narrative"). For my purposes, I'd like to note a specific aspect of this episode that came up with my clients. As soon as I heard this issue had been adapted to TV, I was on edge until I viewed it for myself. I had many clients who would possibly see it without a plan to prepare for viewing the rape content.

And then in a masterful stroke of storytelling, the creators decided not to directly depict the rape act itself, as had been done in the comic. In "*The Sandman* Changed Calliope's Story, And It's a Big Deal" Amelia Emberwing (2022) summarizes it beautifully:

> The team behind Netflix's *The Sandman* elected to distill everything down to a knock on the door, a blinking cursor and one single, gut wrenching, smear of blood on Madoc's cheek. There are no screams, no begging for mercy, simply a singular gash to show what he stole and that she fought. At her most powerless, the decision was made not to exploit her vulnerability and defilation for the sake of realism, but rather to highlight her singular act of defiance.

As Emberwing notes, Calliope's defiance—both implied here and, by the end of the episode, direct—reflects a significant change from the original comic. At the end of issue #17, Morpheus asks Calliope what she plans to do now that she is free, and a defeated-looking Calliope tells him she probably will just go back to "the minds of humanity," noting that the time of the muses is over. In the TV adaptation, however, I was delighted to see Calliope (Melissanthi Mahut) display fire, strength, and dignity. In a significant departure from the original story, Calliope tells Morpheus that she will go back to the muses and work with them make sure what happened to her never happens to anyone else.

This shift was, of course, intentional. The story needed to be adapted for a modern audience. The new Calliope won't stand for injustice—for herself or for anyone else. She is going to take her appropriate rage back to her people and make some changes happen! This felt like such an appropriate update for today's audiences when it first aired, even more so now in light of the assault allegations.

It is hard to overstate the healing power this kind of message can have on a viewer who has experienced sexual trauma. All too often in the media, rape survivors are depicted as weak and submissive, mere victims left broken and powerless by the abuse. As audience members we pay special attention to characters we relate to. People are often curious how someone else would respond to situations similar to what they themselves have been through. We unconsciously look to how characters make sense of their lives and experiences to help us develop insight and gain perspective into our own experiences and reactions. The "Calliope" episode is drama at its best: bringing positive catharsis to real pain, and even adding an empowering model for healing in the conclusion.

Hope's Relationship with Awe and Wonder

When people experience feelings of awe and wonder, it opens the doorway to hope. These feelings are good for our health, both mentally and physically (Allen 2018). And *Sandman* lets the reader/viewer experience awe and wonder in many ways.

One example is the second story paired with "Calliope" in episode 11, "A Dream of a Thousand Cats." (An episode that is examined in more detail in the next two essays of this collection.) In this tale, we meet a cat who travels the world to speak to other cats about her dream and vision for a better future. Audiences of cats from far and wide gather to hear what she has to say. She tells them that once she experienced terrible cruelty from humans and then realized just how little freedom she truly had. She describes how she once prayed and dreamed an answer.

In her dream, she speaks with the King of Cats who tells her about a time when cats once ruled the world. But this all changed when a thousand humans had the same dream together about humans being in charge. Poof! Overnight the humans became the dominant species, and everybody eventually forgot about the way things were and now accepted the current situation as how it always was. She says he told her this story because it means that if she can gather a thousand cats to dream the same dream, they had the power to change the world.

Honestly, the story is pretty tidy. Who's to say this couldn't have happened, really? History, as they say, is written by the victors, and in fact can change once we gain access to the stories of the less powerful players. Life, as we all know well, is a mystery, and nobody truly knows for sure what the bigger picture really is. It's important for us to have our assumptions questioned. There is more to heaven and earth than is in our philosophies—and there are phenomena that cannot be explained with science alone. This is one of the things I love about *Sandman*. It is fantastical, but in a way that makes you almost believe it could happen in real life. And you can't really prove it isn't possible.

The TV adaptation of this story brought it to life in ways I hadn't experienced in the comic version. I attribute part of this to the groundbreaking animation style that was used, which blended oil paintings with computer animation, creating something that feels inexplicably real for the audience. In his essay, "Cautionary Tales: Animation and the Human/Nonhuman Animal in 'Dream of a Thousand Cats,'" Colin Wheeler discusses the impact of this animation style in more depth.

This impact wasn't felt just by the human audience. There was a flurry of activity on social media that involved viewers joining in a collective experience of awe and wonder as their own cats—even the ones who usually never acknowledge the TV—sat and intently "watched" the episode in ways that made their owners nervously ask themselves whether they should worry about just how many cats were watching at the same time (Gaiman 2022).

Gaiman's work often implies and validates the idea that humans don't know everything and there are possibilities outside of what we see with our eyes. As the angel Aziraphale from *Good Omens* might say, some things are ineffable. In my youth, religion wasn't anything we talked about much at home. I was never given a framework for what I was supposed to believe about life and "the bigger picture," so I had to find my own line of spiritual inquiry. For me, spirituality has always been related to the experience of awe and wonder. When I read *Sandman* in my teens, its ideas about the afterlife resonated with me. I was intrigued by the comic's characters and gods from different theologies. I loved the idea that there could be a world where the Muses, and the Greek and even Egyptian gods could all co-exist with the family of the Endless. The very idea that these characters and forces could be impacting our lives without us realizing it fascinated me. And that the interactions could be happening both ways! That a god (or godlike figure) could be impacted by my thoughts, actions, or prayers was exciting. It resonated with my own felt sense that intentions, in a deep way, matter, and that our inner experience is indeed important, even if not in in ways we realize.

This was at the center of my earliest spiritual awakenings. So much healing comes from the idea that there is a bigger picture, or bigger story, and we are being held and loved by it. There is hope in the idea that the Endless serve us and even find us valuable and endearing despite all the faults that make us human.

Hope in Representation

Hope can be especially hard to find for people who have been marginalized for aspects of their identity, such as their race, ethnicity, gender, or sexuality. Many of my clients who identify with marginalized or underrepresented groups speak of a common experience of being "othered" and feeling different than everyone else in the room. This can lead to (or amplify existing) feelings of isolation and hopelessness.

Netflix's *Sandman* has given the world something it desperately needs but has historically been in short supply of: accurate and respectful treatment of marginalized peoples without tokenizing them in any way. When the *Sandman* comics were originally released, the terms "nonbinary" and "genderqueer" weren't in as widespread use as they are today. Traditional binary gender stereotypes were the assumed norm and people who fell outside of that narrow spectrum were often ridiculed. When I was a teenage girl trying to make sense of her own identity as a young woman, walking through the aisles of my favorite comic book store was downright uncomfortable. It seemed like every female character on every cover was a helpless and voluptuous scantily clad damsel in distress calling for her hero to save her. For that reason and more, much of sci-fi before the 1990s can be uncomfortable to read. It doesn't age well. However, *Sandman* has always been ahead of its time. Look for example at the treatment of the character Wanda from "A Game of You." Reading this in the early 1990s was the first time I came across a trans character treated with any respect. My heart opened to see a trans person presented as a fully realized character rather than a caricature. (Although Wanda does not appear in the first season of *Sandman*, viewers eagerly celebrated her promised appearance in Season 2.) Wanda, like many trans people, suffers greatly because of the way people see and treat her. Her story opened me up to more empathy and understanding. Never underestimate the power of this.

Compassionate and accurate representation is essential. Not only so that marginalized people can see themselves represented through media in an accurate way, but also for the audience members who don't identify directly with the character's experience. As one of my gender nonconforming clients put it, "I can't overstate how big it is when we are included in the world of sci-fi and fiction."

As writers in other essays in this volume have noted, some of the casting choices for the TV adaptation shifted dynamics in unexpected ways (for further analysis, see "Fresh-Faced: The Interpretive Impact of Race, Gender, and Ethnicity in the *Sandman* Series"). As the casting announcements were made, I was repeatedly encountering fascinating conversations about people's personal reactions to the announcements, both online and in my sessions. Online, I saw a torrent of angry reactions to the casting of Kirby Howell-Baptiste as Death. We all expected to see the incredibly pale-skinned woman we were so familiar with in the comics, but Howell-Baptiste's performance in the role brought forth all the essential characteristics of the character that I had hoped would be depicted, and more. When Death walks the Earth as a mortal, she takes on whatever is assumed to be the default human form. It feels like poetic justice for the default human form to be Black and female.

Casting Vivienne Acheampong as Lucienne meant that a formerly white, male main character was now a Black woman. In addition to having the show more accurately reflect the diversity in England and the United States, this casting choice opens up possibility for social commentary. Morpheus's librarian is incredibly competent and chronically unappreciated—always working hard to not say the wrong thing to her boss. Casting a Black woman to play this role just makes sense in so many ways. For a more in-depth discussion of this, see "Fresh-Faced: The Interpretive Impact of Race, Gender, and Ethnicity in the Sandman Series" in this volume.

Gwendoline Christie as Lucifer is another great example of a casting choice that opens up the show's relatability to a wider audience. The character of Lucifer, whether in *Sandman, Paradise Lost,* or the Bible, holds great power and gravitas—so much so that it comes as a great shock to Lucifer and the residents of Hell when Morpheus wins the epic battle between them. Almost universally, biblical characters with power are men. In the original *Sandman* comics, Lucifer was depicted as androgynous, modelled after David Bowie. But the *Sandman* television series goes further by casting an actress in the role, an unexpected and welcome twist. One of my clients pointed out that because the show cast Christie instead of a skinny white guy, my client could more easily connect to the concept of the character. She said, "If I don't have to work to relate to the characters, I can engage with it more deeply. It lets me focus on the character and this lets me spend more time with the ideas behind the forms." When my clients can relate to and engage more deeply with the characters on the screen, it lets them have access to the healing value of catharsis in ways they have often been shut out of for too long.

Hope for the Possibility of Change

In the episode "A Hope in Hell," Morpheus evokes the idea of hope as the ultimate checkmate in his duel with Lucifer. He wins, pointing out that Hell could not exist if it were not for the inhabitants' ability to dream of and hope for something better. How exciting and refreshing! Hope has power over even the greatest darkness and pain, perhaps because hope is neither embedded entirely in the lightness or the darkness. Destructive and constructive energies co-exist everywhere and in everything. When these forces are in balance, hope shines through. Therein in lies the potential for change and growth.

In the "Playing House" episode we meet Gault (Ann Ogbomo), the shapeshifting nightmare who always wanted to be a dream. In Morpheus's absence, Gault elected to pose as a little boy's mother in his dreams, offering support and guidance to him since his waking life was so full of abuse and suffering. Morpheus misconstrues Gault's actions and accuses her of manipulating the boy using the power of dreams. Gault tries to explain that she never related to the body and role she was born into, and that she has always wished to be a dream instead of a nightmare.

Morpheus tells Gault, in no uncertain terms, that she has no choice in what she becomes. She must stick with the role she has been given, despite the fact that she doesn't identify with it. He goes on to say that not even the Endless have choices in how they live or do their work. He then banishes her to thousands of years in darkness to learn to feel more fear and remember her place. Throughout this interaction, Lucienne is present and listening, but is clearly uncomfortable with his choice.

My clients relate to this difficult dynamic in a wide variety of ways. There are important threads of representation related to the idea that the life or body someone was born into isn't necessarily congruent with their true identity and felt sense of purpose. There are also parallels with the feelings of burden and hopelessness people can often experience in their harder moments. Many of us can relate to these complicated concepts of destiny and free will.

In the tenth episode, "Lost Hearts," however, we get to be surprised by a different ending that brings the focus back towards hope. We learn that even nightmares can have a choice. After some reflection, Morpheus eventually changes his mind about Gault. He attributes his change of heart to his recent conversations with Lucienne and Gault and states that he has learned from their wisdom. He chooses to grant Gault her wish to become a dream, thus releasing her into her heart's desire. This would be an uplifting story if it ended there but there's more. In a lovely, satisfying twist that evokes a kind of poetic justice, he also gives her wings and the ability to fly.

Lucienne looks on, clearly pleased with Morpheus's choice. He then turns to Lucienne and asks her to cover for him while he is working on rebuilding the Dreaming. Lucienne smiles broadly at this because it is a big moment for them. It demonstrates Morpheus's own ability to evolve and change. When he returned from his imprisonment, he saw how things had fallen apart in his absence. He learned through his interactions with Lucienne and others, including Gault, that even Morpheus, King of Dreams, Lord of the Dreaming, Dream of the Endless can ask for help. In fact, he can embrace Lucienne's competence and allow Lucienne to help with more of his duties, and the whole of the Dreaming can benefit. This story validates the hope that you can always change for the better. It refutes the old idea that you are born into a life and that's just what and who you are. It highlights the fact that everything is a choice, and therein lies hope, the most valuable currency in therapy.

Hope Even in Death

The topic of mortality comes up a lot in therapy. Many of my clients' concerns ultimately boil down to their fears of death and regret. Therapists use the term "existential anxiety" to describe the sense of dread or fear that comes up alongside mortality awareness. This is a powerful force every human needs to reckon with in their own way. Nothing brings us to our knees in quite the same way as brushing with the awareness of our own mortality, a fact that the booming antiaging industry capitalizes on. Wouldn't it be lovely to have some hope that it will all be okay? To know that we will actually feel some sense of peace in the end?

Sandman's approach to the character of Death has always felt like such a delightful take on what has traditionally been represented by menacing male figures, like the Grim Reaper. The comics gave me hope that Death could actually be a kind and loving experience, one where I might even be welcomed with a smile. I have referred to the character and the storyline of "The Sound of Her Wings" in therapy sessions throughout my career. It has opened so many doors for people to shift their relationship with existential anxiety in helpful and meaningful ways. Howell-Baptiste's performance brought to life so many of Death's best possible attributes, such as her kindness and compassion, and her quirky lightness. This has helped so many people relate to their own mortality in a more gentle and positive way. And this changes everything.

I am grateful to the teams who created *Sandman* and brought it to life in all of its forms. While the story is great entertainment, it also has always contained something more, meant something more for its fans. What these stories meant to readers when they first encountered them is meaningful—even if the circumstances around the original author and the reception of his work has changed. Hidden within *Sandman* has always been a call to curiosity and new perspectives for those seeking them. In the moments of emotional release and catharsis, unlimited hope waits for us to dip back into it whenever we need a dose.

REFERENCES

Aristotle. 1982. *The Poetics*. Translated by James Hutton. Norton.
Dickinson, Emily. 1951. "'Hope' is the Thing with Feathers—" from *The Complete Poems*

of *Emily Dickinson*, ed. Thomas H. Johnson. The Belknap Press of Harvard University Press.

Emberwing, Amelia. 2022. "*The Sandman* Changed Calliope's Story, and It's a Big Deal." IGN.com. August 21. https://www.ign.com/articles/the-sandman-changed-calliopes-story-and-its-a-big-deal.

Gaiman, Neil (w). 2011. "The Doctor's Wife." *Doctor Who*. BBC One. BBC, London. 14 May.

Gaiman, Neil. 2017. *The View from the Cheap Seats: Selected Nonfiction*. William Morrow.

Gaiman, Neil (@neilhimself). 2022. "I'm not sure if it was a good idea to let the cats watch it…" Twitter. August 20. https://twitter.com/neilhimself/status/1561056551229693955.

Gaiman, Neil (w), Mike Dringenberg (a), and Malcolm Jones III (a). 1989. "24 Hours." *Sandman* #6. New York: DC Comics. April.

Gaiman, Neil (w), Kelley Jones (a), and Malcolm Jones III (i). 1990. "Calliope." *Sandman* #17. New York: DC Comics. July.

Gaiman, Neil (w), and Shawn McManus (a). 1991. "A Game of You: Part One—Slaughter on Fifth Avenue." *Sandman* #32. November.

Gaiman, Neil, David S. Goyer, and Allan Heinberg, creators. 2022. *Sandman*. Season 1. Netflix.

Hill, Greg. 2022. "Why *The Sandman* Had to Change One of the Comic's Darkest Stories for Netflix." CBR. August 23. https://www.cbr.com/calliope-changed-story-episode-the-sandman-netflix/.

Jackson, Stanley. W. 1994. "Catharsis and Abreaction in the History of Psychological Healing." *Psychiatric Clinics of North America* 17 (3): 471–91.

Stone, Sam. 2022. "The Sandman: Neil Gaiman and Allan Heinberg Explain How the Show's Bonus Episode Came Together." CBR. August 22. https://www.cbr.com/sandman-neil-gaiman-allan-heinberg-interview/.

Cautionary Tails

Animation and the Human/Nonhuman Animal in "Dream of a Thousand Cats"

Colin Wheeler

Two weeks after the announced Season 1 finale of *Sandman* (2022–2025), "Dream of a Thousand Cats" crept into the first part of a two-part episode. Representing the first fully animated segment in the series so far, "Dream of a Thousand Cats" also demonstrates animation's unique potential to construct political parables based on nonhuman-animal (nh) perspectives. While there is no shortage of animated films about nh-animals, most of them anthropomorphize characters to such a degree that their nonhuman aspects are practically erased. Departing from this trope, "Dream of a Thousand Cats" delves into different nh-animal representations and states of consciousness, layering representations of the oneiric. It also serves as a political parable with the specific intention of commenting on animal welfare, expanding depictions of the dream-realm beyond the human-oriented perspective of surrealists and psychoanalysts. This essay offers a close reading of "Dream of a Thousand Cats," presenting it as part of an emerging body of what Alexander Popov (2022) calls "more-than-human" stories that resist hegemonic anthropocentrism through multispecies perspectives (41). Some have criticized these narratives as leading to inaccurate and anthropomorphic assumptions about the animal subject, but the arguments do not appreciate how these texts can teach the ways human and nh-animals are similar (Tarłowski and Rybsk 2021). Just as "Dream of a Thousand Cats" cannot convey what is incomprehensible to human understanding, this study does not explain what it is like to be a cat but instead foregrounds a narrative that centers on the shared vulnerability of being animal denizens making do in a human civilization.

The short episode makes two simple claims: cats are like us, and cats are not like us. Both of these are true; they map onto different ways human-animals perceive nh-animals. Only recently has the study of animal behavior been able to conclude that nh-animals think at all; today, many researchers acknowledge that nh-animals do experience qualitatively different and likely simpler forms of thought (Griffin 2001). Cats, for example, can dream. This was demonstrated in a study by Michel Jouvet (1979), who damaged the brains of cats to disable the neural systems that regulate sleep paralysis during dream-states. His study found that the cat brains displayed a variety of stereotyped motor activity. Although the paper works to avoid anthropomorphizing the cat subjects, it is impossible not to interpret their nocturnal activities as a variety of experiential dream states including stalking, playing, grooming, fighting, and fleeing (281). "Dream of a Thousand Cats" presents an alternative vision of the world, in which the dreams of cats and humans entangle, suggesting that this nebulously defined era of anthropocentrism is just a long dream in all its unruly temporality. The episode challenges the audience to consider the nh-animal perspectives by enfolding them into the animated bodies on screen. In honoring the dreams of nh-animals, human-animals may yet conjure a new reality, else we risk a rude awakening.

In this study, I use the hyphenated terms *human-animal* and *nh-animals* to emphasize the interconnectedness of animal life. While terminology like this may lead to some inelegant prose, the ways that studies represent interactions between nh- and human-animals remain an important opportunity for critical reflection (Hurn 2010, 27). This is common practice in human-animal studies, which explore the ways in which humans and animals interact with and influence each other. Hyphenating the term *human-animal* also helps to avoid the implication that humans are superior to animals, honoring "the entangled labor of humans and animals together in science and in many other domains" (Haraway 2008, 80). This linguistic shift recenters life on earth as a continuum of diverse entities, ensuring that human and nh-animals are not seen as separate entities, but rather as companion species coinhabiting the planet. The hyphen also helps to avoid the use of the term *animal* as a catchall category for all nonhuman creatures, semantically erasing the diversity of animal life. By hyphenating the term *human-animal*, this study acknowledges the many different ways in which nonhuman/human-animals interact, including their representation in human-animal media. Overall, the hyphen is an important part of the term *human-animal* because it helps to emphasize the interconnectedness of humans and animals, the agency exerted by life on earth, and the diversity of animal life.

According to film scholars Kristin Thompson and David Bordwell (2003), people study media to explore the traces of the societies that produced and consumed it, providing insight into a range of issues applicable to contemporary human-animal culture.¹ This also motivates researchers in human-animal studies, delineating the relations between human and animals to achieve a better comprehension of society. French anthropologist Claude Lévi-Strauss (1963) famously said that human-animals garner icons of nh-animals because they are "good to think with" (89), meaning they provide a great lens through which human-animals may better understand themselves. Almost every human culture uses animal species as symbols, a sign of the human-animal's tendency to fetishize and identify with nh-animals. Studying the representation of this continuum in animation yields human-animal animation studies which explores the depiction of animal life in animated media to better define their relation and make inquiry into that human/nonhuman-animal continuum. "Dream of a Thousand Cats" aired as the first part of the episode, followed by "Calliope" (reversing their original order in the comics).² Although seemingly very different stories, when juxtaposed in a single episode, their themes resonate: both focus on the subjugation of the meek by petty, everyday tyrants. Similarly, human-animal studies also harmonize with critical gender studies where both explore social relations to give voice to those in the cultural margins.

The more-than-human narrative may prove challenging for human-animal audiences, as many nonhuman-animals lack emotive faces or relatable anatomy, rendering their appearance and motion uncanny at times. One famous recent example comes from Disney's 2023 live action remake of *The Little Mermaid*. Not even Daveed Diggs's charisma could turn a realistic crab into an appealing sidekick for Ariel. Justin Chang (2023) lamented that traditionally animated characters like Sebastian and Flounder look "creepy and dead-eyed" when rendered to appear photoreal. While photoreal depictions of cats, as seen in *The Lion King* (2019), construct a cohesive yet sterilized view of the natural world, the technical and aesthetic challenges involved in creating the photoreal eclipsed more significant discourses, which were further complicated by the director's refusal to characterize the film as animated (Amidi 2018). The photoreal can often disturb audiences, while highly realistic digital avatars tend to score well in terms of appeal; if their movements reveal their artificial nature then this discordance produces an uncanny sensation. The notoriously panned felines in *Cats* (2019), for example, are uncanny because nothing seems to follow the laws of physics or move the way it should; photoreal ambiguity pervades every second that these humanlike cats gambol across the screen. More stylized animation allows the audience to inhabit the cinematic space as a collective dream, in which human handmade imagery acts as the gateway to nonhuman subjectivity, however anthropomorphic or stylized. Animation imbues the screen with the oneiric, in which animators labor to re-enchant reified images with liberated animal motion, potentially enabling the imagination of new possible worlds informed by more-than-human points of view. "Dream of a Thousand Cats" manages to render such virtual spaces in which new relations might occur through a combination of painted backdrops and cinematography centered on the cat.

The photoreal conundrum became a central issue with the production of "Dream of a Thousand Cats" when Neil Gaiman and showrunner Allan Heinberg insisted that the cats be depicted as "real cats: no anthropomorphic, human-like behavior" (Stone 2022). Warner Bros. approached Hisko Hulsing to direct "Dream," even before they had reached out to directors for their live-action episodes. Hulsing, a Dutch oil painter, film director, and animator, had recently completed *Undone* (2019–2022), a series for Amazon that pushed rotoscope animation to its limits. The only animated episode in the series' first season, "Dream of a Thousand Cats" retains a unique relation to panels of the original comic drawn by Kelley Jones, which Hulsing adapted to a fixed 16:9 horizontal frame. Working with the notes left by Gaiman and Jones, he drew hundreds of storyboards as rough thumbnails for storyboard artist Michael Senarain to adapt into production boards, improving framing and composition when he saw fit. From there, editor Eva Krispijin turned these boards into a rough animatic to get a feel for how the story would progress emotionally, going to Jeroen Nadorp for a detailed temp track. This convinced Gaiman and Heinberg to greenlight the project, but while Location Designer Eelco Siebring got to work, Hulsing had to contend with the photoreal conundrum.

Because the cats needed to be as real as possible, Hulsing collaborated with Untold, a VFX studio that specializes in photoreal animation, such as a turtle on roller skates for an Avanti West Coast Train commercial (2022) and a collection of forest animals in a Frito-Lay ad (2022). They modeled cat skeletons and musculature before calculating and implementing skin weights, much like they did for the *Lion King*. However, Hulsing was also going to hire a team of traditional painters such as Hans Versfelt and J.J. Epping to render each scene with oil paint on massive canvases. The team had been trained in alla prima, a technique that applies wet paint on wet paint, working quickly with broad brushes. This creates a sense of depth that, Hulsing (2022) argues, would be impossible for digital tools. Although digital artists might find this contentious, it is hard to debate the teams' elegant use of *sfumato*, where objects become subtly softer and blurrier as they recede into the distance, applying a kind of air and light that is at once ethereal and precise.

The painted backdrops came with a drawback: the photoreal cat would appear out of place juxtaposed in front of an oil painting. While animators Tim van Hussen and Matthew Kavanagh made the cat models move, Merel van den Broek and Mirte Tas digitally textured them to appear as walking paintings. But this wasn't enough. Tas drew the contours over the body of every single cat to better blend them into a 2D environment and apply a hand-drawn quality Hulsing (2022) describes as "magical." Assistant Director Nora Hoppener collected a wide variety of reference material for the animators to study, as they abstained from using motion-capture technology for the nonhuman characters (Hulsing 2022). Instead, the animators restricted themselves to acting out behaviors cats are already known to demonstrate, adapting this nh-animal motion to the screen.

Opening on a longshot of a stone cottage in the country, "Dream of a Thousand Cats" positions the audience outside in the twilight, the glow of the window more inviting than what a photograph could allow. Cutting to the interior of the home, the shot positions the camera at kitten's-eye view so the human-animal, Don (David Tennant), appears gargantuan, so much so that the upper frame of the screen cuts him off above the knees ("Dream of a Thousand Cats"). Don reaches down toward the Tabby Kitten (Rosie Day) to put her to bed, prompting the kitten to tuck in her tail and lower her ears, one of many moments in which human pantomime is eschewed in favor of naturalistic feline motion. Barely registering her fear, Don places the kitten in a wicker cat bed, demonstrating the communicative divide between human and nh-animals. This is contrasted by the telepathy the kitten shares with other cats. For example, an adult gray cat (David Gyasi) beckons the Tabby Kitten to join him on a nocturnal sojourn. More shots keep the camera low as the Tabby Kitten makes her escape, dramatizing the alien scale of the human-animal's home environment, such as a daunting climb up the staircase and a vertiginous leap from the second story of their home. Many animal narratives romanticize the power and freedom of the non-human, to allow the human a chance to engage in some imaginative escapism, but "Dream of a Thousand Cats" follows the Tabby Kitten's struggle through what would be an otherwise mundane home rendered expansive by her scale, presenting a space at once familiar yet imposing.

Arriving in a graveyard, the two encounter the Black Cat (Joe Lycett), who wonders about the point of gathering cats together but attends out of curiosity nevertheless. Dozens of cats appear around a tall gravestone shaped like an angel, some hissing and batting at each other to establish seating. These scenes reinforce the cat's fiercely independent nature, mythologizing their aloofness and tendency to affect disinterested curiosity. The cats' bewilderment regarding the point of a public gathering proves especially poignant in a time of hyperindividualism, in which an increasing number of people become "the politically indifferent private person," who embraces living a life of their own rather than forming community (Beck and Beck-Gernsheim 2002, 9). This ideology articulates the ways human-animals interpret feline behavior; ethnographic observation of feral cat communities reveal that cats are social creatures which hunt, sleep, and share meals together (for more information about feral cat communities, see the next essay in this collection, by Sara Misato Aoki). Here the cat functions as a liminal figure, representing independence while providing glimpses of communal possibilities beyond the human-animal imagination.

A blue point Siamese, known as the Prophet (Sandra Oh), steps onto the angel's crown and addresses her audience, backlit by the full moon. She explains to her audience that she used to live as a pet; the film flashes back to a living room with a fireplace flanked by a square-armed sofa on which the Prophet dozes. As her former owner, Paul (Michael Sheen), walks on screen to pet her, she explains in voiceover to her audience that her humans worshiped her. The silhouette of a large tabby cat appears in the reflection of the window; they lock eyes and blink at each other slowly, presenting a complex moment of anthropomorphic layering. Cats developed slow blinking as an interspecies method of communication with human-animals, expressing friendship, but here it stands in for a moment of courtship (Humphrey et al. 2020). Although the animators chose an appropriate expression for their presumably human-animal audience to understand as feline affection, the film does not romanticize their relationship in a manner typical of anthropomorphic depictions of nh-animals. In the next scene, she nurses her kittens inside Paul's closet, her maternal rapture interrupted by Paul bickering with his partner Marion (Anna Lundberg) about keeping the kittens. As he drowns them in the lake, the Prophet describes the agony she felt when they slipped from this world, realizing her subordinated status to the human-animal in that moment. Anat Pick (2011) defines creaturely poetics as texts which highlight the similarities between human and nh-animals by centering the shared vulnerability of our temporal bodies (5). "A Dream of a Thousand Cats" illustrates not only our shared vulnerability to physical harm and death but also our capacity to grieve for the loss of our kin.

The cat, as the chosen subject of the story, reflects our own liminal relationship to the animal as well. Only cohabitating with human-animals beginning around 9,500 years ago, the human-animal desires the cat's domestication yet romanticizes their nightly sojourns (Wade 2007).[3] Feral cats also occupy an unusual intersection between the wild and the domesticated, as many receive food and shelter from human-animals without becoming pets, retaining the status of a denizen free to roam and hunt (as explored in the next essay). Traditionally depicted as a force external to human-animal manipulation, nature, according to hegemonic narratives, must be captured and commodified. Although animals such as the dog and horse have entire historical genres of art dedicated to them, the cat remained in the margins of visual culture prior to the invention of the mechanically reproduced image, likely due to the fact that few would cooperate with an oil painter long enough to capture their sinuous, ever-shifting form on canvas (Galt 2015, 43). Cat imagery proliferated in the modern era, before becoming memes on the internet, tokens of sweetness and innocence to be passed around (Ibid.). In this way, the cat is never itself but is instead an image mediated through presentation and human perception. Whether nh-animals are in a zoo enclosure or the subject of a photograph, nature and culture remain partitioned, and the civilized human-animals are allowed to move freely while the unspeaking nh-animals remain sequestered (Massumi 2014, 66). Like the zoo's displays, which recall natural habitats without recreating them, the nature documentary allows the environmental elements to serve as the frame for the animal, while the audience remains safely remote. Human-animal culture proves replete with pleasures regarding nh-animals, with children's media functionally a cornucopia of anthropomorphic depictions of nh-animals, for example. Household pets, similarly, possess a genuine if somewhat infantilized status in the human-animal household. These pleasures may reinforce this division between nature and culture, as Gilles Deleuze and Félix Guattari (1980) argue, describing individual nh-animals with names and histories as sentimental projections (241). These nonhuman pets allow a kind of playtime in which the human-animal imagines a filial relationship with the nh-animal without acknowledging their differences. These arguments evoke a common criticism regarding anthropomorphism, which some studies suggest leads to inaccurate projections of human-animal characteristics, suggesting such media is a poor method for teaching biological differences (Waxman et al. 2014; Bonus 2019, as cited in Tarłowski and Rybsk 2021, 2).

One could argue that the performances of nh-animals depicted in animation constitute mere pantomime, overlaying human-animal behaviors onto the image of the nonhuman. As Sara Misato Aoki (2024) observes in the next essay, an animated short about talking cats may be "too cartoony" to belong in a collection of otherwise serious narratives, functioning as a "fun" excursion that may delight the audience while failing to take on social meaning. However, Hulsing's aesthetic decisions reflect a delicate balancing act inherent to the depiction of animals in animation, encouraging identification with the creatures through careful stylization, while abstaining from the overly cartoony to discourage over-projection of human-animal sentimentality onto the nh-protagonists. Temple Grandin argues that nh-animals interpret sensory stimuli in a manner similar to neurodivergent human-animals; animators can achieve this perception through the careful observation and reenactment of animal motion (Grandin 2006, as cited in Wells 2009, 36). Anthropomorphic representations of animals may not benefit students learning about the ways human-animals differ from nh-animals, but it is a useful tool for educating others about interspecies similarities (Tarłowski and Rybsk 2021, 8). While animators must work toward anthropomorphism to render the nh-animal intelligible to the human-animal audience, the very language of animation insists on exploring representations of the animal and nature. This is because animation enables the exploration of the inherent distinction and similarity of the animal. Introducing a variety of viewpoints that reconfigure the human-animal-nature relation, more-than-human media makes the mundane strange by exploring perspectives outside anthropocentric perspectives and bending back to render them familiar again (Murphet 2015, 153).

Flashing back to the evening after she lost her kittens, the Prophet prays for justice in front of the fireplace as the embers reflect in her eyes. Cutting to her point of view, the fire in the fireplace begins to morph into trees and hills covered in human skulls, the flames dying back to reveal an ashen plane coated in thick black clouds. Rather than remaining literal, "Dream of a Thousand Cats" attempts to depict what live-action recordings cannot, the nh-animal's reverie. This oneiric logic still follows a human-animal centered understanding of the psyche, however. The Prophet finds herself on a pile of bones, for example, likely an illustration of the psychoanalytic theory that unconscious thoughts remain buried below the surface of conscious reality. A partially skeletonized Crow (Neil Gaiman) acts as a herald for her quest and a harbinger of her many challenges, sending her to a distant mountain where the Cat of Dreams (Tom Sturridge) may offer revelation. This section of the story departs from the "real world," but it also reminds the human-animal about this trait shared with all biological life, the aspiration to not merely survive but flourish (Massumi 2014, 9). After braving the elements and mythological beasts, she reaches the Cat of Dreams, and she is permitted to look into his eyes and receive her reward in the form of a vision within a dream.

The layering of dream states only compounds the surreal quality of the episode's unfolding images, cutting to a cat the size of a school bus lounging with a group of nude women in grooming attendance. At first glance, this appears to be a kind of interspecies Eden, but at night, a cat resembling the Tabby Kitten chases a human, playfully tossing him in the air a few times before catching him in his mouth with a sickly crunch. A shot of the full moon cross fades to the sun. A man stands in front of it, proselytizing to his fellow human-animals that if enough dream of a new world, it will come into existence. Standing on the edge of a low cliff, the composition mirrors the scene in which the Prophet speaks to her audience of cats. The film augments its oneiric narrative through the use of visual motifs tied to mythological imagery, such as the moon for the feminine Prophet and cats, versus the masculine sun with the human-animal standing under its rays. His vision comes to pass and the trees in the forest morph into skyscrapers, the cat on-screen shrinks as human-animals sprout clothing. A speeding car forces the now diminutive cat to leap out of its path, avoiding the feet of oncoming pedestrians as she tucks her tail under her body in terror, illustrating the many dangers nh-animals face in a world dominated by human-animals. The dream of human-animal dominance has come true, or rather, it was and always will be true until enough other creatures can dream something else.

The Anthropocene is a temporality caught up in industrialization and the apparent inevitability of technological progress, but "Dream of a Thousand Cats" argues this period took form through a collective desire for human-animals to flourish. The strange temporality of the dream highlights the ways myths and legends distort the past, rendering human-animals alienated from nature while prognostications regarding the end of human-animal dominance become a scotoma of the collective imagination. Most narratives about the Anthropocene center on criticizing ecocidal hegemony, presenting a facts-to-outrage structure that regrettably fails to open avenues for creative solutions or suggest the possibility for transformation. Notoriously, capitalism often finds ways to incorporate criticism into its market, in which dystopia represents conforming to global capitalist hegemonic practices, suggesting there can be no alternative (Oziewicz 2022, 4). At the same time, "Dream of a Thousand Cats" scrutinizes the power relations of non-human/human-animals through a juxtaposition of ordinary and oneiric scenes, presenting imagery intended to inspire critical reflection on pet-ownership, rather than a straightforward criticism of specific power-structures. In this way, the episode slips into the gaps between a polemic and pop-cultural commodity, like a cat making do in a world where the human-animal dominates.

Walking alongside the Cat of Dreams, the Prophet learns that she must spread her message as the two ascend toward the opening of the cave, through which she steps and awakens, departing from her home to begin her quest. The episode offers no simple solution for her; while those in power need only exist within the dream to maintain it, those without power must cultivate grassroots support. Before she can enter the cave, the stone guardians warn her that every dream has a price, hinting that every hope for a new future comes with the burden of expressing or enacting it and the many risks that may entail. But it is promised that this combination of dream and enactment, theory and praxis, may one day bring about a new beginning, an outcome human-animals may or may not be around for to appreciate.

As the Tabby Kitten and the Gray Cat return from their session in the graveyard to the kitten's domicile, the little one asks if the dream could really manifest. The Gray Cat responds, "I'd like to see anyone, prophet, god, or king, make a thousand cats do anything at the same time." The cat's reputation for self-reliance becomes a metaphor for the human-animal's political struggle in an era of rugged individualism, but this independence is also treated as an asset, as the Cat of Dreams warmly observes that "a cat may look at a king." This refusal to acknowledge status, wealth, or power renders the cat immune to the posturing that leads human-animals astray, reducing the problem of liberation to simply making the case to a large-enough audience.

At home, Don and his wife Laura Lynn (Georgia Tennant) notice the Tabby Kitten twitching in her sleep. Don wonders what cats dream about, echoing the opening scene in which the desires of the Tabby Kitten remain obscure to her owner, and the audience is left to speculate as the camera cuts close on her to mirror the scene in which a tabby cat caught and ate a man. As she sleeps, her meow deepens to a jungle cat's before she chomps down on the imaginary subject. "Dream of a Thousand Cats" presents the twist that the familiar cuddly pet remains a predator first and foremost, their dreams representing a frontier that has fascinated writer and poet alike.[4] Inscribing new meaning onto nh-animals is possible in human-animal symbolic culture because of the changing and conflicting ways we view other species. In *Manwatching*, Desmond Morris (1977) suggests, "Man has viewed other species of animals in many lights. He looked upon them as predators, prey, pests, partners, and pets. He has exploited them economically, studied them aesthetically, and exaggerated them symbolically" (260). This succinct explanation illustrates some of the many symbolic positions animals occupy in human-animal culture, in which shared narratives serve as the inspiration for what an animal is and what that means. Cats, for example, are often depicted as cruel hunters in opposition to an innocent mouse or bird protagonist, dramatizing the tension between predatory animals and the prey they consume. They take on the qualities of a swarm in animated media depicting stereotypical crazy cat ladies and become pests when their population outdoors goes unchecked, contributing to the global extinction of birds while attracting more dangerous predators like coyotes (Dauphine and Cooper 2009, 210, and Aoki 2024). Cats enjoy a special privilege among nh-animals because of their status as "pest-destroyers" (Morris 1977, 260) and sustain emotional bonds formed between pets in the domestic setting. "Dream of a Thousand Cats" follows them throughout many of these roles, contrasting the cat across their symbolic positions, beginning with the familiar pet. Paul prizes his blue point Siamese because her pedigree carries economic and cultural value, but her mixed kittens are regarded as pests to be discarded. The episode concludes with a meditation on the cat as predator, problematizing their supposedly domesticated status in the first place.

It is imperative to adapt and fabricate new narratives to interrupt the ongoing monologue about capitalism and eternal progress, in favor of interspecies dialogue centered on the diverse organisms living on the planet. Myths and legends have long explored heroism, power, and identity, and "Dream of a Thousand Cats" does this through the eyes of the nh-animal to criticize human/nonhuman-animal relations and to speculate about unknown futures. This episode combines mythological imagery and animation to enhance its oneiric qualities while centering on the cats, making new relations to our nonhuman-animal kith imaginable. "Dream of a Thousand Cats" allows for greater empathic connection on behalf of human-animals, because the episode's animation reveals the nuances of feline form and motion, allowing the audience to imaginatively enfold themselves into narratives which give voice to the nh-animal. This "more-than-human" story delivers a message of increasing urgency in an era defined by intensifying ecological crises amidst petrochemical strangulation, while also serving an important political function. A study on the relationship between the belief in human evolution and bigotry indicated that believing in evolution was positively related to the participant's perceived similarity to nh-animals and negatively associated with prejudice, racism, and negative intergroup attitudes, even when controlling for religious beliefs, political views, and other demographic variables (Syropoulos et al. 2023). A civilization that becomes ecologically aware will likely also become a more just one, but this can only come to pass through stories that address the Anthropocene with counternarratives that give voice to nh-animals, allowing collective dreams to shape lived realities.

Dominant cultural narratives re-establish the mythological conquest of nature by civilization, in which human-animals must compete with nature to commodify it into fungible resources. These myths have enabled a wide range of racist, colonialist, and imperialist perspectives that imagine the human-animal as removed from nature, as an observer detached from a physical world. The various emergencies brought about by climate change and loss of biodiversity demand that these myths receive scrutiny, and more-than-human narratives represent a valid method for challenging ecocidal fatalism. The Prophet's revelation suggests that the success of the human-animal is always razor thin, as we are only a few dreamers away from finding ourselves in a new world altogether, illustrating a political reality through the language of myth. While a warning, "Dream of a Thousand Cats" retains the hopeful note that change is only a vision away, provided enough share it, reminding humanity that they are not the only animal that dreams of a better future, and challenging them to imagine a reality in which human and nonhuman-animal life can flourish on earth together.

Notes

1. Eric S. Jenkins (2014) coined the term *animistic mimesis* to describe a character's capacity to allow the subject to enfold themselves imaginatively and affectively into the sensations of the character as if subject and object were one (8). This is how animation produces a wondrous sensation, in which everything is explainable yet what unfolds defies explanation, hovering on the edge of the uncanny valley.
2. The narrative arc *Dream Country* contained four standalone issues: "Calliope," "A Dream of a Thousand Cats," "A Midsummer Night's Dream," and "Façade."
3. In contrast, Larson et al. argue that the dog was domesticated in Europe 16,000 years ago, while Germonpré et al. (2009) have found dog bones dating back to approximately 30,000 BC.
4. Gaiman may have been inspired by the poem "Cat" by J.R.R. Tolkien, published in *The Adventures of Tom Bombadil* (2014): "The fat cat on the mat / may seem to dream / of nice mice that suffice [...] his kin, lean and slim, / or deep in den / in the East feasted on beasts / and tender men."

References

Amidi, Amid. 2018. "Top Disney Executive Believes Disney's New 'Lion King' Isn't Animation or Live-Action." Cartoon Brew. December 28. https://www.cartoonbrew.com/ideas-commentary/top-disney-executive-believes-disneys-new-lion-king-isnt-animation-or-live-action-168342.html.
Bazin, André, and Hugh R. Gray. 1960. "The Ontology of the Photographic Image." *Film Quarterly* 13 (4): 4–9. https://doi.org/10.2307/1210183.
Beck, Ulrich, and Elisabeth Beck-Gemsheim. 2002. *Individualization: Institutionalized Individualism and Its Social and Political Consequences*. Sage.
Berland, Jody. 2008. "Cat and Mouse." *Cultural Studies* 22 (3–4): 431–54. https://doi.org/10.1080/09502380802012559.
Bonus, James Alex. 2019. "The Impact of Pictorial Realism in Educational Science Television on U.S. Children's Learning and Transfer of Biological Facts." *Journal of Children and Media* 13 (4): 433–51. https://doi.org/10.1080/17482798.2019.1646295.
Chang, Justin. 2023. "Is It See-Worthy? The New 'Little Mermaid' Is Not That Bad ... but Also Not That Good." NPR. May 26. https://www.npr.org/2023/05/26/1177917346/the-little-mermaid-review-remake-disney-halle-bailey.
Dauphiné, Nico, and Robert G. Cooper. 2009. "Impacts of Free-Ranging Domestic Cats (*Felis catus*) on Birds in the United States: A Review of Recent Research with Conservation and Management Recommendations." *Proceedings of the Fourth International Partners in Flight Conference: Tundra to Tropics*. September 25. http://abcbirds.org/abcprograms/policy/cats/pdf/impacts_of_free_ranging_domestic_cats.pdf.
Gaiman, Neil, David S. Goyer, and Allan Heinberg, creators. 2022. *Sandman*. Season 1. Netflix.
Galt, Rosalind. 2015. "Cats and the Moving Image: Feline Cinematicity from Lumière to Maru." In *Animal Life and the Moving Image*, edited by Michael S. Lawrence and Laura MacMahon, 42–54. British Film Institute. https://doi.org/10.5040/9781838711467.

George, Joe. 2022. "The Sandman: What Is 'A Dream of a Thousand Cats' and 'Calliope'?" *Den of Geek*. August 22. https://www.denofgeek.com/tv/the-sandman-what-is-a-dream-of-a-thousand-cats-and-calliope/.

Germonpré, Mietje, Mikhail V. Sablin, Rhiannon E. Stevens, Robert E. M. Hedges, Michael Hofreiter, Mathias Stiller, and Viviane R. Després. 2009. "Fossil Dogs and Wolves from Palaeolithic Sites in Belgium, the Ukraine and Russia: Osteometry, Ancient DNA and Stable Isotopes." *Journal of Archaeological Science* 36 (2): 473–90. https://doi.org/10.1016/j.jas.2008.09.033.

Grandin, Temple, and Catherine L. Johnson. 2005. *Animals in Translation: Using the Mysteries of Autism to Decode Animal Behavior*. Simon & Schuster. http://ci.nii.ac.jp/ncid/BA74297737.

Griffin, Donald R. 2001. *Animal Minds: Beyond Cognition to Consciousness*. University of Chicago Press.

Guattari, Félix, and Gilles Deleuze. 1980. *A Thousand Plateaus: Capitalism and Schizophrenia*. University of Minnesota Press.

Hosea, Birgitta. 2019. "Made by Hand." In *The Crafty Animator: Handmade, Craft-Based Animation and Cultural Value*, edited by Paul Ward and Caroline Ruddell, 17–45. Palgrave Macmillan. http://research.aub.ac.uk/id/eprint/131/.

Hulsing, Hisko. 2022. "Anatomy of a Shot: 'A Dream of a Thousand Cats' from 'The Sandman.'" *Animation Magazine*. August 6. https://www.animationmagazine.net/2022/08/anatomy-of-a-shot-a-dream-of-a-thousand-cats-from-the-sandman-exclusive/.

Humphrey, Tasmin, Faye Stringer, Leanne Proops, and Karen McComb. 2020. "Slow Blink Eye Closure in Shelter Cats Is Related to Quicker Adoption." *Animals* 10 (12): 2256. https://doi.org/10.3390/ani10122256.

Jenkins, Eric S. 2014. *Special Affects: Cinema, Animation and the Translation of Consumer Culture*. http://ci.nii.ac.jp/ncid/BB18525628.

Jouvet, Michel. 1979. "What Does a Cat Dream About?" *Trends in Neurosciences* 2 (January): 280–82. https://doi.org/10.1016/0166-2236(79)90110-3.

Larson, Greger, Elinor K. Karlsson, Angela R. Perri, Matthew T. Webster, Simon Y.W. Ho, Joris Peters, Peter D. Stahl, Philip J. Piper, Frode Lingaaas, Merete Fredholm, et al. 2012. "Rethinking Dog Domestication by Integrating Genetics, Archeology, and Biogeography." *Proceedings of the National Academy of Sciences of the United States of America* 109 (23): 8878–83. https://doi.org/10.1073/pnas.1203005109.

Lawrence, Michael S., and Laura MacMahon. 2015. "Introduction." In *Animal Life and the Moving Image*, 1–27. London: British Film Institute. https://doi.org/10.5040/9781838711467.

Lévi-Strauss, Claude. 1963. *Totemism*. Merlin Press.

Massumi, Brian. 2014. *What Animals Teach Us about Politics*. Duke University Press. https://doi.org/10.1215/9780822376057.

Morris, Desmond. 1977. *Manwatching: A Field Guide to Human Behavior*. http://ci.nii.ac.jp/ncid/BA14024237.

Murphet, Julian. 2015. "King Kong Capitalism." In *Animal Life and the Moving Image*, edited by Michael S. Lawrence and Laura MacMahon, 153–71. British Film Institute. https://doi.org/10.5040/9781838711467.

Oziewicz, Marek. 2023. "Introduction: The Choice We Have in the Stories We Tell." In *Fantasy and Myth in the Anthropocene: Imagining Futures and Dreaming Hope in Literature and Media*, edited by Marek Oziewicz, Brian Attenbery, and Tereza Dědinová, 1–13. Bloomsbury.

Pick, Anat. 2011. *Creaturely Poetics: Animality and Vulnerability in Literature and Film*. Columbia University Press.

Popov, Alexander. 2022. "Staying with the Singularity: Narrators and More-Than-Human Mythologies." In *Fantasy and Myth in the Anthropocene: Imagining Futures and Dreaming Hope in Literature and Media*, edited by Marek Oziewicz, Brian Attebery, and Tereza Dědinová, 41–54. Bloomsbury.

Stolworthy, Jacob. 2023. "The Little Mermaid's Flounder and Sebastian Posters Lampooned by Film Fans." *The Independent*. April 28. https://www.independent.

co.uk/arts-entertainment/films/news/flounder-poster-the-little-mermaid-b2328603.html.

Stone, Sam. 2022. "The Sandman: Hisko Hulsing Delivers a Gorgeous Adaptation of *A Dream of a Thousand Cats*." CBR. August 24. https://www.cbr.com/sandman-hisko-hulsing-interview/.

Tarlowski, Andrzej, and Eliza Rybska. 2021. "Young Children's Inductive Inferences within Animals Are Affected by Whether Animals Are Presented Anthropomorphically in Films." *Frontiers in Psychology* 12 (June): 634809. https://doi.org/10.3389/fpsyg.2021.634809.

Thompson, Kristin, and David Bordwell. 2003. *Film History: An Introduction*. 2nd ed. McGraw-Hill. http://ci.nii.ac.jp/ncid/BA59757412.

Tolkien, J.R.R. 2014. *The Adventures of Tom Bombadil*. HarperCollins.

Wade, Nicholas. 2007. "Study Traces Cat's Ancestry to Middle East." *New York Times*. June 29. https://www.nytimes.com/2007/06/29/science/29cat.html.

Waxman, Sandra R., Patricia A. Herrmann, Jennie Woodring, and Douglas L. Medin. 2014. "Humans (Really) Are Animals: Picture-Book Reading Influences 5-Year-Old Urban Children's Construal of the Relation between Humans and Non-human Animals." *Frontiers in Psychology* 5 (March). https://doi.org/10.3389/fpsyg.2014.00172.

Wells, Paul. 2009. *The Animated Bestiary*. Rutgers University Press.

A Cat of a Thousand Dreams
A Research Assistant's Perspective

Sara Misato Aoki

Field Notes 2/5/23: When the feeder whistles, cats come in droves, slipping out from behind dumpsters, alleyways, and abandoned warehouses. The feeder looks akin to an urban Snow White, with one orange cat rubbing along her ankles as about sixty other cats mill about, meowing. I am collecting ethnographic research for the Feral Cats Project, part of the Labyrinth Project, headed by Dr. Christopher Kelty, a Professor at the Institute for Society and Genetics at UCLA. Currently, I am in Los Angeles at the feral cat colony that resides in the overlooked spaces between Washington and 10th, right off the 10 freeway. I will remain here for the better part of two hours writing down my observations. My research aims to better understand human-cat interactions and cat-cat interactions and to get a glimpse into the incredibly complex lives of feral cats.

This essay is not a typical literary essay, nor is it a typical research paper. Much like the creatures I observe as a research assistant, this essay will deftly wander, from the sciences to the humanities and back again, among my own field notes and research and Neil Gaiman's stories, before curling around *Sandman*'s most curious episode, "Dream of a Thousand Cats." As a cat lover and researcher, I was immediately drawn to Gaiman's feline characters when I first encountered his work. Initially, it was easy to assume that these characters were simply the result of his love of cats. It's obvious from his online writing, published stories, and film and TV adaptations that he loves animals, and in particular, cats, fiercely. But it is also easy to see that, with their long history, elusive behavior, capacity for world-walking, and mysterious relationships, cats make for appealing, complex characters. Gaiman's cats are a homage to the multifaceted nature of felines.

Cats have long been a subject of deep fascination for many people. Their role in human culture and imagination dates as far back as 2890 BCE with legends of the Egyptian cat goddess, Bast (Nikolajeva 2009). At the time, cats were revered and respected in temple spaces across Egypt, and the ancient Egyptians mistakenly believed that cats were close descendants of reptiles (Nikolajeva 2009). Over time, our understanding of cats has evolved both in terms of science (including feline anatomy and behavior) as well as terms of culture (how we think and write about cats and consider their meaning in our lives). The impact of long term scientific and cultural investments in cats has resulted in a comprehensive understanding of domestic cat biology down to a molecular level. Their entire genome has been completely sequenced, with information on the specific single nucleotide polymorphisms that contribute to breed variety and appearance widely available (O'Brien et al. 2008). Yet even as we learn more and more about their biology, cat behavior is still not fully understood. Anthropologically, they remain an enigma. This may point to cats' long literary history as symbols used by writers and storytellers. Historically, the cat has been synonymous with both good and evil, closely associated with witchcraft, Satanism, rodent control, and also viewed as a beloved, if independent, pet (Nikolajeva 2009). Modern literature often depicts cats as mystical guides (Nikolajeva 2009), with famous examples including the heroic Puss in Boots, the enigmatic Cheshire Cat, Harry Potter's Crookshanks (a pet only Hermione could love), and the newest members of the feline family: Neil Gaiman's literary cats. Still, so much about cats remains a mystery. Indeed, in order to properly appreciate the complexity of cats in research and literature, we must follow the lead of the cats themselves, and allow our research and analysis to wander and explore.

There are dozens of cats that make brief appearances in Gaiman's stories, but perhaps the most prominent examples appear in the novella *Coraline*, the short story "The Price," and *Sandman* issue #18, "Dream of a Thousand Cats," which has just been adapted for the Netflix TV series. These cats occupy a peculiar space, embodying some of the more traditional cat tropes while also aligning with some real-world behaviors observed in feral cat research. Gaiman's cats transcend singular feline qualities to become complex characters that alter the course of his stories.

Field Notes 1/17/23: As dusk settles, I wait in front of the StorQuest Self Storage on National Blvd in Los Angeles. Slowly, they begin to creep out. The shades of their coats vary—from a pale ginger to a deep, inky black. The small black kitten, no more than a few weeks old, closely follows a larger black tom. He stops in front of a gray tabby to touch noses in greeting. They eat, sleep, and hunt together.

Literary depictions of cats, particularly feral ones, reinforce the notion of cats as solitary, aloof, independent creatures (Nikolajeva 2009). Gaiman's depictions of cats tend to play off this trope as well. For example, in *Coraline*, the unnamed black cat, arguably the most famous of all Gaiman's cats, is portrayed as a loner, and the 2009 stop-motion film adaptation directed by Henry Selick notes that he is feral. The black cat is described as "irritatingly self-centered" (Gaiman 2006, 34), the embodiment of the conventional egotistical, independent cat. This fits with the common perception of cats, but in reality, extensive research has demonstrated that the opposite is true: cats are deeply social creatures with complex friendships and relationships (Vitale et al. 2022). Indeed, cats tend to congregate in groups and make deliberate choices to be social with other cats and humans (Vitale et al. 2022). My experience and research with stray cats have reinforced the importance of cat social relationships; the cats we observe live in groups upward of ten to fifteen. In fact, our cat observations are largely centered around recording cat-cat interactions to better understand their complicated relationships. Over time, I have witnessed many intricacies of cat dynamics. For example, I observed one cat that would selectively swat at certain cats, but completely ignore others.

Even before Netflix adapted *Sandman*, the "Dream of a Thousand Cats" issue had a certain notoriety among fans for its unusual nature. This issue, illustrated by Kelley Jones and Malcolm Jones III, was collected as part of the *Dream Country* narrative arc, published alongside a tale of a suicidal woman with superhero powers, a story about a Greek muse held captive for inspiration, and an adaptation of a Shakespeare play that became the only comic to win a World Fantasy Award for Best Short Story. It was an unlikely place for an entire story about cats. In a culture that makes jokes about "crazy cat ladies," it is perhaps even more unlikely that Netflix would choose to adapt this issue for the television series, especially since it is a "one shot" story that can easily be skipped without affecting the main plot.

But the episode, like the cats themselves, has more going on than initially meets the eye. Clearly, the creators behind this episode took the process of adapting it very seriously, investing a great deal of creative energy into a story "just" about cats. The cast is stacked with award-winning actors, including Sandra Oh, as well as actors visiting from other Gaiman adaptations, including James McAvoy (Morpheus for Audible's *Sandman*), Michael Sheen (Lucifer in Audible's *Sandman* and Aziraphale in *Good Omens* for Amazon Prime), and David Tennant (Crowley in *Good Omens* and the Tenth Doctor from *Doctor Who*—featured in an episode written by Gaiman, "The Doctor's Wife"). And there's an early clue that this story is near and dear to Gaiman's heart: he provides a cameo as the voice of the Crow/Skull Bird.

The story embraces the intricacies of cat relationships and social dynamics, presenting an animal prophet who encourages others to dream of a world free from human control. The Siamese prophet (Sandra Oh) is familiar with human brutality; her owners drowned her kittens because they were not purebred. After the death of her kittens, the Siamese cat vowed to travel across the world, advocating for radical change to the human-cat hierarchy. For the Siamese cat, change starts with dreaming of a world where cats are not at the mercy of humans.

"Dream of a Thousand Cats" features many different cats gathering in a graveyard at night. Cats have long been associated with graveyards due to their shared associations with witchcraft, death, and darkness (Łogożna-Wypyc 2018). And beyond the imaginative reasons, there are in fact well-documented, practical reasons that real cats favor graveyards. Hollywood Forever, the iconic Los Angeles cemetery where many actors, musicians, and celebrities have been laid to rest, is home to five cat colonies containing hundreds of cats. At sixty-two acres, containing a pond and many trees in an otherwise dense urban area, Hollywood Forever is attractive to cat colonies because of the abundance of available prey and relatively protected open space. Similar to the cats in "Dream of a Thousand Cats," the free-roaming Hollywood Forever cats have dynamic relationships and social hierarchies (Vitale et al. 2022).

Field Notes 3/17/23: Tonight, I am observing an atypical pair of stray cats. They have been named Fred and Ginger by the residents of the apartment building at the intersection of National and Cheviot Place. Although Fred and Ginger are technically stray cats, they spend their days sunning on soft outdoor beds and eating wet food provided by the tenants of the building. I watch as Fred and Ginger swat and hiss at Penny, a domesticated cat owned by the landlord of the building.

"Dream of a Thousand Cats" presents interesting interactions between feral and domestic cats. The Siamese cat forms an intimate relationship with a stray tom cat, and eventually, they have kittens. She has a deep, loving attachment to her kittens, vowing to teach them to hunt and love. Unbeknownst to the cat, her human owners are furious. Because the kittens aren't purebred, they're worthless to the owners. Her owners drown her kittens, leaving her heartbroken and distraught. The male owner (James McAvoy) tries to rationalize his horrific action by saying he's doing the Siamese cat a favor, relieving her from the burden of kittens.

From a literary perspective, this interaction highlights the contrast between freedom and captivity. The tom cat is the epitome of freedom, separate from humanity and the responsibility of parenthood. On the other hand, the Siamese cat sits in a gray area; although she has reproductive freedom and the tom cat was her "choice for lover" (Gaiman 1990, #18), she has no choice when her kittens are taken from her. She had no power, no autonomy, and no control when her humans deemed her kittens "worth diddly squat." Her sense of freedom and choice was an illusion.

From a research perspective, there are several noteworthy components to this interaction. The first is that both the orange tom cat and the Siamese cat are able to reproduce, so they have not been spayed or neutered. Research estimates that around 80 percent of all domesticated cats living in households are spayed (Chu et al. 2009). Most states in the U.S. require new pet owners to spay or neuter their cats before they are allowed to bring them home unless they have applied for a special breeding permit (Chu et al. 2009). However, the Siamese cat's prestigious pedigree may have contributed to the absence of spaying; given her owners' anger at her "mongrel" kittens, they likely intended to use her for breeding.

The importance of spaying and neutering is part of a much larger conversation about cat management. Cats reproduce quickly and frequently, leading to several negative consequences, both for the cats themselves and for the environment they inhabit. These worries are primarily centered around non-neutered and spayed stray cats, as their populations can quickly grow when unchecked. There are an estimated thirty to forty million stray cats in the United States (Chu et al. 2009). The former, non-spayed house cat in the story, is somewhat unusual by today's standards, but the depiction of the stray tom cat certainly tracks. Currently, the number of neutered stray cats hovers at around 3 percent. The number may be even lower; it can be very hard to keep track of feral cat numbers especially if they are not dependent on feeders for food (Chu et al. 2009).

In an effort to curb cat populations, some cities, like Los Angeles, have tried to promote robust trap, neuter, and return (TNR) operations with varying levels of success. Indeed, the debate around TNR's ability to manage Los Angeles' cat population is raging. Recent media reports paint a complicated picture: although TNR can be successful on a local level, its impact on total cat population is questionable, with even Los Angeles city officials expressing doubts about TNR's effectiveness (Franzen 2023). Beyond cat welfare, there are a number of added variables too consider: feral cats can have devastating impact on native wildlife populations, carry disease, and attract more dangerous predators to local neighborhoods, like coyotes.

These numbers and the speed of reproduction have been corroborated by my own observations. Over a few weeks, I saw the number of cats in one of our colonies jump from eight to fifteen cats. None of the cats in this colony have been spayed or neutered; we spotted three new kittens and one pregnant cat the last time we visited. The colony is growing with no signs of slowing or stopping. Beyond the insight that "Dream of a Thousand Cats" offers on stray cat reproduction, it also reinforces how little we know about cats and their secret lives. The Siamese cat's owners misinterpret her feelings, believing that these kittens were not her choice. They assume they know what she wants, and clearly, that they know best. This reflects the human tendency to prioritize themselves as the smartest entities at the top of the food chain, and the way they fail to recognize intelligence in animals. The callousness of the man's actions and disregard for the life of the kittens is emblematic of larger patterns.

In research, I spend weeks trying to glean information from small gestures and movements between stray cats and am still far from understanding cat-cat relationships. Even in the literature on cat behavior, there are many experts that remain perplexed. We are using observations to make inferences and well-informed guesses. Despite centuries of cat research, they are a mystery.

Field Notes 3/5/23: Tonight, at the corner of Wills and Lull, there are only seven cats that emerge. This colony is known to be particularly skittish, only coming out when they see one specific feeder, a young, middle-school-aged girl. One of the older feeders hangs back. When I ask her why she is remaining behind, she informs me that the colony does not trust her. She has trapped and neutered almost all the cats present, and if she approaches them, they will flee. They remember her and their brush with caged life.

"Dream of a Thousand Cats" also sheds light on human-cat interactions. The episode raises an interesting question of trust and freedom, with the Siamese cat declaring she was once "in the thrall of human beings: plaything, possession, and toy" (Gaiman, 1990, #18). She exchanged food, comfort, and warmth for her freedom. Then, she regretted it. In this scene, there is particular emphasis on the trust that was formed over food. In research, most of the connections formed with stray cat populations begin with food. Veteran feeders recommend starting with distanced interactions and letting the cats become accustomed to a human presence before making contact. Dona Cosgrove Baker, a veteran feeder and founder of Feral Cat Caretakers Coalition, an LA-based TNR organization, suggests using a tentative, food-inspired bond with the cats to trap and neuter them. However, once the cat has been trapped, the trusting relationship completely evaporates. Like the Siamese cat with her former owners, stray cats remember their former captors. Although there is no formal research that has been conducted on the bond between a feeder and a stray cat, the general understanding among the local feeder population is that the bond is very delicate. For example, cats in a colony located in Koreatown will only emerge when they hear the specific sputtering noise made by the very old truck that one of the feeders drives. He reports that the cats will not come out if he drives a different car. Even around him, the cats are very skittish and will flee at the first sign of outside human presence. These cats are so hesitant to trust that even their feeder cannot establish a relationship with them.

Gaiman's black cat in *Coraline* also exhibits some interesting human-cat behavior. In this novel, the black cat acts as a guide for Coraline, a young girl, fighting against an otherworldly force, her Other Mother. The Other Mother has imprisoned Coraline's real family in a different dimension known as the Other World, trying to trap Coraline forever. The black cat is able to travel between Coraline's world and the Other World, helping Coraline craft a plan to get her life back. Although the black cat communicates through speech with Coraline in the Other World, in her "real" world he cannot talk. Instead, the cat "talks" to Coraline in a series of slow blinks, an action that Coraline interprets "as a yes" (Gaiman 2006, 46). This is not that far from the way that domestic cats communicate with owners in real life. Research has demonstrated that cats employ different forms of eye movement in order to communicate with humans (Humphrey et al. 2020). In fact, the slow blink seen in Coraline's cat is the same blink used by cats to communicate with humans in a positive way (Humphrey et al. 2020). In the past, cat-human communication went largely ignored due to preconceived, incorrect notions about cats' preference for independence (Humphrey et al. 2020). However, researchers found that when humans directed a slow blink toward cats, cats that slowly blinked in response were friendlier and more likely to approach the human (Humphrey et al. 2020). It turns out Gaiman's use of nonverbal cat movements in *Coraline* surprisingly aligns well with actual cat communication.

Field Notes 2/27/23: Tonight, I can only see a few cats. I am in South LA, waiting on the 57th Avenue post–6 p.m. cat colony feeding. Soon after finishing the food in the bowls, the cats began to disperse. Out of curiosity, I follow a small, striped cat. It walks along a concrete pipe, only pausing briefly to glance at me before disappearing into a crevice where I cannot follow.

During observational research, cats often disappear. They slip into narrow crevices, between bars, crossing boundaries with ease. Even in the household, most cats are easily able to shift between domestic life and free-roaming life when they get the chance (Wandesforde-Smith et al. 2021). They jaunt back and forth as they please, spending time indoors and outdoors. They dine on prey and human-supplied cat food. Cats are beyond restrictions. Even in research, they are regarded as an inherently semi-wild species, always at the intersection of domesticated and untamed (Wandesforde-Smith et al. 2021).

Gaiman has leaned into cats' ability to transverse between spaces, fully building on and expanding this quality in his literary cats. The most obvious example is his black cat in *Coraline*. When Coraline asks the cat how it managed to move between dimensions, the cat replies matter-of-factly, "I walked" (Gaiman 2006, 41). Coraline attempts to monitor the cat's movements and finds that when she goes to check the location she thought the cat went, "the cat was gone" (Gaiman 2006, 42). Indeed, Gaiman's cat is able to travel beyond the limits of human understanding.

Gaiman's black cat in *Coraline* is not the only one of his cats to cross boundaries. In "Dream of a Thousand Cats," the Siamese cat travels from reality into the "heart of the dreamworld" (Gaiman 1990 #18). The residents of the Dreaming are incredulous, impressed that this small cat was able to achieve such a feat. Throughout the narrative, characters refer to the Siamese as a "walker" and she even calls herself a "walker in the night places" (24). Similar to the black cat in *Coraline*, the Siamese transverses realms by walking. Indeed, Gaiman's literary cats are world walkers, similar to cats traversing through hidden spaces and doorways in our world.

In my own research, I work with cats that have been trapped, neutered, and released. These cats occupy an interesting intersection between captivity and freedom. They know what it is like to be free, to be trapped and physically altered, and released into their old environment. Even though their environment stays the same, the cats change. They experience hormonal behavior changes that come from spaying and neutering and afterwards, feeders report that these cats are less likely to hunt and are more inclined to rely on humans for food. Indeed, these cats are technically "free" but spaying/neutering has taken away their freedom to make certain choices. Their personalities will be forever changed.

Joe Federico, the founder of Stray Paws Animal Haven, has noted additional behavioral changes he has observed in cats pre/post-catch and release. According to Federico, cats were much less aggressive in terms of hunting and mating after TNR, and these cats appear "sharper" and better equipped to survive in the wild. The research seems to support Joe's observations: some studies have shown that neutered/spayed cats are less stressed and aggressive (Finkler and Terkel 2010). Can humans control the "wildness" in cats, altering their territorial, mating, and social behavior, by spaying and neutering? Surprisingly, based on Joe's observations, it would seem that the more humans try to tame the "wildness" in feral cats (like spaying and neutering to reduce territorial behaviors), the better equipped that cat actually is to survive in the wild.

Field Notes 2/28/23: I have been waiting here for an hour, hoping to catch sight of the kittens that normally play in the foliage behind the bars. Finally, I see a tiny black kitten. As I watch, it pounces on something—possibly a rodent or a litter mate's tail. It is no more than three months old, a small hunter in training.

The black cat has long been associated with bad luck, a phenomenon known as "black cat bias" (Jones and Hart 2020). In his short story "The Price," Gaiman subverts this stereotype, casting his unnamed black cat in the role of savior, battling evil to protect his human family. The story begins with the human protagonist encountering a new visitor, a black cat that appears at their house one night. The black cat goes unnamed, simply known as the Black Cat. Despite being feral, the animal is "well-fed … jaunty … very friendly" (Gaiman 1998, 1), at odds with typical descriptions of black cats as mangy or demonic. At night, the Black Cat faces "The Devil," protecting the main character's family. The Black Cat sustains significant injuries with every encounter, and it is implied that the cat is protecting the family at great cost to itself, leaving the main character "wonder[ing] what we did to deserve [him]" (3). The cats in this story have an autobiographical basis. Gaiman writes about the unnamed Black Cat's relationship with Princess, Furball, Hermione, and Pod—all real cats in Gaiman's life that he frequently blogs about (Gaiman 2023). In the past, Gaiman has blogged about the power of cats and the fierce love they inspire. He has written about loving Princess's ferocious spirit, Zoe's unconditional affection, Pod's uncertainty, and Hermione's craziness. His animals have taught him many lessons and comforted him in dark times. Perhaps "The Price" is a tribute to the power of cats; the Black Cat protects against a visible demon while his other cats help him fend off invisible ones.

The most interesting comparisons "The Price" brings up are not found in research but in culture. In Western culture, the color black has many negative connotations, with links to evil and death (Jones and Hart 2020). Due to these superstitions, research shows black cats have a much harder time getting adopted and are euthanized more frequently (Jones and Hart 2020).

Tracing this bias, these associations may stem from racism directed toward people with darker skin tones (Jones and Hart 2020). On the contrary, many other cultures and religions deeply respect and admire black cats for their perceived luck and prosperity. For example, black cats are considered symbols of protection and luck in Japan. Despite cultural perceptions of black cats, research shows that there are no color-associated personality differences among cat populations (Anwar 2020).

The black cat figure appears in several Gaiman stories. For example, the cat guide in *Coraline* is also described as "a large black cat" (Gaiman 2006, 39). Like the Black Cat in "The Price," the Coraline's cat guide is a protective force. When Coraline was in danger with the Other Mother, the cat guide attacked with "claws flailing, teeth bared, fierce and angry" (Gaiman 2006, 121). Coraline and the cat guide face the Other Mother together; without the cat guide's help, Coraline would have been unprepared to fight the Other Mother. The Other Mother is a dark and ancient spirit, rather like the Devil in "The Price."

Like the Black Cat in "The Price," the cat guide in *Coraline* also goes unnamed. Even when prompted, the cat guide simply says, "Cats don't have names" (Gaiman 2006, 40). Cats do not need names because "[cats] know who we are" (41). The Black Cat is the only cat in "The Price" that does not have a name. Without a name tying the black cat to a specific story, an interesting possibility emerges. Both of Gaiman's black cats are unnamed, notorious world-walkers, and face off against demon-like characters. It is not out of question to wonder whether these black cats are the same cat, waltzing between Gaiman's stories similar to the way they walk between worlds. Regardless of the merit behind this theory, Gaiman has written two powerful black cat characters that challenge traditional black cat stereotypes.

Gaiman's depiction of the black cat falls in line with non–Western interpretations of the black cat as a protective force. It rejects the evil harbinger trope black cats are often forced to embody. Additionally, Gaiman's subverted black-cat trope is also more in line with the research on human-cat behavior. Indeed, past research has demonstrated that there is a secure attachment that can form between a cat and its owner, similar to the relationship between a dog and its owner (Vitale et al. 2019). This makes it very plausible that a cat would choose to protect their family, like the Black Cat from "The Price" or the black cat in *Coraline*.

Field Notes 3/22/23: The sun is setting in Palms. These cats are unbothered by my presence; they are puddled together underneath a green-grey shrub, tracking me with bright, yellow eyes. This is my last night conducting stray cat observations for the winter quarter. I will return; we have decided to include this colony in our rotation of weekly observations in the spring. Professor Kelty and Professor Lynch, a biological anthropologist, are creating an ethnographic manual, informed by hormone-mediated changes to cat behavior pre- and post-spay and neuter, over the course of the next year.

We will track both cat-cat and human-cat, paying particular attention to cat responses to human communication and cat hunting behavior. My specific role will continue to be primarily fieldwork, collecting and recording my observations at each of the colonies. We will also expand our network, reaching out to more trap and neuter organizations in Los Angeles to find a colony composed of only cats that have already been spayed/neutered.

On the surface, "Dream of a Thousand Cats" may seem too light-hearted, too fun, too *cartoony* to belong to the serious first season of the live-action *Sandman*. This is an argument, misguided as it may be, that Gaiman is familiar with. He has had to defend light-hearted genres before. For example, Gaiman (2007) described an early interview about *Stardust*, an adult fairytale comedy romance:

> [The journalist] had turned *Stardust* upside down and shaken it, looking for social allegories, and found absolutely nothing of any good purpose.
> "What's it for?" he had asked, which is not a question you expect to be asked when you write fiction for a living.
> "It's a fairytale," I told him. "It's like an ice cream. It's to make you feel happy when you finish it."

Like the fairytale *Stardust*, the cat characters in Gaiman's stories, and in turn, their film and television adaptations, are there because they are fun. You don't have to be a cat person to be captivated by "Dream of a Thousand Cats." In the final scene of the episode, we all can delight in watching an adorable kitten chomping down on an imagined human victim, dreaming of a time when cats will rule once more.

References

Anwar, Yasmin, and Media Relations. 2012. "Don't Be so Fast to Judge a Cat by Its Color, Study Warns." *Berkeley News*, October 23, 2012. https://news.berkeley.edu/2012/10/23/cat-color/.

Chu, Karyen, Wendy M. Anderson, and Micha Y. Rieser. 2009. "Population Characteristics and Neuter Status of Cats Living in Households in the United States." *Journal of the American Veterinary Medical Association* 234 (8): 1023–30. https://doi.org/10.2460/javma.234.8.1023.

Finkler, Hilit, and Joseph Terkel. 2010. "Cortisol Levels and Aggression in Neutered and Intact Free-Roaming Female Cats Living in Urban Social Groups." *Physiology & Behavior* 99 (3): 343–47. https://doi.org10.1016/j.physbeh.2009.11.014.

Franzen, Jonathan. 2023. "How the No-Kill Movement Betrays its Name." *The New Yorker*. December 25. https://www.newyorker.com/magazine/2024/01/01/how-the-no-kill-movement-betrays-its-name.

Gaiman, Neil. 1998. "The Price." In *Smoke and Mirrors*, 1–3. William Morrow.

———. 2006. *Coraline*. HarperCollins.

———. 2007. "Happily Ever After." *Guardian*. October 13. https://www.theguardian.com/books/2007/oct/13/film.fiction.

———. 2023. "Neil Gaiman's Journal." Cats (blog). Accessed January 31, 2023. https://journal.neilgaiman.com/search/label/Cats.

Gaiman, Neil (w), Kelley Jones (a), and Malcolm Jones III (i). 1990. "A Dream of a Thousand Cats." *Sandman* #18. DC Comics. August.

Gaiman, Neil, David S. Goyer, and Allan Heinberg, creators. 2022. *Sandman*. Season 1. Netflix.

Humphrey, Tasmin, Leanne Proops, Jemma Forman, Rebecca Spooner, and Karen McComb. 2020. "The Role of Cat Eye Narrowing Movements in Cat–Human Communication." *Scientific Reports* 10 (1): 16503. https://doi.org/10.1038/s41598-020-73426-0.

Jones, Haylie D., and Christian L. Hart. 2020. "Black Cat Bias: Prevalence and Predictors." *Psychological Reports* 123 (4): 1198–1206. https://doi.org/10.1177/0033294119844982.

Nikolajeva, Maria. 2009. "Devils, Demons, Familiars, Friends: Toward a Semiotics of Literary Cats." *Marvels & Tales* 23 (2): 248–67.

O'Brien, Stephen J., Warren Johnson, Carlos Driscoll, Joan Pontius, Jill Pecon-Slattery, and Marilyn Menotti-Raymond. 2008. "State of Cat Genomics." *Trends in Genetics* 24 (6): 268–79. https://doi.org/10.1016/j.tig.2008.03.004.

Vitale, Kristyn R., Alexandra C. Behnke, and Monique A. R. Udell. 2019. "Attachment Bonds between Domestic Cats and Humans." *Current Biology* 29 (18): R864–65. https://doi.org/10.1016/j.cub.2019.08.036.

Wandesforde-Smith, Geoffrey, Julie K. Levy, William Lynn, Jacquie Rand, Sophie Riley, Joan E. Schaffner, and Peter Joseph Wolf. 2021. "Coping with Human-Cat Interactions beyond the Limits of Domesticity: Moral Pluralism in the Management of Cats and Wildlife." *Frontiers in Veterinary Science* 8: 1–11. https://www.frontiersin.org/articles/10.3389/fvets.2021.682582.

A Dreaming of Our Own
How Fandom Adapts Multiple Canons to Create a New Fanon

Adrienne E. Raw

In the weeks following the release of Netflix's *Sandman* adaptation, its online fandom exploded—particularly in the creation of transformative fanworks. This subset of fandom engages with media through the invention of new creative and metatextual works that borrow the characters, plots, settings, themes, and/or imagery from the original. These works include critical analysis, fanfiction that rewrites or continues the original, fan art, and more. Transformative fandoms vary in size according to the passions of the fans in them, but some, like *Sandman*, grow rapidly and host significant amounts of creative work. As of May 2023, the massive, popular fanfiction site Archive of Our Own (AO3) hosted over 7,600 works of *Sandman* fanfiction, with individual stories ranging in length from less than 100 to nearly 420,000 words. Nearly 85 percent of those works were written after the show's August 2022 release. This growing fandom activity offers a place to consider how fans negotiate *Sandman*'s multiple canons and how they develop their own fannish adaptation of the material.

I joined *Sandman*'s fandom in its early days, diving gleefully into the show version of the comics I had loved as a child. I reached the end of the first season yearning for more, so, like many fans, I turned immediately to my dependable source of new content—the fanfiction archives of AO3—and consumed them with a voracious appetite. As a longtime participant in the transformative fandom community, I read with an eye for the developing trends that inevitably emerge as a fandom grows: the characters that become fan favorites, the plot moments that fans remix over and over, the narrative tropes repeated so often that they become ubiquitous. These repeated narrative tropes distinguish fans' version of *Sandman* from the versions that actually appeared on the page and on the screen. I argue, first, that these repeated narrative tropes define the body of work created by transformative fandom as a unique adaptation of *Sandman* and, second, that positioning fan work as adaptation highlights how fans mirror Gaiman's practice of revisionist writing and offers a new lens for analyzing collaborative authorship.

Pairing Fanon and Adaptation Studies

To facilitate my analysis of transformative fandom, I bring together the fandom concept of "fanon" with the film studies field of adaptation theory, which can help explain the various techniques visible in fanon activity. Fanon, a portmanteau of "fan" and "canon," is a fan-authored story element such as a character quirk or backstory that is "so perfect, so convincing or fun that other fan-authors simply adopt it wholesale," despite it having little or no basis in that text's established canon (Coppa 2017, ix). A fanon detail can develop in several ways; some are extensions of canon (such as a small canon event or detail that gets exaggerated in transformative fanworks) while others are invented by fans (such as a canonically unnamed character being named for a piece of fanfiction). Fan studies scholars have analyzed fanon for the sense of agency it gives fans in their relationship to a text and particularly as a point of tension in the producer/consumer relationship between author and fan (Amsler 2019; Gonzalez 2016; Winter 2020). However, even as it has been acknowledged that, for fans, "canon and fanon stand on a par," scholars have rarely considered fanon as a distinct text in its own right (Amsler 2019).

To reconsider fanon in this new light, I draw from the film studies field of adaptation theory, "the systematic study of films based on literary sources" (Leitch 2007, 1). Though the field of adaptation theory is typically concerned with the study of films based on literary sources, particularly the novel, its theoretical framework is equally useful for examining how fans adapt an original text for transformative fanworks. In particular, this similarity can be seen in the changes of scale that so often concern film studies scholars who consider how a written work must be reshaped to fit a genre that might not be able to contain or adequately convey its original ideas. For example, scholars of Peter Jackson's adaptation of *The Lord of the Rings* film series often consider the necessity of Jackson's cuts, such as the removal of Tom Bombadil for a faster plot progression (Thompson 2011; Rateliff 2011), or of Jackson's changes, such as the re-characterization of Aragorn or the revisualization of his love story with Arwen to suit film-oriented themes (West 2011). Transformative fandom operates on a similar discrepancy of scale to its original text. Even a small fandom with only a few hundred works may eclipse in length the original text those works were based on. The content of a large fandom, as *Sandman*'s fandom is rapidly becoming, likely already outpaces the amount of content in the TV show and may also have produced more content than the original comics. Using adaptation theory to examine fanon as a collective of disparate fanworks highlights that fans are using the same techniques as filmmakers when dealing with differing scales of content and mediums of consumption.

Further, adaptation theory provides a framework for considering the relationship between the original canonical texts and transformative fandom without the hierarchy of power that typically exists between a fan and a creator. Through much of the field's history, film adaptations have been studied in relation to and serving their literary originating texts: a successful adaptation is one which is deemed to have communicated in some way the intent of the author of the original literary text, regardless of any changes necessitated by a shift in medium (Leitch 2007). More recently, though, adaptation theory scholars have pushed for the field to step away from fidelity as the primary focus of analysis and instead elevate the writing process—particularly revision—as the connection between an adaptation and its originating text. As Leitch (2007) argues, "this alternative approach to adaptation study does not approach adaptations as either transcriptions of canonical classics or attempts to create new classics but rather as illustrations of the incessant process of rewriting as critical reading" (16). This approach resonates powerfully with fans' motivations for creating transformative fanworks; for fans, absolute fidelity is *rarely* the concern. Instead, fanworks are created in response to fans' critical engagement with the original texts: to address what they feel are mistakes, to explore the unexplored paths, to introduce new ideas, and to transpose the story into new contexts. Transformative fandom is, at its heart, an incessant rewriting of the original canonical texts. By studying the emergence of fanon as an adaptation, we can analyze how fans engage in that process of rewriting, particularly in a collaborative writing context, and evaluate what fanon themes suggest about fans' response to both the original text (the comics) and its most recent adaptation (the Netflix show).

A Survey of Fandom Adaptation Techniques

I first noticed the trends that I analyze in this essay through the fanfiction I read and wrote. Among the trends that emerged, one stood out: fans' fascination with Hob Gadling (Ferdinand Kingsley), a minor character who only appeared in one episode of the first season ("The Sound of Her

Wings") but who quickly became a fan favorite and received considerable attention in fanfiction. The development of his character, in the particular the consistency in that collective development, exemplifies the fandom practice of creating fanon. To support my observations as a member in the community, I surveyed sixty-five fanfiction stories featuring Hob Gadling gathered randomly from work posted in the ten months following the show's release. I searched each story for the elements of fanon that I had identified through my personal reading, tallying the trends across the sample. The goal of this survey was to assess whether my sense of the emerging fanon was a true trend across fandom and not influenced by my personal reading preferences, as well as to articulate how widespread each fanon element had actually become.

The survey also gave me the foundation to describe these trends without quoting from particular pieces of fanfiction. I refrain from citing fanfiction directly for this essay because of the history of contention within fandom when fanworks are transported outside fan communities (Fanlore 2018a; Fanlore 2018b; Kelley 2016). While many fanfiction archives, including AO3, are publicly accessible, they are typically only used by community members. Most fans, therefore, expect these works only to be accessed by other fans and many are uncomfortable with the idea of non-fans interacting with the work. Further, there have been several contentious instances where fanworks have been accessed and exploited by non-fans, including one where the inclusion of specific works on a class syllabus resulted in fans receiving unsettling comments from student readers who were not part of the fandom community (Fanlore 2018b). Most recently, many fans have been incensed by the discovery that AI software has likely used fanfiction to train its programs (Leishman 2022). To preserve the anonymity of fan authors and to avoid the implication that I am scrutinizing specific iterations of a fanon trope, in this essay I speak generally about elements of fanon and, where excerpts from fanfiction would be useful to support my analysis, have written my own or summarized common narrative plot points.

In this analysis, I identified four techniques that characterize fans' development of fanon within transformative fanworks:

1. Interpreting a component of the original text in a way that is not explicitly stated in the original text.
2. Expanding a component of the original text with new content.
3. Inventing completely new components not present in the original text.
4. Borrowing elements from multiple related texts to create a unified fanon.

In the following sections, I use Hob Gadling as a focus through which I explore how each of these techniques function within fandom and fanon.

The Curious Case of (Fanon) Hob Gadling

Hob Gadling is a minor character in both *Sandman*'s comics and Netflix adaptation canons, yet he has become wildly popular among fans. His character, particularly Ferdinand Kingsley's portrayal of him in the Netflix adaptation, features in the majority of *Sandman*'s fanfiction. Hob is a peasant who encounters Dream and Death in 1389 in the White Horse tavern where, unbeknownst to him, Dream and Death overhear him denouncing death and claiming that he will live forever. The Endless siblings take him up on this claim; Death withholds her gift until Gadling requests it as Dream is curious to see how long it will be before Gadling begs to die. However, Gadling defies Dream's expectations and so the pair meet every one hundred years, where Gadling regales Dream with his experiences since their last meeting.

Hob first appears in the comics in *Sandman* issue #13, "Men of Good Fortune" (1990). In the Netflix adaptation, his relationship with Dream (Tom Sturridge) is the subject of the second half of the sixth episode, "The Sound of Her Wings," wherein, following his day with Death (Kirby Howell-Baptiste), Dream goes looking for Hob at the White Horse. In both canons, Gadling's first appearance is a series of vignettes chronicling his centennial meetings with Dream. While there are minor differences between the episode and the comic, the only substantial difference is the 1989 meeting between Hob and Dream. In the comics, Dream escapes his imprisonment by Alex Burgess in 1988, shown in *Sandman* issue #1: "Sleep of the Just" and collected in *Sandman, Vol 1: Preludes and Nocturnes*, and makes it to the planned meeting with Hob, shown in *Sandman* issue #13: "Men of Good Fortune" and collected in *Sandman, Vol 2: The Doll's House*. In the Netflix adaptation, however, while Dream is still captured in 1916, he doesn't escape until 2021, lengthening his imprisonment to 105 years and more closely aligning his in-story escape with the show's release date. As a result of this extended imprisonment, Dream misses his 1989 meeting with Hob—which changes that vignette in the show—and he must then deliberately seek out the immortal outside of their normal meeting schedule. "The Sound of Her Wings" is, as yet, Gadling's only appearance in the Netflix adaptation, but he appears several additional times in the comics: in *Sandman* issue #22: "Season of Mists, Chapter One" where Dream visits Hob before descending into Hell; in *Sandman* issue #53: "Hob's Leviathan" where Hob recounts one of his many adventures as an immortal independent of Dream; in *Sandman* issue #59: "The Kindly Ones: Part 3" where Dream speaks with Hob after the death of Hob's lover in a car accident; and in *Sandman*, Vol 10: "The Wake" (issues #70, #72, and #73) where Hob learns of Dream's death, attends his wake, and decides not to give up his immortality. Though recurring throughout Dream's narrative, Hob's stories are interludes that do not affect or often intersect with the main arc of the comics series.

Despite his status as a minor character in both the comics and the Netflix adaptation, Hob Gadling rapidly became a fan favorite, particularly after the Netflix show's release. Of the over 7,600 pieces of fanfiction published since the show's release, Hob appears in over 3,900 of them, second only in popularity to Dream himself. The reasons for Hob's popularity likely include his status as an "ordinary guy" in a story of supernatural creatures, his sense of humor and joie de vivre, the role he plays in changing Dream's perceptions of life and living, and, perhaps most crucially, his potential as a fanfiction romantic partner for Dream. Shipping—the imagining of a romantic and/or sexual relationship between two characters that may or may not be in a relationship within the text's canon—has long been a staple and driving force of transformative fandom (Massey 2019; Warner 2018). Fans' reasons for shipping two characters are myriad, but fans are often drawn to characters that have an existing relationship on-screen, especially if that relationship is emotionally charged. Of the fanfiction in which Hob appears, nearly 3,400 stories (over 86 percent) feature a romantic and/or sexual relationship between Hob and Dream.[1] Using fanon Hob as a case study, the following sections explore how a minor character can be consistently developed by fans to create someone noticeably different from the original canon—and consequently, become foundational to a fan canon distinctly different from either the show or comics canon.

Interpretation: Hob Gadling Hates Shakespeare

According to *Sandman*'s fanfiction writers, Hob Gadling loathes Shakespeare. Yet neither the comics nor the Netflix show include any overt or explicit animosity from the immortal toward the bard. In its first season, the Netflix adaptation only shows the series of vignettes that comprise Hob's meeting with Dream up to the modern day ("The Sound of Her Wings"). Hob Gadling hating Shakespeare is an interpretation by *Sandman* fanfiction writers of two key scenes in those vignettes that mention Shakespeare: in 1589 when Dream walks away from Hob mid-conversation to make a bargain with Shakespeare about inspiring the bard's plays and in 1789 when Hob brings up having recently seen Shakespeare's work to divert the conversation once Dream chastises him for engaging in the trafficking of enslaved people. Close examination of these two scenes reveals no overt hostility on Hob's behalf toward Shakespeare, yet it is from these scenes that fandom has interpreted Hob Gadling as a man who hates Shakespeare.

Shakespeare is first referenced in the 1589 meeting between Hob and Dream, where he is present in the White Horse tavern where Dream and Hob are meeting. At the beginning of this meeting, Dream sits with Hob only a little while, listening as he brags about his new wealth and family. Dream's attention is quickly drawn, though, by a conversation in which Shaxbeard/Shakespeare praises Kit Marlowe and loudly wishes he were capable of writing work as good. Hob appears disappointed that Dream's attention is so clearly turned away from him, but nevertheless answers Dream's questions about the playwright:

> DREAM: Who is he?
> HOB: His name's Will Shaxberd. Acts a bit. Wrote a play.
> DREAM: Is he good?
> HOB: No, he's crap. Now, that chap next to him, with the broken leg, he is a good playwright ["The Sound of Her Wings"].

Hob's statement that Shakespeare is "crap" is the most direct and overt critique he makes in the episode. It does not seem directed at the man himself, though, nor solely the result of Dream's attention toward someone other than Hob. In the same statement in which he dismissed Shakespeare, Hob acknowledges and praises Marlowe's skill, though he does then attempt to recapture Dream's attention with another story about his exploits. Dream, however, is uninterested, leaving the meeting to speak with Shakespeare. As Dream guides Shakespeare out of the White Horse, Hob looks disappointed to have lost Dream's attention but turns back to his own feast, reassuring himself that he has "everything to live for. And nowhere to go but up." While clearly disappointed, Hob does not appear to be particularly contemptuous toward Shakespeare nor significantly bothered by Dream's engagement with the bard. It is this scene in particular, though, that has formed the basis of fans' interpretation of Hob's feelings toward Shakespeare.

For fans, the 1589 meeting between Hob and Dream is a pivotal moment in the relationship between the two. Their 1389 meeting was fleeting, as was their 1489 meeting where Hob seemed more concerned with understanding his deal than conversing with Dream. In the 1589 meeting, though, Hob actively attempts to forge a closer relationship with Dream by openly welcoming him with a feast and revealing personal details. Fans—especially those who imagine a romantic relationship between Hob and

Dream—interpret Hob's actions as a desire for a long, deep conversation and Dream's subsequent abandonment of the conversation as emotionally painful for Hob. Both the show and the comics give audiences some visible evidence of Hob's disappointment, so this is not an unrealistic interpretation regardless of the fannish impulse toward shipping. Transformative fans take this a step further, though, directly connecting Hob's disappointment at the meeting's rapid end with Shakespeare: Dream abandoned Hob to talk with Shakespeare and subsequently left with him, Hob is disappointed and hurt, Hob blames Shakespeare for stealing Dream's attention, Hob subsequently hates Shakespeare.

There is, understandably, no mention of Shakespeare at Dream and Hob's 1689 meeting because Hob has lost everything and spent the 80 years before the meeting in poverty and privation. However, when they meet again in 1789, Shakespeare once again comes up in conversation. By this time, Hob has regained his wealth by trafficking in enslaved people—an occupation Dream disapproves of and chastises Hob for. Hob, clearly uncomfortable with the conversation, abruptly changes the topic to Shakespeare, which he also uses to try to learn more about his own bargain with Dream:

> Hob: That lad, Will Shakespeare. He turned out to be a half-decent playwright after all. You made some kind of deal with him, didn't you?
> Dream: Perhaps.
> Hob: What kind of deal? His soul?
> Dream: Nothing so crude.

Hob says nothing critical of Shakespeare in this exchange; his only critique is for a recent performance of *King Lear* that had given the play a happy ending. He calls the creators of the interpretation "idiots," seeming angered at the misinterpretation, implying he both knows and appreciates the work well enough to know its intended meaning. Additionally, just a moment later he praises Shakespeare as a "half-decent playwright," highlighting not only a lack of hatred toward the bard but perhaps even a sense of appreciation. It is, perhaps notably though, faint praise for a man widely regarded today as an extraordinary playwright. Fans may be taking the faintness of Hob's praise as a basis on which to interpret his feelings toward Shakespeare as negative. They may also be drawn by a sense of schadenfreude in the opportunity to take down one of the pillars of English literature or the potential drama that a hatred of Shakespeare introduces to Dream and Hob's relationship.

In my systematic review of *Sandman* fanfiction, I found that, of the stories in which Hob Gadling was a character and Shakespeare was mentioned (over a third of my sample), over 75 percent also included reference to Hob having explicit, often powerful, negative feelings toward the bard. In some stories, this hatred is a minor character quirk, a throwaway descriptor of Hob's personality. For example, Hob might be introduced thus: "Robert Gadling, immortal, pub owner, professor, and notorious Shakespeare critic, was having one of *those* days." This kind of brief mention might be the *only* reference to Shakespeare or Hob's antipathy toward him in the entire story. It might have no bearing on the plot, on Hob's character, or on his interactions with any other character. Yet many fans still find it important to mention, the detail having become a fundamental and important aspect of Hob's fanon characterization—as fundamental as Dream's identity as one of the Endless or Rose's as the Dream Vortex.

In other stories, the intersection of Hob Gadling, Dream, and Shakespeare becomes a major element of the story. In some cases, this is humorous; many stories that focus on Hob's modern-day career as a teacher incorporate this imagined hatred of Shakespeare into Hob's classroom behavior. For example, an author writing a story featuring Hob in the classroom might include a scene of Hob's students goading him into a rant about Shakespeare to get out of a test. In other cases, Hob's antipathy becomes a point of tension in his developing romantic relationship with Dream. In *Sandman*'s fandom, a romantic relationship between Hob and Dream rapidly became the most-written pairing. As of May 2023, this pairing is featured in nearly 3,400 pieces of fanfiction on AO3. For comparison, the next most common relationship is a romantic relationship between Dream and the story's reader with over 475 stories, followed by a relationship between Dream and the Corinthian with just over 350 stories. In fanfiction stories where Hob and Dream develop a romantic relationship—most often after their 2021 reunion—the 1589 meeting often comes up as a point of contention or insecurity on Hob's part. For example, a story where Dream and Hob are admitting their feelings to each other and working out the boundaries of a new romantic relationship might include a conversation where Hob expresses insecurities about not living up to Shakespeare, who he assumes was Dream's previous romantic partner.

Fans' interpretation that Hob hates Shakespeare has become so persistent and prevalent that it is rare to see a mention of Shakespeare that is mild or neutral. I have never read a story in which Hob has an overtly positive feeling toward Shakespeare, though I acknowledge the possibility of such a story existing. However, though I'm able to recognize the lack of overt animosity in the original texts, I admit that, as a part of the transformative fandom, if I saw Hob having a positive relationship to Shakespeare in a piece of fanfiction, I would find it strange and unsettling. Such is the power of fanon that a single interpretation can become the subjective truth for most fans.

While fanon interpretations demonstrate the remarkable ability for massive transformative fandoms with thousands of authors to negotiate a consensus, this consensus-making can pose challenges within the community. Fandom's interpretations are often the result of overemphasizing a canon detail—for example, a character who is clumsy for a single gag in a single episode can suddenly be tripping over something in a multitude of circumstances in every single piece of fanfiction (Busse 2017). In overemphasizing a single character trait or backstory detail, fanon's adaptation runs the risk of flattening the character and stripping away the complexity created by the original canon. Conversely, fanon can *build* complexity for secondary or tertiary characters who, by the constraints of the original canon, were not deeply developed. This produces a rich sandbox and a ready-made backstory for fanfiction writers who might want to use these secondary characters in their own work. However, the emergence and repeated reinforcement of a single interpretation often comes at the expense of all other interpretations. Possibilities which might be equally supported by the canon are no longer explored in transformative fandom, either because they feel strange and unnatural to fans or because fans have come to see the fanon as canon and no longer accept any other interpretation.

Expansion: Hob Gadling Is a Professor

Hob Gadling has held many jobs over the centuries of his acquaintance with Dream—a bandit, a printer, a noble/knight, a merchant/trafficker of enslaved people, and unemployed among them. In the twenty-first century, Hob Gadling is a teacher—at least, he is in fandom's expansion of a paratextual comment from Gaiman himself, one of the show's creators. While Hob Gadling is not explicitly named as a teacher in the twenty-first century, some fans noticed that he appeared to be grading papers during his reunion with Dream. In this scene, Dream enters The New Inn and stands opposite from Hob's table. The camera focuses briefly on a small stack of papers on the table before Hob, showing his hand making check marks down one side of the top-most paper, before panning up to his face. Tumblr user thenightling posted a screenshot of this moment with the note, "I just now realized Hob was grading papers in the 2022 scene. How much you want to bet he's a history teacher now?" Neil Gaiman subsequently confirmed this interpretation on his Tumblr blog, reblogging thenightling's post with the additional comment, "Well spotted" (2022). Hob Gadling the teacher has since become a staple of fanfiction set in the modern day. In my fanfiction sample, over 55 percent include reference to him as a teacher or professor.

Though thenightling's post speculates that Hob was a history teacher, Gaiman's response was not as specific and provided no other detail about Hob's profession. This lack of additional detail has not deterred fans in the slightest; they have taken what little the show and Gaiman's comment have provided and, as fandom does, run with it. Fans have subsequently cast Hob as a teacher of either history (58 percent) or literature (17 percent) and as teaching at either the elementary/secondary (11 percent) or college/university (89 percent) levels. There are currently over 215 works tagged with "Professor Hob Gadling," over 75 tagged with "Teacher Hob Gadling," and many more that use this fanon without tagging it.[2] Hob's profession as a teacher, most typically a college professor, has become an established part of *Sandman*'s fanon.

Though fans have almost no material to work with in the original texts, they have expanded that minute detail, giving it considerable attention in fanfiction. While some fanfiction mentions Hob's profession only in passing, many stories center it. The specific story elements are myriad, but some of the trends include the following:

- Dream visits Hob's campus and/or classroom, sitting in on his lectures and interacting with his students.
- Hob has to cancel classes to help Dream deal with a crisis.
- As Hob and Dream develop a romantic relationship, Hob discusses these developments with fellow professors and/or is questioned by students about his new romantic partner.
- Following the end of Season 1, Rose meets Hob when she starts taking classes at his university, often as a prelude to encountering Dream again and building a familial relationship with him.

In expanding, like interpreting, fans are using a technique often deployed by filmmakers, particularly in the creation of films based on short stories such as *The Killers* (1946) based on an Ernest Hemingway short story of the same name (Leitch 2007); *2001: A Space Odyssey* (1968), developed from Arthur C. Clarke's "The Sentinel"; *Stand by Me* (1986), based on Stephen King's "The Body"; or *How to Talk to Girls at Parties* (2007), based on a Gaiman short story by the same name. While expansion in filmmaking is often used to render a text more suitable for film (Leitch 2007), fandom often uses expansion differently. In some ways, fans' use of expansion *does*, as Leitch suggests, render the story more suitable for fanfiction as a medium with no word count limits and in which stories are often posted episodically over a long period of time—features which allow space for more meandering plots, stories that are primarily slice-of-life, and a sense of familiar speed to the episodic nature of comics and pre-streaming TV shows. However, that does not entirely encapsulate fans' motivations for expanding these kinds of detail. Fans' expansion of the fanon of Hob as a professor primarily shifts the story away from Dream's trials and tribulations with his realm, his family, and the supernatural, and instead tells stories set primarily in the waking, mortal world and primarily concerned with mundane, mortal lives. These narratives completely shift the context of Dream's story but, interestingly, often retain what many fans see as the thematic focus of the series: Dream's emotional growth and developing relationships with other characters. Interpersonal relationships—whether romantic/sexual shipping or platonic friendship/family—are often the spark of inspiration for fans, so it is unsurprising that fans' adaptation of *Sandman* would build increased space for these intimate, relationship-building interactions.

Invention: Hob Gadling Owns the New Inn

The Netflix adaptation introduces one new element to Hob and Dream's story: the New Inn, the place of their twenty-first-century meeting following Dream's imprisonment. Fans have also taken up the New Inn, completely inventing a relationship between Hob Gadling and this establishment that has no foundation in the original text: fans have decided that Hob built or owns this new pub. The New Inn originates because of the extension of Dream's captivity by Burgess, which causes Dream to miss his 1989 meeting with Hob. Instead of the meeting from the comics where Dream acknowledges his feelings of friendship toward Hob, show viewers are treated to a vignette of Hob arriving to the White Horse tavern in the rain and sitting alone at a table for hours, waiting fruitlessly for Dream to come. The scene is reminiscent of being stood up for a date; the show furthers this allusion when Hob, realizing that Dream is coming, confides in the bartender that he thinks he's "been stood up," whereupon he learns that reuniting with Dream is about to become even more complicated:

> BARTENDER: I've seen plenty of friends get in fights in pubs. Even more of them laugh about it together later.
> HOB: Maybe in another one hundred years.
> BARTENDER: Ah. You'll have to have found a new pub by then. This place has been sold to make room for new flats ["The Sound of Her Wings"].

Hob is clearly disturbed by this news. After the bartender reveals the forthcoming closure of the White Horse, the camera returns to Dream in 2021, staring in dismay at the White Horse that has been boarded up, surrounded by fences, and presumably slated for demolition. As he stares through the fence, he also finds the words "The New Inn" in red spray paint above a series of painted arrows. Following the arrows, Dream finds The New Inn and Hob waiting for him.

While the episode implies that Hob was the one to leave the arrows and that they were meant to direct Dream to the New Inn, the show is not explicit about this. Hob *owning* the New Inn is not even implied in the show. Additionally, as the New Inn itself—and the closure of the White Horse—is an original fabrication for the show, fans are likewise not drawing anything from the comics to support this invention. Yet Hob's ownership of the New Inn is just as widespread and enduring a fanon detail as his hatred of Shakespeare or job as a professor. Over 45 percent of stories in my sample included references to the New Inn; Hob owned, and often built, the pub in all but one.

Much like the other fanon elements, Hob's ownership of the New Inn, often paired with him living in a flat above it, might be a minor mention or an important plot element in a fanfiction story. It might be mentioned as an aside in a story where Dream and Hob begin to meet more frequently than their centennial pattern and migrate their meetings to Hob's home—above the pub. The New Inn might also become an important plot element; in one popular trope, the New Inn is a temple to Dream: the fanon explanation is that Hob participated in the labor of the New Inn's construction, built it explicitly as a place to meet Dream, spends a great deal of time there hoping to reunite with Dream, and facilitates offerings (the consumption of food and drink) in a place dedicated to Dream. These combined actions take on a supernatural weight that consecrates the New Inn as a temple and gives it power that Dream feels. In some alternate universe stories, where fans narrate a significant divergence from canon, this power manifests by drawing Dream to the New Inn rather than the Dreaming after his escape from Burgess. Nearly thirty stories have used some variation of the "the New Inn is a temple" trope.

What's notable about this invention is that while fans have created something new for the fanon adaptation of *Sandman*, they have not significantly revised the original. While neither the show nor the comics support this invention, they also do not contradict it. In this particular invention, we also see fans retaining the thematic and emotional resonances of the original: Hob and Dream's friendship is a powerful journey and clearly matters deeply to both of them. It is therefore not surprising or out of character for Hob, a man prone to the occasional excess particularly in relation to Dream, to buy or build a meeting place specifically for them. Consequently, the invention retains a sense of plausibility, suggesting that the process of adaptation in the development of fanon is more of a patch or addition than a replacement—canon itself remains fundamental to fanon despite fans' revisionist tendencies.

Borrowing: Comics as Source Material

Fans' final technique of adaptation is less visible in the case of Hob Gadling, likely because he has so little content in both the show and the comics. In cases like *Sandman*, where multiple canons exist, often because of adaptations from one medium to another or because of reboots (e.g., the Marvel Cinematic Universe versus the Marvel comics), fans often begin their work of adapting their own version by negotiating its existing canons. In this situation, fans freely borrow from one version of canon to fill in the holes of another or to help them explore in fanfiction aspects of the story that the newer version of canon has not yet gotten to. For *Sandman*, we see this most often in fans borrowing plotlines and character histories from the comics that have not yet been addressed in the show. In the case of Hob Gadling, this is visible in stories that deal with the events of *Sandman, Vol. 9: The Kindly Ones* or *The Wake* that the Netflix show did not reach in its first season. In general, the Netflix adaptation sparked a resurgence of interest in the comics, with new fans buying them and previous readers returning to them. It's a story that I saw again and again in the paratextual notes that authors attached to their fanfiction: "I love the show so I'm buying the comics," "I love the show so I'm re-reading the comics," "I was inspired to write this detail into this story because of the comics." The comics are clearly a canon equally loved by fans, as much as they are also an explicit source of backstory.

More commonly, *Sandman* fanfiction incorporates backstory revealed in later comics (after *The Doll's House* arc) into stories about the events of the show. A common example of this is the background of the enmity between Dream and Desire, which is only hinted at in the show's first season but explained in detail in the comics. In the show, we learn only that Dream and Desire have a contentious relationship because Desire believes their brother looks down on them ("Chapter 7: The Doll's House"), that they often get into heated debates at family dinners ("The Sound of Her Wings"), and that the key story arcs of the first season (Dream's imprisonment and the Dream Vortex) were orchestrated by Desire as plots against Dream ("The Doll's House"; "Chapter 10: Lost Hearts"). The show does not reveal *why* the relationship between the two siblings is so contentious, how long it has been this way, or the true scope of that enmity. Presumably, the show will address this backstory in future seasons, but until then, fans have turned back to the comics for explanations, drawing on Desire influencing Killala of the Glow away from Dream and toward Sto-Oa in *Endless Nights* and Desire being angered by Dream winning a bet against Despair in *Sandman, Vol. 6: Fables & Reflections*. Fans have incorporated this backstory into their fanfiction about Dream, particularly stories in which Dream and Desire interact or their relationship is central to the plot. In this situation, rather than interpreting an explanation from the available show scenes or inventing an explanation to suit the plot needs of the fanfiction story, fans have consistently returned to a different version of *Sandman*'s canon for their explanation. The Netflix adaptation, then, is not positioned as a separate reboot of the comics canon. Rather, fans perceive the two as existing within the same universe—companion rather than competing canons.

What's interesting is that while the show has thus far been a fairly faithful adaptation of the major plot points of Dream's story, it has already made some not-insignificant changes: the extension of Dream's captivity, the increased role of the Corinthian in the first story arc, the change in location and participants for the duel over Dream's helm, and several gender and race changes for characters, among others. At the end of Season 1, audiences did not know if Season 2 would hew as close to the existing comics canon. Also, Gaiman has a tendency of supporting new story directions during adaptations. In his most recent adaptation before *Sandman*, the Amazon TV show version of *Good Omens*, Gaiman made a significant change to the final confrontation in the story. In the book version, first Adam dramatically disavows Satan as his father, then his human father arrives. In the Amazon TV show, Adam's human father is missing from this scene; instead, Satan himself arises from the ground and Adam makes the declaration to his biological father's towering form, a significant change as Satan was never physically present in the book. Responding to a Tumblr question about the reason for this change, Gaiman (2023) cited the challenge of making the book's version satisfying to watch, but also emphasized the importance of originality, writing, "I didn't ever want people who had read the book to assume they knew everything that would happen." Similarly, we could not assume that *Sandman* Season 2 would not make even more significant changes to the story. Fans can't know that the comics backstory will remain applicable to fanfiction written primarily in response to the show. Fanon, therefore, may require another iteration to incorporate new information revealed in *Sandman* Season 2; it will be interesting, as a fan and scholar, to see how fanon develops as the show does.

Fanon as Adaptation

Fans' practice of creating a new adaptation through fanon is very much in keeping with Gaiman's own tendency toward work that adapts the work of others, from the centering of Orchid's consciousness in his *Black Orchid* (Cantrell 2012) to the temporal dislocation in his *Marvel 1602* (Dalmaso 2012) to the origins of Dream himself in early DC comics, as well as playing in the sandbox of other writers as he does in his *Doctor Who* episodes "The Doctor's Wife" and "Nightmare in Silver." As Gaiman scholars have previously argued, Gaiman's practice of adaptation is also one of revisioning, "the act of looking back, of seeing with fresh eyes, of entering an old text from a new critical direction" (Rich 1972, 18, quoted in Dalmaso 2012, 116). Fans are also notoriously revisionist, but here I want to make a distinction between revisioning as Rich and Dalmaso describe—the re-engagement with a text using a new critical lens—and revisioning as Leitch uses in his grammar of adaptation techniques. According to Leitch (2007), revisions "differ from updates to the extent that they seek to rewrite the original, not simply improve its ending or point out its contemporary relevance" (106). Fans frequently revise the original text, from minor tweaks to major overhauls; a particular fan favorite is the "fix-it fic" in which the author fixes what they feel is broken in the original, often the death of a favorite character. While popular in fandom broadly, this kind of revision is rare in fanon, which tends to cleave more closely to the original canon. In this way, fans also align with Gaiman's own views of playing in others' sandboxes, which he describes as different from original writing for two reasons: "One, you know, you're not going to break anything you want to leave the toys for them. You're in the sandbox and you're playing with the toys that somebody left for you, but you're not going to break the toys. That's one of them. And I think the other is. Honestly, the sandbox thing, it is the fact that your inner kid gets happy, right?" (Tennant, 2020). Fanon inhabits this same philosophy of not breaking others' toys while taking joy in the process of creation. It is often less about revising an element of canon than about filling a gap that may have been elided in canon: creating something that *could* plausibly fit with canon and rarely directly contradicting it.

Analyzing fanon as an adaptation also facilitates new perspectives on collaborative authorship. Gaiman is as well-practiced at collaboration as he is at revisionist adaptation: his visual texts, from comic books to *Who Killed Amanda Palmer* (2009), are collaborations between storyteller and visual artist; his work with other writers includes his notable cowritten novel *Good Omens* (1990) with Terry Pratchett and the crowd-inspired collection *Calendar of Tales* (2013) collaboratively generated with his Twitter fans; and his recent projects include a collaboration with the Fourplay string quartet to create the album *Signs of Life* (2023). Scholars have also considered the nature of collaborative authorship in studies of Gaiman, particularly how it can result in the generation of new ideas, driving a project to new heights. Miller's (2012) study of *Who Killed Amanda Palmer*, for example, highlights how the collaboration between Gaiman and Palmer transformed a series of photos intended as album liner notes into a 119-page coffee table book of images and stories. When we think of such collaboration, though, it is typically imagined as an intentional process between a limited number of individuals: an author working with a team of artists on a comic, two authors cowriting a novel. Considering fanon as a collaboratively authored adaptation suggests a new model of collaborative authorship: a collective of authors writing a story without collaboration in the drafting or idea generation phases of creation where such collaboration typically occurs. Instead, collaborative authorship of fanon becomes an iterative process, with each fanfiction author building on the work of other fans, reinforcing or tweaking their ideas until they reach a point of stability that becomes a collectively accepted fanon.

The adaptation itself, then, is not a single work that revisions another, but the *process* of rewriting and re-visioning. In critiquing the history of adaptation studies, Leitch (2007) writes that the field has not, for most of its history, taken up what he says "one might have expected to be the primary lesson of film adaptation: that texts remain alive only to the extent that they can be rewritten and that to experience a text in all its power requires each reader to rewrite it" (13). Fans seem to have taken this to heart, gleefully rewriting *Sandman* again and again and again to suit their own tastes and critical perspectives on both the story and the world around them. In recognizing fanon as a legitimate adaptation, then, we are also celebrating the ways that this fan practice enables transformative fandom to empower and deeply experience a text.

Notes

1. Hob Gadling and Dream are not the first pair of Gaiman's characters to be heavily shipped by fans. The angel Aziraphale and demon Crowley from Gaiman and Pratchett's collaboration *Good Omens* have long been a popular couple among fans, who have dubbed their relationship the "Ineffable Husbands" and published more than 46,000 stories about their romance on AO3. While regarded as largely subtextual in the original novel, the Amazon adaptation partially canonized their relationship with both Michael Sheen (Aziraphale) and David Tennant (Crowley) saying that their characters loved each other (Showbiz Junkies 2018) and Gaiman (2019) confirming on Twitter that "Whatever Crowley and Aziraphale are, it's a love story."

2. AO3 uses a system of author-generated tags to allow readers to search for specific works. Fan authors typically tag the main characters and relationships in their stories, as well as additional details like emotional tone (e.g., "angst" or "fluff"), content warnings, and common plot elements (e.g., "alternate universe" or "canon divergence").

References

Amsler, Monika. 2019. "The Making of Ḥanina ben Dosa: Fan Fiction in the Babylonian Talmud." In "Fan Fiction and Ancient Scribal Cultures," edited by Frauke Uhlenbruch and Sonja Ammann, special issue, *Transformative Works and Cultures* 31. https://doi.org/10.3983/twc.2019.1647.

Busse, Kristina. 2017. *Framing Fan Fiction: Literary and Social Practices in Fan Fiction Communities*. University of Iowa Press.
Cantrell, Sarah. 2012. "Feminist Subjectivity in Neil Gaiman's *Black Orchid*." In Prescott and Drucker, *Feminism in the Worlds of Neil Gaiman*, 102–15.
Coppa, Francesca. 2017. *The Fanfiction Reader: Folk Tales for the Digital Age*. University of Michigan Press.
Dalmaso, Renata. 2012. "When Superheroes Awaken: The Revisionist Trope in Neil Gaiman's *Marvel 1602*." In Prescott and Drucker, *Feminism in the Worlds of Neil Gaiman*, 116–30.
Fanlore. 2018a. "SurveyFail." Fanlore, July 13,. https://fanlore.org/wiki/SurveyFail.
———. 2018b. "Theory of FicGate." Fanlore, July 28. https://fanlore.org/wiki/TheoryofFicGate.
Gaiman, Neil (@neilhimself). 2019. "I wouldn't exclude the ideas that they are ace, or aromantic, or trans. They are an angel and a demon, not as make humans, per the book. Occult/Ethereal beings don't have sexes, something we tried to reflect in the casting. Whatever Crowley and Aziraphale are, it's a love story." Twitter, June 8. https://twitter.com/neilhimself/status/1137370226931228672.
Gaiman, Neil. 2022. "Well spotted." Tumblr, August 6. https://neil-gaiman.tumblr.com/post/691865264928768000/thenightling-i-just-now-realized-hob-was.
———. 2023. "Because I couldn't figure out…" Tumblr, March 12. https://neil-gaiman.tumblr.com/post/711594555045298176/as-i-awoke-this-morning-i-was-struck-by-a.
Gaiman, Neil (w), et al. 1990–1994. *Sandman*. Trade paperback vols. 1–10. DC Comics/Vertigo.
Gaiman, Neil (w), et al. 2003. *Sandman: Endless Nights*. DC Comics.
Gonzalez, Victoria M. 2016. "Swan Queen, Shipping, and Boundary Regulation in Fandom." *Transformative Works and Cultures* 22. http://dx.doi.org/10.3983/twc.2016.0669.
Kelley, Brittany. 2016. "Toward a Goodwill Ethics of Online Research Methods." *Transformative Works and Cultures* 22. https://doi.org/10.3983/twc.2016.0891.
Leishman, Rachel. 2022. "Fanfiction Writers Scramble to Set Profiles to Private as Evidence Grows That AI Writing Is Using Their Stories." *The Mary Sue*, December 12. https://www.themarysue.com/fanfiction-writers-scramble-to-set-profiles-to-private-as-evidence-grows-that-ai-writing-is-using-their-stories/.
Leitch, Thomas. 2007. *Film Adaptation and Its Discontents: From* Gone with the Wind *to* The Passion of the Christ. Johns Hopkins University Press.
Marwick, Alice E., and danah boyd. 2010. "I tweet honestly, I tweet passionately: Twitter Users, Context Collapse, and the Imagined Audience." *New Media and Society* 13 (1). https://doi.org/10.1177%2F1461444810365313.
Massey, Erica Lyn. 2019. "Borderland Literature, Female Pleasure, and the Slash Fic Phenomenon." *Transformative Works and Cultures* 30. https://doi.org/10.3983/twc.2019.1390.
Miller, Monica. 2012. "Feminist Fairy Tales in *Who Killed Amanda Palmer*." In Prescott and Drucker, *Feminism in the Worlds of Neil Gaiman*, 206–20.
Prescott, Tara, and Aaron Drucker, eds. 2012. *Feminism in the Worlds of Neil Gaiman: Essays on the Comics, Poetry and Prose*. McFarland.
Rateliff, John D. 2011. "Two Kinds of Absence: Elision and Exclusion in Peter Jackson's *The Lord of the Rings*." In *Picturing Tolkien: Essays on Peter Jackson's* The Lord of the Rings *Film Trilogy*, edited by Janice M. Bogstad and Philip E. Kaveny, 54–69. McFarland.
Showbiz Junkies. 2018. "Good Omens—Michael Sheen and David Tennant Interview (NYCC)." YouTube, 6:39, October 6. https://www.youtube.com/watch?v=Ut-Ex94P8hw&t=180s.
Tennant, David, host. 2020. "Neil Gaiman." Produced by Sony Music Entertainment and No Mystery. *David Tennant Does a Podcast With…*, October 12. Podcast, streaming audio, 53:23, https://podcasts.apple.com/gb/podcast/neil-gaiman/id1450005207?i=1000494521236.
thenightling. 2022. Tumblr, "I just realized… " August 6. https://thenightling.tumblr.com/post/691854020656119808/i-just-now-realized-hob-was-grading-papers-in-the.

Thompson, Kristin. 2011. "Gollum Talks to Himself: Problems and Solutions in Peter Jackson's Film Adaptation of *The Lord of the Rings*." In *Picturing Tolkien: Essays on Peter Jackson's* The Lord of the Rings *Film Trilogy*, edited by Janice M. Bogstad and Philip E. Kaveny, 25–45. McFarland.

Warner, Kristen. 2018. "(Black Female) Fans Strike Back: The Emergence of the Iris West Defense Squad." In *The Routledge Companion to Media Fandom*, edited by Melissa A. Click and Suzanne Scott, 253–61. Routledge.

West, Richard C. "Neither the Shadow nor the Twilight: The Love Story of Aragorn and Arwen in Literature and Film." In *Picturing Tolkien: Essays on Peter Jackson's* The Lord of the Rings *Film Trilogy*, edited by Janice M. Bogstad and Philip E. Kaveny, 227–37. McFarland.

Winter, Rachel. 2020. "Fanon Bernie Sanders: Political Real Person Fan Fiction and the Construction of a Candidate." In "Fandom and Politics," edited by Ashley Hinck and Amber Davisson, special issue, *Transformative Works and Cultures* 32. https://doi.org/10.3983/twc.2020.1679.

Sandman Episode Guide

Netflix's *Sandman* Season 1 covers issues #1–8 (collected in *Preludes and Nocturnes*), issues #9–14 (collected in *The Doll's House*) and a bonus two-part episode covering issues #17 and #18 (collected in *Dream Country*).

The first ten episodes became available on August 5, 2022. A bonus two-part episode, episode #11, was released on August 19, 2022.

Performers portraying key characters are listed in order of appearance.

S1.E1 | Chapter 1: Sleep of the Just

Based on: Gaiman, Neil (w), Sam Kieth (a), and Mike Dringenberg (a). 1989. "The Sleep of the Just." *Sandman* #1. DC Comics. January 1989.

> 54 minutes
> Directed by Mike Barker.
> Teleplay, developed by, and executive produced by Neil Gaiman, David S. Goyer, and Allan Heinberg. Story editing by Lauren Bello with staff writers Catherine Smyth-McMullen and Vanessa Benton.
> Based on the DC comic by Neil Gaiman, Sam Kieth, and Mike Dringenberg.
> Includes performances by Tom Sturridge (Dream), Boyd Holbrook (the Corinthian), Vivienne Acheampong (Lucienne), Bill Patterson (Dr. John Hathaway), Laurie Kynaston (Alex Burgess), and Charles Dance (Roderick Burgess).

The pilot episode introduces the waking world and the Dreaming, ruled by a powerful god-like entity known as the King of Dreams. In 1916, an order of occultists in England led by "the magus" Roderick Burgess attempt to ensnare Death but accidentally capture the King of Dreams instead. Held captive for over a century, Dream must break free, track down the tools of his power in the waking world, fix his broken realm, and consequently, save humanity.

S1.E2 | Chapter 2: Imperfect Hosts

Based on Gaiman, Neil (w), Sam Kieth (a), and Mike Dringenberg (a). 1989. "Imperfect Hosts." *Sandman* #2. DC Comics. February 1989.

37 minutes
Directed by Jamie Childs.
Teleplay by Allan Heinberg.
Story editing by Lauren Bello with staff writers Catherine Smyth-McMullen and Vanessa Benton.
Based on the DC comic by Neil Gaiman, Sam Kieth, and Mike Dringenberg.
Includes performances by Tom Sturridge (Dream), Boyd Holbrook (the Corinthian), Vivienne Acheampong (Lucienne), Jenna Coleman (Johanna Constantine), Joely Richardson (Ethel Cripps), Sanjeev Bhaskar (Cain), Asim Chaudhry (Abel), Nina Wadia (Fate Mother), Souad Faress (Fate Crone), Dinita Gohil (Fate Maiden), and David Thewlis (John Dee).

Severely weakened, Dream returns to his realm, the Dreaming, and finds it in ruins. With the support of his loyal librarian, Lucienne, Dream makes a plan for finding and reclaiming the tools of his power. But first, he must pay a visit to some of his oldest creations—the Biblical brothers Cain and Abel. Meanwhile, an escaped nightmare called the Corinthian pays a call on stolen antiquities dealer Ethel Cripps. She and her son John are not what they appear.

S1.E3 | Chapter 3: Dream a Little Dream of Me

Based on: Gaiman, Neil (w), Sam Kieth (a), and Mike Dringenberg (a). 1989. "Dream a Little Dream of Me." *Sandman* #3. DC Comics. March 1989.

46 minutes
Directed by Jamie Childs.
Teleplay by Jim Campolongo.
Developed by Neil Gaiman, David S. Goyer, and Allan Heinberg.
Story editing by Lauren Bello with staff writers Catherine Smyth-McMullen and Vanessa Benton.
Based on the DC comic by Neil Gaiman, Sam Kieth, and Mike Dringenberg.
Includes performances by Tom Sturridge (Dream), Boyd Holbrook (the Corinthian), Patton Oswalt (voice of Matthew the Raven), Jenna Coleman (Johanna Constantine), Joely Richardson (Ethel Cripps), Clare Higgins (Mad Hettie), David Thewlis (John Dee), and Eleanor Fanyinka (Rachel).

Accompanied by his raven Matthew, Dream seeks out exorcist and magician Johanna Constantine to help locate his pouch of sand. Together, they visit the last human to have the pouch in her possession and find that it is eating her alive. Ethel Cripps visits her son John in a psychiatric hospital, gifting him the amulet that protects against all harm. John escapes and sets out to recover Dream's ruby, a stone that makes dreams and nightmares come alive.

S1.E4 | Chapter 4: A Hope in Hell

Based on: Gaiman, Neil (w), Sam Kieth (a), and Mike Dringenberg (a). 1989. "A Hope in Hell." *Sandman* #4. DC Comics. April 1989.
———. "Passengers." *Sandman* #5. DC Comics. May 1989.

44 minutes
Directed by Jamie Childs.
Teleplay by Austin Guzman.
Developed by Neil Gaiman, David S. Goyer, and Allan Heinberg.
Story editing by Lauren Bello with staff writers Catherine Smyth-McMullen and Vanessa Benton.
Based on the DC comic by Neil Gaiman, Sam Kieth, and Mike Dringenberg.
Includes performances by Tom Sturridge (Dream), Patton Oswalt (voice of Matthew the Raven), Gwendoline Christie (Lucifer), Sarah Niles (Rosemary), and David Thewlis (John Dee).

Matthew the Raven and Dream travel to Hell in search of Dream's helm. While there, they see Dream's former lover Nada, but he refuses to come to her aid. Dream must face Lucifer Morningstar, ruler of Hell, in a battle of wits for his helm, with his life on the line.

Once armed with both the helm and the sand, he can pursue the final tool of power: the ruby. Meanwhile, John Dee hitches a ride with the unwitting Rosemary. Dream reaches the ruby first and quickly realizes it has been altered.

S1.E5 | Chapter 5: 24/7

Based on: Gaiman, Neil (w), Mike Dringenberg (a), and Malcolm Jones III (a). 1989. "24 Hours." *Sandman* #6. DC Comics. June 1989.
_____. "Sound and Fury." *Sandman* #7. DC Comics. July 1989.

44 minutes
Directed by Jamie Childs.
Teleplay by Ameni Rozsa.
Developed by Neil Gaiman, David S. Goyer, and Allan Heinberg.
Story editing by Lauren Bello with staff writers Catherine Smyth-McMullen and Vanessa Benton.
Based on the DC comic by Neil Gaiman, Sam Kieth, and Mike Dringenberg.
Includes performances by David Thewlis (John Dee), Emma Duncan (Bette), Steven Brand (Marsh), Daisy Head (Judy Talbot), Laurie Davidson (Mark Brewer), Lourdes Faberes (Kate Fletcher), James Udom (Gary Fletcher), Tom Sturridge (Dream), Patton Oswalt (voice of Matthew the Raven), and Mason Alexander Park (Desire).

John Dee heads into a diner to test his powers on the staff and patrons. The ruby forces everyone in the diner to share their secrets. Gradually, over the 24 hours that they are trapped inside the diner together, the staff and patrons descend into infidelity, jealousy, resentment, lust, anger, torture, self-harm, and murder, until everyone but John is dead. Dream invites John to meet him in the Dreaming, where John attempts to take over Dream's power as well. Instead, he unintentionally restores Dream to power.

S1.E6 | Chapter 6: The Sound of Her Wings

Based on: Gaiman, Neil (w), Mike Dringenberg (a), and Malcolm Jones III (i). 1989. "The Sound of Her Wings." *Sandman* #8. DC Comics. August 1989.
Gaiman, Neil (w), Mike Zulli (a), and Steve Parkhouse (i). 1990. "Men of Good Fortune." *Sandman* #13. DC Comics. February 1990.

>53 minutes
>Directed by Mairzee Almas.
>Teleplay by Lauren Bello.
>Developed by Neil Gaiman, David S. Goyer, and Allan Heinberg.
>Story editing by Lauren Bello with staff writers Catherine Smyth-McMullen and Vanessa Benton.
>Based on the DC comic by Neil Gaiman, Sam Kieth, and Mike Dringenberg.
>   Includes performances by Tom Sturridge (Dream); Kirby Howell-Baptiste (Death); Curtis Kants (Franklin); Jon Rumney (Harry the violinist); Leemore Marrett, Jr. (Sam the swimmer); Ferdinand Kingsley (Hob Gadling); Samuel Blenkin (William Shakespeare); Jenna Coleman (Johanna Constantine); and Mason Alexander Park (Desire).

Death checks in on her little brother Dream. He joins her for the day on her rounds, meeting humans who are dying and accompanying them into the Sunless Lands. Dream then heads to a centennial appointment with his friend, Hob Gadling, and learns what it means to be human.

S1.E7 | Chapter 7: The Doll's House

Based on: Gaiman, Neil (w), Mike Dringenberg (a), and Malcolm Jones III (i). 1989. "The Doll's House: Part 1." *Sandman* #10. DC Comics. November 1989.
_____. 1989. "The Doll's House: Part 2—Moving In." *Sandman* #11. DC Comics. December 1989.

>49 minutes
>Directed by Andrés Baiz.
>Teleplay by Heather Bellson.
>Developed by, and executive produced by Neil Gaiman, David S. Goyer, and Allan Heinberg. Story editing by Lauren Bello with staff writers Catherine Smyth-McMullen and Vanessa Benton.
>Based on the DC comic by Neil Gaiman, Sam Kieth, and Mike Dringenberg.
>   Includes performances by Vanesu Samunyai / Kyo Ra (Rose Walker), Aryel Tsoto (Young Jed Walker), Andi Osho (Miranda Walker), Mason Alexander Park (Desire), Donna Preston (Despair), Razane Jammal (Lyta Hall), Lloyd Everitt (Hector Hall), Asim Chaudhry (Abel), Vivienne Acheampong (Lucienne), Tom Sturridge (Dream), Patton Oswalt (voice of Matthew the Raven), Sandra James-Young (Unity Kincaid), Kerry Shale (Nimrod), Jill Winternitz (The Good Doctor), Danny Kirrane (Fun Land), Nina Wadia (Fate Mother), Souad Faress (Fate Crone), Dinita Gohil (Fate Maiden), Boyd Holbrook (The Corinthian), Mark Hamill (Merv Pumpkinhead), John Cameron Mitchell (Hal Carter), Richard Fleeshman (Ken), Lily Travers (Barbie), Daisy Badger (Chantal), Stephen Fry (Gilbert), Eddie Karanja (Jed Walker), Lisa O'Hare (Aunt Clarice), and Sam Hazeldine (Uncle Barnaby).

Dream learns that three important members of his realm have gone AWOL: Gault, the Corinthian, and Fiddler's Green. He knows they will be drawn to Rose Walker because she is a vortex: a powerful being that can destroy the world. He sends Matthew the Raven to watch her. Rose is an orphan looking for her lost little brother Jed. After meeting her great-grandmother Unity Kincaid, Rose and her friend Lyta Hall travel to Florida in search of Jed. They find a room in a lodging house filled with eccentric neighbors, including a benevolent protector named Gilbert. Meanwhile, a trio of "collectors" plan a convention for serial killers, seeking a guest speaker: the Corinthian.

S1.E8 | Chapter 8: Playing House

Based on: Gaiman, Neil (w), Mike Dringenberg (a), and Malcolm Jones III (i). 1989. "The Doll's House: Part 2—Moving In." *Sandman* #11. DC Comics. December 1989.
_____. 1990. "The Doll's House: Part 3—Playing House." *Sandman* #12. DC Comics. January 1990.

> 50 minutes
> Directed by Andrés Baiz.
> Teleplay by Alexander Newman-Wise.
> Developed by, and executive produced by Neil Gaiman, David S. Goyer, and Allan Heinberg. Story editing by Lauren Bello with staff writers Catherine Smyth-McMullen and Vanessa Benton.
> Based on the DC comic by Neil Gaiman, Sam Kieth, and Mike Dringenberg.
> Includes performances by Vanesu Samunyai / Kyo Ra (Rose Walker), Tom Sturridge (Dream), Vivienne Acheampong (Lucienne), Andi Osho (Miranda Walker), Ann Ogbomo (Gault), Patton Oswalt (voice of Matthew the Raven), Eddie Karanja (Jed Walker), Lisa O'Hare (Aunt Clarice), Sam Hazeldine (Uncle Barnaby), Sandra James-Young (Unity Kincaid), Boyd Holbrook (The Corinthian), John Cameron Mitchell (Hal Carter), Lily Travers (Barbie), Richard Fleeshman (Ken), Daisy Badger (Chantal), Razane Jammal (Lyta Hall), and Lloyd Everitt (Hector Hall).

Rose meets Dream and starts to learn how to harness her power to walk through the dreams of others. She hunts for Jed, who is hidden as "The Sandman," living in a dream made by the nightmare Gault. This helps him mentally escape from his reality as a prisoner in his foster parents' basement. Lyta Hall is also escaping into her dreams, visiting her dead husband Hector, and returns to the waking world pregnant with their baby. Dream finds and punishes Gault, who makes a case for change. And finally, the Corinthian finds Jed, getting one step closer in his quest to defeat Dream.

S1.E9 | Chapter 9: Collectors

Based on: Gaiman, Neil (w), Mike Dringenberg (a), and Malcolm Jones III (i). 1990. "The Doll's House: Part 5—Collectors." *Sandman* #14. DC Comics. March 1990.

188 *Sandman* Episode Guide

49 minutes
Directed by Coralie Fargeat.
Teleplay by Vanessa Benton.
Developed by, and executive produced by Neil Gaiman, David S. Goyer, and Allan Heinberg. Story editing by Lauren Bello with staff writers Catherine Smyth-McMullen and Vanessa Benton.
Based on the DC comic by Neil Gaiman, Sam Kieth, and Mike Dringenberg.
Includes performances by Vanesu Samunyai / Kyo Ra (Rose Walker), Razane Jammal (Lyta Hall), Patton Oswalt (voice of Matthew the Raven), Vivienne Acheampong (Lucienne), Tom Sturridge (Dream), Boyd Holbrook (the Corinthian), Eddie Karanja (Jed Walker), Stephen Fry (Gilbert), Lloyd Everitt (Hector Hall), Mark Hamill (Merv Pumpkinhead), Kerry Shale (Nimrod), Jill Winternitz (The Good Doctor), Danny Kirrane (Fun Land), and Lewis Reeves (The Bogeyman / Philip Sitz).

Rose and Lyta realize that what's happening in their dreams is becoming real—and that Rose is the reason why. The Corinthian, Jed, Rose, and Gilbert all converge on the "cereal" convention, where regular humans are far more dangerous than nightmares. Meanwhile, seeking the source of his fracturing realm, Dream confronts Hector and Lyta in their dream, sending Hector back to the dead and making the haunting promise that he will someday return for Lyta's child. Gilbert / Fiddler's Green returns to the Dreaming, unwittingly putting Rose in even more danger.

S1.E10 | Chapter 10: Lost Hearts

Based on: Gaiman, Neil (w), Mike Dringenberg (a), and Malcolm Jones III (i). 1990. "The Doll's House: Part 7—Lost Hearts." *Sandman* #16. DC Comics. June 1990.

46 minutes
Includes performances by Boyd Holbrook (the Corinthian), Vanesu Samunyai / Kyo Ra (Rose Walker), Eddie Karanja (Jed Walker), Jill Winternitz (The Good Doctor), Kerry Shale (Nimrod), Tom Sturridge (Dream), Patton Oswalt (voice of Matthew the Raven), Sandra James-Young (Unity Kincaid), Razane Jammal (Lyta Hall), John Cameron Mitchell (Hal Carter), Daisy Badger (Chantal), Richard Fleeshman (Ken), Lily Travers (Barbie), Vivienne Acheampong (Lucienne), Stephen Fry (Gilbert), Mason Alexander Park (Desire), Ann Ogbomo (Gault), and Gwendoline Christie (Lucifer).

The Corinthian finds Rose and reveals that Dream is planning to kill her. Once Rose falls asleep, she takes Dream's place at the center of the Dreaming, causing dreams to collide. Both Dream and the Corinthian try to manipulate Rose—but she resists them both and awakes. Meanwhile, a sleeping Unity meets Lucienne in the Library of the Dreaming and discovers a way to sacrifice herself to save Rose. Lyta delivers her baby, who Dream now knows is a descendant of Desire. Dream recreates Gault as a dream. And Lucifer makes a plan.

S1.E11 | Dream of a Thousand Cats / Calliope

64 minutes

"Dream of a Thousand Cats"

Based on: Gaiman, Neil (w), Kelley Jones (a), and Malcolm Jones III (i). 1990. "A Dream of a Thousand Cats." *Sandman* #18. DC Comics. August 1990.

> 16 minutes
> Directed by Hisko Hulsing.
> Teleplay by Catherine Smyth-McMullen.
> Developed by, and executive produced by, Neil Gaiman, David S. Goyer, and Allan Heinberg.
> Based on the DC comic by Neil Gaiman, Sam Kieth, and Mike Dringenberg.
> Performances by Rosie Day (Tabby Kitten), David Tennant (Don), Georgia Tennant (Laura Lynn), David Gyasi (Grey Cat), Joe Lycett (Black Cat), Sandra Oh (the Prophet), Neil Gaiman (Crow / Skull Bird), Tom Sturridge (the Cat of Dreams), James McAvoy (Golden-Haired Man), Anna Lundbert (Marion), and Michael Sheen (Paul).

A young domestic kitten sneaks out of her home to hear a speech from a feline prophet. The Prophet tells a tale of suffering at the hands of her owners and how she traveled to the Heart of the Dreaming to gain audience with Cat of Dreams. Now she travels to share what she has learned: if enough cats share a common dream, they can turn the tables on humanity and change the world.

"Calliope"

Based on: Gaiman, Neil (w), Kelley Jones (a), and Malcolm Jones III (i). 1990. "Calliope." *Sandman* #17. DC Comics. July 1990.

> 48 minutes
> Directed by Louise Hooper.
> Teleplay by Catherine Smyth-McMullen.
> Developed by, and executive produced by Neil Gaiman, David S. Goyer, and Allan Heinberg.
> Based on the DC comic by Neil Gaiman, Sam Kieth, and Mike Dringenberg.
> Performances by Tom Sturridge (Dream), Melissanthi Mahut (Calliope), Arthur Darvill (Richard Madoc), Nina Wadia (Fate Mother), Souad Faress (Fate Crone), Dinita Gohil (Fate Maiden),
> Kevin Harvey (Larry), Amita Suman (Nora) and Derek Jacobi (Erasmus Fry).

Richard Madoc, a writer and college professor suffering from writer's block and an impending deadline, discovers a horrifying cure: by imprisoning and abusing the ancient muse Calliope, he can steal inspiration to write. Desperate to escape, Calliope pleads with Madoc; begs the Fates to intercede; and then, as her last resort, begs for help from her former lover: Dream of the Endless.

About the Contributors

Sara Misato **Aoki** is a law student at the University of Chicago Law School and a recent graduate of the University of California, Los Angeles, with a major in human biology and society and a minor in geography/environmental studies. Her research experience spans a wide variety of fields, from the study of schizophrenia to an exploration of the intersection between art and science in museum settings.

Alexis **Brooks de Vita** is the author of several books, including *Mythatypes: Signatures and Signs of African/Diaspora and Black Goddesses*, and essays in a variety of edited collections and journals such as *God Is Change: Religious Practices and Ideologies in the Works of Octavia Butler, Fourth Wave Feminism in Science Fiction and Fantasy, Extrapolation, The Griot*, and *Journal of the Fantastic in the Arts*.

Novella **Brooks de Vita** has presented on literature including comics, film, theater, literacy, andragogy, and pedagogy. She has published on pedagogy; literacy; children's literature; spirit children; and the works of Octavia Butler, Ben Okri, Tina McElroy Ansa, and Edwidge Danticat. Recent publications include the Neil Gaiman interview "Building Inclusive Worlds and Global Representations in the Works of Neil Gaiman."

Naveen Kelvin **Dalmeida** is a teacher of English at Apollo Education and Training (International House), Hanoi, Vietnam. His master's thesis is on reading abjection in selected works of Neil Gaiman. He has research experience in new historicism and post-structuralist literary theory and he is interested in the relationship between language acquisition and adapting authentic texts to be used in ESL classrooms in the South East Asian context.

Angela Carmela Uy **Fantone** is a Filipino literary scholar and writer born and raised in the Philippines. She is also a graduate instructor at Weber State University and teaches undergraduate composition courses. She received her bachelor's degree in English from Brigham Young University-Hawai'i and is pursuing a Master of Arts in English from Weber State. Her scholarly interests include the intersection of memory studies and literature.

Melisa Maryann **Goveas** is an associate professor at the Department of Postgraduate Studies and Research in English, which she chairs, at St. Aloysius (Deemed to Be University), Mangalore, India. Her PhD dissertation is *"Who Murdered the Detective?" Subversion and Erasure in Postmodern Crime Fiction*. She has research experience in abjection and postmodernism as well as gender sensitization in children via "New Age" Disney princesses.

Drea **Letamendi** is a licensed psychologist and suicide interventionist at UCLA. As an educator, writer, and media consultant, she uses storytelling as a vehicle for teaching psychological science and fostering positive mental health outcomes. In her private practice, Drea provides technical consultation and creative content for the gaming, VFX, film, and television industries. She co-hosts *The Arkham Sessions*, a podcast about the psychology of superheroes and other pop culture narratives.

Pinky Chung-Man **Lui** is a literary scholar and university lecturer based in Hong Kong. She received her PhD from the Chinese University of Hong Kong with a thesis on the feminist autofiction of Anaïs Nin and Zelda Sayre. Her work has been published in *CSS Working Paper Series*, *Cha: An Asian Literary Journal*, and *Hong Kong Review of Books*. Her research focuses on feminist criticism, modernism, and literary censorship.

Tara **Prescott-Johnson** is a continuing lecturer and distinguished teacher in Writing Programs at UCLA, where she served for nine years as a Faculty in Residence. She is the author of *Poetic Salvage: Reading Mina Loy*, editor of *Neil Gaiman in the 21st Century*, and co-editor of *Gender and the Superhero Narrative* and *Feminism in the Worlds of Neil Gaiman*. Her TEDxUCLA talk, "Hike Your Own Hike," is available on YouTube.

Adrienne E. **Raw** is an assistant professor of professional writing at SUNY Cortland where she teaches professional and creative writing, young adult literature, and rhetorical thinking about everything from disability to video games. When she's not writing about the construction of community, identity, and consensus in online spaces, she is lurking on Tumblr and reading and writing fanfiction.

Samara V. **Serotkin**, Psy.D. is a psychologist, personal coach, and mindfulness meditation teacher based in Seattle, Washington. She is the author of *Mindful Willpower: Powerful Mindfulness Practices to Increase Self-Control, Get Focused, and Build Good Habits*. She has more than twenty years' experience providing mindfulness-based therapy and coaching to help people discover meaningful paths forward.

Aayushi **Shah** is a research associate at the Gladstone Institutes studying Alzheimer's Disease and a recent graduate of the University of California, Los Angeles, with a major in microbiology, immunology, and molecular genetics and a minor in biomedical research. Her work on antivirals for pandemic potential viruses was published in *Cell Reports Medicine*.

Joseph Michael **Sommers** is a professor of English at Central Michigan University where he teaches courses in children's and young adult literature, popular culture, and comics. He has published essays, articles, books, and interviews on topics in YACL literature and culture, comics, movies, video games and Neil Gaiman, including *Critical Insights on Neil Gaiman*, *Conversations with Neil Gaiman*, and *The Artistry of Neil Gaiman*.

Colin **Wheeler** designs motion media and animates as a freelancer and teaches animation at Kennesaw State University, researching the theory and practice of creativity as a discipline and a discourse. He completed his MFA in animation at the Savannah College of Art and Design and received his doctorate in communications at Georgia State University. He has a lifelong passion for the critical exploration of animation as an art form and an industry.

Index

Abel 46, 184
Acheampong, Vivienne *see* Lucienne
adaptation 5, 9-12, 34, 44-49, 49n1, 53, 62-65, 68, 78-90, 102, 106, 111-112, 153, 163-165, 175-179
African descent 3, 8-9, 12, 15, 17, 19-29, 30n1, 46, 79, 96, 133
AI (artificial intelligence) 166
allegations (against Neil Gaiman) 1-12, 115, 120, 126, 129, 135
American Gods 12, 53, 80, 124
Amos, Tori 4
Anansi Boys 12, 45, 53
anthropomorphism 143-144
antiracist 16, 103; *see also* racism
AO3 *see* Archive of Our Own
Archive of Our Own 163, 166
Ariel *see The Little Mermaid*
Audible 102, 153
Aziraphale 131, 153, 179n1; *see also* Sheen, Michael

Barbie 61
Batman 80, 86, 90n7, 96
Berger, Karen 6
Black *see* African descent
Black Lives Matter 12
Black Orchid 177
Blackwell, Urania 42, 70
Bod *see* Owens, Nobody "Bod"
Brief Lives (issue and/or story arc) 58, 73
Brute 85-89
Buffy the Vampire Slayer 5, 11, 105, 108
Burgess, Alex 118, 167, 174-175, 183
Burgess, Roderick 80, 110, 183
Butler, Octavia 29

Cain 46, 184
Calendar of Tales 178
"Calliope" (character and/or issue and/or television episode) 2, 5, 10-11, 16, 24, 41, 44, 46, 54, 102-120, 124, 129-130, 139, 148n2, 189
casting 8-10, 15-16, 18, 20, 22-24, 46, 68, 75-76, 132-133
cats 11, 75, 130, 137-148, 151-161
Christie, Gwendoline *see* Morningstar, Lucifer
Cinnamon 49n1
Coleman, Jenna *see* Constantine, Johanna
"Collectors" (issue and/or episode) {em}90n8, 187-188
colonialism 8-9, 16-17, 33-35, 42, 44-48, 147
Comic-Con 10
Constantine, Johanna 109, 124
Constantine, John 80
continuity 10
Convocation of Jacks *see* Jacks of All Trades
Coraline (character and/or novel and/or film) 68, 73, 152-153, 157-158, 160
the Corinthian 26-29, 89, 103, 171, 177, 183-184, 186-188
Covid-19 *see* pandemic
Cripps, Ethel 184
Crowley 153, 179n1; *see also* Tennant, David

DC Comics 6, 10, 25, 78-83, 86, 177
Dead Boy Detectives 2, 12, 33
Death (character) 9-10, 15-18, 33, 42, 46, 57, 59, 67-76, 79, 90n2, 92-100, 109, 132-133, 135, 167, 183, 186
Dee, John 28, 103, 127-129, 185-186
Deleuze, Gilles 143
Delight *see* Delirium
Delirium 57-59, 71
Desire (character) 9-10, 18-19, 57-58, 60, 67-76, 79, 85, 89, 110, 126, 176, 185-186, 188
Despair (character) 56-58, 73, 126, 176, 186

196 Index

Destruction (character) 57–58
Disney 46–47, 49n1, 106, 139
diversity 8–9, 15–16, 30, 45–46, 68, 76, 133, 138
Doctor Who 123, 153, 178
"The Doctor's Wife" 123, 153, 178
Dodds, Wesley 10, 78, 82, 90n1
The Doll's House (story arc and/or episode) 6, 85, 110, 167, 176
Dream (character) 10, 18–22, 25, 29, 41, 54, 56–61, 69, 71–75, 78, 85–89, 90n8, 94, 96–99, 109–110, 115–119, 129–130, 133–134, 153, 167–177, 179n1, 183–189
"Dream a Little Dream of Me" (issue and/or episode) 109, 184
Dream Country (story arc and/or episode) 6, 44, 46, 102, 119, 148n2, 153, 183
The Dream King *see* Dream (character)
"A Dream of a Thousand Cats" (issue and episode) 10–11, 90n9, 130–131, 137–148, 151–161, 189
"Dream of a Thousand Cats / Calliope" *see* "A Dream of a Thousand Cats"; "Calliope"
the Dreaming 29, 61, 75, 85–89, 96, 110, 134, 158, 175, 183–185, 188–189

Endless 10–11, 17–18, 57–61, 67–76, 78–79, 86, 93, 98, 110, 131, 134, 167, 171, 176, 189; *see also* Death (character); Desire (character); Despair (character); Destiny (character); Destruction (character); Delirium (character); Dream (character)
enslavement: fictional 109, 118, 169–170, 172; historical 17–18, 21–23
Eumenides *see* Fates

"Façade" (issue) 9, 42, 44, 46, 70, 93, 148n2
Faerie 36–38
Fanfiction 11, 163–179
fantasy 2, 9, 18, 27, 35–36, 39, 41–44, 48–49, 51, 55, 57, 61–65, 93, 96, 106, 116, 123, 153
Fates 74, 111, 115, 189
feminism 67, 116
Fiddler's Green 186–188
fidelity 20, 81–82, 84, 89, 165
folklore 53–54, 84
Freud, Sigmund *see* the uncanny
Frost, Jack 39–40
Fun Land 103, 186, 188
Furies *see* Fates

Gadling, Hob 98, 165–176, 179n1, 186
Game of Thrones 11, 106–108
"A Game of You" (issue and/or story arc) 132
Gault 25–27, 29, 85–89, 134, 187–188
gender 8–10, 15–19, 46, 68, 71, 79, 94, 103, 109, 131–133, 139, 177; *see also* nonbinary
ghosts 33, 38, 41, 68, 73, 88
Gilbert *see* Fiddler's Green
Glob 85–89
grief 4, 10, 24, 92–100
Good Omens (novel and/or television series) 2, 12, 44–45, 131, 153, 177–178, 179n1; *see also* Aziraphale; Crowley
The Graveyard Book 2, 9, 12, 34–35, 38–41, 46–49, 73, 80

Hall, Hector 25, 81, 86–89, 186–188
Hall, Lyta 25–26, 86, 88–89, 110, 186–188
Harry Potter 3, 34, 152
HBO 106–108, 114
Hecate *see* Fates
Hector *see* Hall, Hector
Heinberg, Allan 140, 183–189
Hell 20–21, 29, 39, 119, 133–134, 167, 184–185
Hob *see* Gadling, Hob
Holbrook, Boyd *see* the Corinthian
homophobia 69, 103
Hooper, Louise 109, 189
"A Hope in Hell" (issue and/or episode) 133, 184
How to Talk to Girls at Parties (film) 173
Howell-Baptiste, Kirby *see* Death (character)
Hulsing, Hisko 140–141, 143, 189

I May Destroy You 11, 114, 118
"Imperfect Hosts" (issue and/or episode) 74, 183
"In Which We Wake" (issue) 73
Indigenous 9, 18–19

Jed *see* Walker, Jed
Johnson, Rachel *see* allegations (against Neil Gaiman)
The Jungle Book see Kipling, Rudyard

Kincaid, Unity 23–26, 110, 116, 186–188
The Kindly Ones (issue and/or story arc) 72–73, 168, 176
Kipling, Rudyard 33–34, 38, 47
Kirby, Jack 80–82, 85–86, 88–89
Klapcsik, Sándor 53, 67–68, 93
Kristeva, Julia 9, 67–72, 75

Larsen, Kristine 25, 56
LGBTQ+ 8–9, 69, 103
Library of the Dreaming 19–20, 188

Lilim *see* Fates
liminal spaces 51, 55, 57, 61, 68, 93, 100
The Little Mermaid 139
The Lord of the Dreaming *see* Dream (character)
The Lord of the Rings (books and/or films) 122–123, 164
Lorde, Audre 119
"Lost Hearts" (issue and/or episode) 71, 75, 89, 110, 134, 176
Lucienne 19–20, 29, 74, 85–86, 89, 109, 133–134, 183–184, 186–188
Lucifer *see* Morningstar, Lucifer
Lyta *see* Hall, Lyta

Madoc, Richard 16, 46, 102, 111–120, 129, 189
male gaze 107–108
man Jack *see* Frost, Jack
Marvel 1602 177
Master: The Allegations Against Neil Gaiman (podcast) *see* allegations (against Neil Gaiman)
Matthew the Raven 72, 184–188
Mahut, Melissanthi *see* "Calliope"
McAvoy, James 153–154, 189
McKean, Dave 6–7
#MeToo 2, 12, 104–105, 115, 126
"Men of Good Fortune" (issue and/or episode) 99, 167, 186
Mendlesohn, Farah 57
"A Midsummer Night's Dream" (issue) 148n2
Miller, Monica 178
misogyny 16, 69
Morningstar, Lucifer 133, 153, 185, 188
Morpheus *see* Dream (character)

Nada 20–22, 29, 54, 119, 185
Neil Gaiman in the 21st Century 10
nonbinary 9, 41, 46, 68, 71, 76, 125, 132
nonhuman 137–148
Norse Mythology 53

The Ocean at the End of the Lane 3, 73
Odd and the Frost Giants 53
Oneiros *see* Dream (character)
Orientalism *see* Said, Edward
Orpheus 54, 73
Overture see Sandman: Overture
Owens, Nobody "Bod" 39–41

Palmer, Amanda 2, 178
pandemic 56, 93, 99, 126
parasocial relationships 3, 10, 99
Park, Mason Alexander *see* Desire (character)

"Passengers" (issue) 184
"Playing House" (issue and/or episode) 86, 134, 187
postmodernism 67
poststructuralism 67–68
Pratchett, Terry *see Good Omens*
pregnancy 25, 110, 156, 187
Preludes and Nocturnes 6, 80, 167, 183

Queen Nada *see* Nada
queer 9, 18–19, 132

racism 9, 17–18, 20–22, 24, 26–27, 47, 69, 76, 119, 147, 159
Rainie *see* Blackwell, Urania
"Ramadan" (issue) 9, 42–43, 54
rape 2, 10, 20–23, 25, 44, 102–120, 126, 129
Rose *see* Walker, Rose
Rowling, J.K. *see Harry Potter*
Russell, P. Craig 33

Said, Edward 9, 33–34, 43, 48
Sandman (audiobook) 51–52, 72, 102
Sandman (character) *see* Dream (character)
Sandman: Endless Nights 176
Sandman: Overture 71
Season of Mists (issue and/or story arc) 119, 167
sexual assault *see* rape
Shakespeare, William 45, 56, 153, 168–171, 175
Shapiro, Lila *see* allegations (against Neil Gaiman)
Sheen, Michael 142, 153, 179n1; *see also* Aziraphale
Signs of Life 178
Silas 40–41
Simon, Joe 80, 82, 85, 90n5, 90n7
slavery *see* enslavement
"Sleep of the Just" (issue and/or episode) 7, 167, 183
"The Song of Orpheus" 54
"Sound and Fury" 185
"The Sound of Her Wings" (issue and/or episode) 10, 69, 72, 74, 92–100, 109, 135, 167–169, 174, 176, 186
Stardust (novel and/or film) 9, 34–39, 45–49, 80, 161
Stark, Sansa 107–108
Sturridge, Tom *see* Dream (character)
the Sunless Lands 33, 70, 94, 186

"Tales in the Sand" (issue) 54
Tennant, David 141, 146, 153, 178, 179n1, 189; *see also* Crowley

"There Is No Safe Word" *see* allegations (against Neil Gaiman)
Thewlis, David *see* Dee, John
Thompson, Craig 33
The Threshold 60, 71, 75, 89
Tristran 36–38, 45
"24 Hours" (issue and/or "24/7" episode) 28, 75, 124, 128–129, 185

uncanny 70, 93, 139, 148n1
Unity *see* Kincaid, Unity

Vess, Charles 6
Vertigo 6, 81
vortex *see* Walker, Rose

The Wake (issue and/or story arc) 168, 176
Walker, Jed 22–29, 81, 86–89, 90n4, 186–188
Walker, Rose 23–26, 73, 86–88, 110, 171, 173, 186–188
Wanda 132
Weinstein, Harvey 3, 105
Weird Sisters *see* Fates
Whedon, Joss *see* Buffy the Vampire Slayer
Who Killed Amanda Palmer? 178
The Wolves in the Walls 4
Wylde, Vera 1–2

Yvaine 36–38, 45

www.ingramcontent.com/pod-product-compliance
Lightning Source LLC
LaVergne TN
LVHW041807060526
838201LV00046B/1161